History of Egypt

Chaldea, Syria, Babylonia, and Assyria

IN THE LIGHT OF RECENT DISCOVERY

By L. W. KING, M. A., F. S. A., and H. R. HALL, M. A.
Department of Egyptian and Assyrian Antiquities, British Museum.

CONTAINING OVER TWELVE HUNDRED
COLORED PLATES AND ILLUSTRATIONS

ISBN: 978-1-63923-900-9

All Rights reserved. No part of this book maybe reproduced without written permission from the publishers, except by a reviewer who may quote brief passages in a review to be printed in a newspaper or magazine.

Printed: March 2023

Published and Distributed By:
Lushena Books
607 Country Club Drive, Unit E
Bensenville, IL 60106
www.lushenabks.com

ISBN: 978-1-63923-900-9

PUBLISHERS' NOTE

It should be noted that many of the monuments and sites of excavations in Egypt, Mesopotamia, Persia, and Kurdistan described in this volume have been visited by the authors in connection with their own work in those countries. The greater number of the photographs here published were taken by the authors themselves. Their thanks are due to M. Ernest Leroux, of Paris, for his kind permission to reproduce a certain number of plates from the works of M. de Morgan, illustrating his recent discoveries in Egypt and Persia, and to Messrs. W. A. Mansell & Co., of London, for kindly allowing them to make use of a number of photographs issued by them.

PREFACE

The present volume contains an account of the most important additions which have been made to our knowledge of the ancient history of Egypt and Western Asia during the few years which have elapsed since the publication of Prof. Maspero's *Histoire Ancienne des Peuples de l'Orient Classique,* and includes short descriptions of the excavations from which these results have been obtained. It is in no sense a connected and continuous history of these countries, for that has already been written by Prof. Maspero, but is rather intended as an appendix or addendum to his work, briefly recapitulating and describing the discoveries made since its appearance. On this account we have followed a geographical rather than a chronological system of arrangement, but at the same time the attempt has been made to suggest to the mind of the reader the historical sequence of events.

At no period have excavations been pursued with more energy and activity, both in Egypt and Western Asia, than at the present time, and every season's work obliges us to modify former theories, and extends our

PREFACE

knowledge of periods of history which even ten years ago were unknown to the historian. For instance, a whole chapter has been added to Egyptian history by the discovery of the Neolithic culture of the primitive Egyptians, while the recent excavations at Susa are revealing a hitherto totally unsuspected epoch of proto-Elamite civilization. Further than this, we have discovered the relics of the oldest historical kings of Egypt, and we are now enabled to reconstitute from material as yet unpublished the inter-relations of the early dynasties of Babylon. Important discoveries have also been made with regard to isolated points in the later historical periods. We have therefore attempted to include the most important of these in our survey of recent excavations and their results. We would again remind the reader that Prof. Maspero's great work must be consulted for the complete history of the period, the present volume being, not a connected history of Egypt and Western Asia, but a description and discussion of the manner in which recent discovery and research have added to and modified our conceptions of ancient Egyptian and Mesopotamian civilization.

CONTENTS

CHAPTER		PAGE
I.	THE DISCOVERY OF PREHISTORIC EGYPT	1
II.	ABYDOS AND THE FIRST THREE DYNASTIES	55
III.	MEMPHIS AND THE PYRAMIDS	91
IV.	RECENT EXCAVATIONS IN WESTERN ASIA AND THE DAWN OF CHALDÆAN HISTORY	143
V.	ELAM AND BABYLON, THE COUNTRY OF THE SEA AND THE KASSITES	221
VI.	EARLY BABYLONIAN LIFE AND CUSTOMS	265
VII.	TEMPLES AND TOMBS OF THEBES	317
VIII.	THE ASSYRIAN AND NEO-BABYLONIAN EMPIRES IN THE LIGHT OF RECENT RESEARCH	388
IX.	THE LAST DAYS OF ANCIENT EGYPT	428

LIST OF ILLUSTRATIONS

	PAGE
Statue of Rui, High Priest in the Reign of Ramses II	*Frontispiece*
The bed of an ancient watercourse in the Wadiyên, Thebes	7
Palæolithic Implements of the Quaternary Period	8
Palæolithic Implements	9
Upper desert plateau, where Palæolithic Implements are found	12
Flint Knife mounted in a gold handle	15
Buff Ware Vase, predynastic period	17
Camp of the expedition of the University of California at Nag' ed-Dêr, 1901	27
Portion of the "Stele of Vultures" found at Telloh, representing the burial of the dead after a battle	38
Obverse of a slate relief representing the King of Upper Egypt in the form of a Bull	50
Reverse of a slate relief	51
Obverse of a slate relief with representations of the Egyptian nomes	52
Reverse of a slate relief representing animals	53
Professor Petrie's camp at Abydos, 1901	60
The Tomb of King Den at Abydos	65
Examples of conical vase-stoppers taken from Abydos	67
The Tomb of King Tjeser at Bêt Khallâf	82
False Door of the Tomb of Teta, an official of the IVth Dynasty	86
The Shûnet ez-Zebîb: the fortress-town of the IId Dynasty at Abydos	89
Statue No. 1 of the Cairo Museum	100
Exterior of the southern Brick Pyramid of Dashûr: XIIth Dynasty	109
The Pyramids of Gîza during the inundation	111
List of Archaic cuneiform signs	147
Fragment of a list of Archaic cuneiform signs	150
Obelisk of Manishtusu, King of the City of Kish	155
Babil, the most northern mound which marks the site of the ancient city of Babylon	160
"Stele of Victory," representing Narâm-Sin conquering his enemies	160

LIST OF ILLUSTRATIONS

	PAGE
Roughly hewn sculpture of a lion standing over a fallen man, found at Babylon	161
General view of the excavations on the Kasr at Babylon	163
View within the palace of Nebuchadnezzar II	165
Excavations in the temple of Ninib at Babylon	166
The principal mound of Birs Nimrud, which marks the site of the ancient city of Borsippa	167
The principal mound at Sherghat, which marks the site of Ashur, the ancient capital of the Assyrians	168
The mound of Kuyunjik, one of the palace mounds of the ancient Assyrian city of Nineveh	169
Winged bull in the palace of Sennacherib on Kuyunjik, the principal mound marking the site of Nineveh	170
Clay memorial-tablet of Eannadu, viceroy of Shirpurla	173
Marble gate-socket bearing an inscription of Entemena, a powerful Patesi of Shirpurla	175
Stone gate-socket bearing an inscription of Ur-Engur, an early king of the city of Ur	188
Statue of Gudea, viceroy of Shirpurla	191
Tablet inscribed in Sumerian with details of a survey of certain property	192
Clay tablet, found at Susa, bearing an inscription in the early proto-Elamite character	230
Clay tablet, found at Susa, bearing an inscription in the early proto-Elamite character	231
Block of limestone, found at Susa, bearing inscriptions of Karibu-sha-Shushinak	233
Brick stamped with an inscription of Kudur-mabug	241
Semitic Babylonian contract-tablet, inscribed in the reign of Hammurabi with a deed recording the division of property	245
A Kudurru, or Boundary-stone, inscribed with a text of Nazimaruttash	256
A Kudurru, or Boundary-stone, inscribed with a text of Melishikhu	260
Upper part of the Stele of Hammurabi, King of Babylon	265
Clay contract-tablet and its outer case, First Dynasty	280
A track in the desert	282
A camping-ground in the desert, between Birejik and Urfa	283
Approach to the city of Samarra, situated on the left bank of the Tigris	284
A small caravan in the mountains of Kurdistan	285
The city of Mosul	286
The village of Nebi Yunus	287
Portrait-sculpture of Hammurabi, King of Babylon	289
A modern machine for irrigation on the Euphrates	293
Kaiks, or native boats, on the Euphrates at Birejik	297
The modern bridge of boats across the Tigris opposite Mosul	298

LIST OF ILLUSTRATIONS

	PAGE
A small Kelek, or raft, upon the Tigris at Baghdad	299
Statue of Mera, Chief Steward, IXth Dynasty	320
Wall of XIth Dynasty: Dêr el-Bahari	324
Wall of XVIIIth Dynasty: Dêr el-Bahari	325
Excavation of the north lower colonnade of the XIth dynasty temple, Dêr el-Bahari, 1904	326
The granite threshold and sandstone pillars of the XIth dynasty temple, at Dêr el-Bahari	327
Excavation of the tomb of a priestess, on the platform of the XIth Dynasty temple, Dêr el-Bahari, 1904	328
Cases of antiquities leaving Dêr el-Bahari for transport to Cairo	330
Shipping cases of antiquities on board the Nile steamer at Luxor, for the Egypt Exploration Fund	331
Statue of Queen Teta-shera	339
The two temples of Dêr el-Bahari	344
The upper court and trilithon gate of the XVIIIth Dynasty temple at Dêr el-Bahari	346
The tomb-mountain of Amenhetep III in the western valley, Thebes	350
The tomb-hill of Shêkh 'Abd el-Kûrna, Thebes	356
Wall painting from a Tomb at Shêkh 'Abd el-Kûrna, Western Thebes	358
Fresco in the tomb of Senmut, at Thebes	360
The valley of the Tombs of the Queens at Thebes	372
The Nile-Bank at Luxor	374
The Great Temple at Karnak	376
M. Legrain's excavation of the Karnak statues	379
Portrait-group of a great noble and his wife, of the time of the XVIIIth Dynasty	381
A tomb fitted up as an Explorer's Residence	382
Stone Object Bearing a Votive Inscription of Arik-dên-ilu	396
Entrance into one of the Galleries or Tunnels of the principal mound at Sherghat	397
Stone tablet of Tukulti-Ninib I, King of Assyria	408
The Ziggurat, or Temple Tower, of the Assyrian city of Calah	409
Work on one of the Rock-Inscriptions of Sennacherib, near Bavian in Assyria	413
The Principal Rock Sculptures in the Gorge of the Gomel near Bavian	414
The rock and citadel of Van	415
Ancient Flight of steps and gallery on the face of the Rock-citadel of Van	417
Part of the ancient fortifications of the city of Van	419
Within the Shrine of E-makh, Temple of the Goddess Nin-makh	425
Trench in the Babylonian Plain, between the mound of the Kasr and Tell Amran ibn-Ali, showing a section of the paved sacred way	426
The Great Dam of Aswân, showing water rushing through the sluices	447

LIST OF ILLUSTRATIONS

                                                                                       PAGE

The Kiosk at Philæ in process of underpinning and restoration, January, 1902 449
The Ancient Quay of Philæ, November, 1904 450
The Rock of Konosso in January, 1902, before the building of the Dam . 452
The Isle of the Konosso, with its inscriptions, November, 1904 . . . 454

EGYPT AND MESOPOTAMIA
In the Light of Recent Excavation and Research

CHAPTER I

THE DISCOVERY OF PREHISTORIC EGYPT

DURING the last ten years our conception of the beginnings of Egyptian antiquity has profoundly altered. When Prof. Maspero published the first volume of his great *Histoire Ancienne des Peuples des l'Orient Classique,* in 1895, Egyptian history, properly so called, still began with the Pyramid-builders, Sneferu, Khufu, and Khafra (Cheops and Chephren), and the legendary lists of earlier kings preserved at Abydos and Sakkâra were still quoted as the only source of knowledge of the time before the IVth Dynasty. Of a prehistoric Egypt nothing was known, beyond a few flint flakes gathered here and there upon the desert plateaus, which might or might not tell of an age when the ancestors of the Pyramid-builders knew only the stone tools and weapons of the primeval savage.

Now, however, the veil which has hidden the beginnings of Egyptian civilization from us has been lifted, and we see things, more or less, as they actually were, unobscured by the traditions of a later day. Until the last few years nothing of the real beginnings of history in either Egypt or Mesopotamia had been found; legend supplied the only material for the reconstruction of the earliest history of the oldest civilized nations of the globe. Nor was it seriously supposed that any relics of prehistoric Egypt or Mesopotamia ever would be found. The antiquity of the known history of these countries already appeared so great that nobody took into consideration the possibility of our discovering a prehistoric Egypt or Mesopotamia; the idea was too remote from practical work. And further, civilization in these countries had lasted so long that it seemed more than probable that all traces of their prehistoric age had long since been swept away. Yet the possibility, which seemed hardly worth a moment's consideration in 1895, is in 1905 an assured reality, at least as far as Egypt is concerned. Prehistoric Babylonia has yet to be discovered. It is true, for example, that at Mukayyar, the site of ancient Ur of the Chaldees, burials in earthenware coffins, in which the skeletons lie in the doubled-up position characteristic of Neolithic interments, have been found; but there is no doubt whatever that these are burials of a much later date, belonging, quite possibly, to the Parthian period. Nothing that may rightfully be termed prehistoric has yet been found in the Euphrates valley, whereas in Egypt prehistoric antiquities are now almost as well known and as well represented in our museums as are the prehistoric antiquities of Europe and America.

With the exception of a few palæoliths from the surface of the Syrian desert, near the Euphrates valley, not a single implement of the Age of Stone has yet been found in Southern Mesopotamia, whereas Egypt has yielded to us the most perfect examples of the flint-knapper's art known, flint tools and weapons more beautiful than the finest that Europe and America can show. The reason is not far to seek. Southern Mesopotamia is an alluvial country, and the ancient cities, which doubtless mark the sites of the oldest settlements in the land, are situated in the alluvial marshy plain between the Tigris and the Euphrates; so that all traces of the Neolithic culture of the country would seem to have disappeared, buried deep beneath city-mounds, clay and marsh. It is the same in the Egyptian Delta, a similar country; and here no traces of the prehistoric culture of Egypt have been found. The attempt to find them was made last year at Buto, which is known to be one of the most antique centres of civilization, and probably was one of the earliest settlements in Egypt, but without success. The infiltration of water had made excavation impossible and had no doubt destroyed everything belonging to the most ancient settlement. It is not going too far to predict that exactly the same thing will be found by any explorer who tries to discover a Neolithic stratum beneath a city-mound of Babylonia. There is little hope that prehistoric Chaldæa will ever be known to us. But in Egypt the conditions are different. The Delta is like Babylonia, it is true; but in the Upper Nile valley the river flows down with but a thin border of alluvial land on either side, through the rocky and hilly desert, the dry Sahara, where rain falls but once in two or three years. Antiquities buried in this soil in the most remote ages are preserved intact as they were first interred, until the modern investigator comes along to look for them. And it is on the desert margin of the valley that the remains of prehistoric Egypt have been found. That is the reason for their perfect preservation till our own day, and why we know prehistoric Egypt so well.

The chief work of Egyptian civilization was the proper irrigation of the alluvial soil, the turning of marsh into cultivated fields, and the reclamation of land from the desert for the purposes of agriculture. Owing to the rainless character of the country, the only means of obtaining water for the crops is by irrigation, and where the fertilizing Nile water cannot be taken by means of canals, there cultivation ends and the desert begins. Before Egyptian civilization, properly so called, began, the valley was a great marsh through which the Nile found its way north to the sea. The half-savage, stone-using ancestors of the civilized Egyptians hunted wild fowl, crocodiles, and hippopotami in the marshy valley; but except in a few isolated settlements on convenient mounds here and there (the forerunners of the later villages), they did not live there. Their settlements were on the dry desert margin, and it was here, upon low tongues of desert hill jutting out into the plain, that they buried their dead. Their simple shallow graves were safe from the flood, and, but for the depredations of jackals and hyenas, here they have remained intact till our own day, and have yielded up to us the facts from which we have derived our knowledge of prehistoric Egypt. Thus it is that we know so much of the Egyptians of the Stone Age, while of their contemporaries in Mesopotamia we know nothing, nor is anything further likely to be discovered.

But these desert cemeteries, with their crowds of oval shallow graves, covered by only a few inches of surface soil, in which the Neolithic Egyptians lie crouched up with their flint implements and polished pottery beside them, are but monuments of the later age of prehistoric Egypt. Long before the Neolithic Egyptian hunted his game in the marshes, and here and there essayed the work of reclamation for the purposes of an incipient agriculture, a far older race inhabited the valley of the Nile. The written records of Egyptian civilization go back four thousand years before Christ, or earlier, and the Neolithic Age of Egypt must go back to a period several thousand years before that. But we can now go back much further still, to the Palæolithic Age of Egypt. At a time when Europe was still covered by the ice and snows of the Glacial Period, and man fought as an equal, hardly yet as a superior, with cave-bear and mammoth, the Palæolithic Egyptians lived on the banks of the Nile. Their habitat was doubtless the desert slopes, often, too, the plateaus themselves; but that they lived entirely upon the plateaus, high up above the Nile marsh, is improbable. There, it is true, we find their flint implements, the great pear-shaped weapons of the types of Chelles, St. Acheul, and Le Moustier, types well known to all who are acquainted with the flint implements of the "Drift" in Europe. And it is there that the theory, generally accepted hitherto, has placed the habitat of the makers and users of these implements.

The idea was that in Palæolithic days, contemporary with the Glacial Age of Northern Europe and America, the climate of Egypt was entirely different from that of later times and of to-day. Instead of dry desert, the mountain plateaus bordering the Nile valley were supposed to have been then covered with forest, through which flowed countless streams to feed the river below. It was suggested that remains of these streams were to be seen in the side ravines, or *wadis*, of the Nile valley, which run up from the low desert on the river level into the hills on either hand. These *wadis* undoubtedly show extensive traces of strong water action; they curve and twist as the streams found their easiest way to the level through the softer strata, they are heaped up with great water-worn boulders, they are hollowed out where waterfalls once fell. They have the appearance of dry watercourses, exactly what any mountain burns would be were the water-supply suddenly cut off for ever, the climate altered from rainy to eternal sun-glare, and every plant and tree blasted, never to grow again. Acting on the supposition that this idea was a correct one, most observers have concluded that the climate of Egypt in remote periods was very different from the dry, rainless one now obtaining. To provide the water for the *wadi* streams, heavy rainfall and forests are desiderated. They were easily supplied, on the hypothesis. Forests clothed the mountain plateaus, heavy rains fell, and the water rushed down to the Nile, carving out the great watercourses which

THE BED OF AN ANCIENT WATERCOURSE IN THE WADIYÊN, THEBES.

remain to this day, bearing testimony to the truth. And the flints, which the Palæolithic inhabitants of the plateau-forests made and used, still lie on the now treeless and sun-baked desert surface.

This is certainly a very weak conclusion. In fact, it seriously damages the whole argument, the watercourses to the contrary notwithstanding. The palæoliths are there. They can be picked up by any visitor. There they lie, great flints of the Drift types, just like those found in the gravel-beds of England and Belgium, on the desert surface where they were made. Undoubtedly where they were made, for the places where they lie are the actual ancient flint workshops, where the flints were chipped. Everywhere around are innumerable flint chips and perfect weapons, burnt black and patinated by ages of sunlight. We are taking one particular spot in the hills of Western Thebes as an example, but there are plenty of others, such as the Wadi esh-Shêkh on the right bank of the Nile opposite Maghagha, whence Mr. H. Seton-Karr has brought back specimens of flint tools of all ages from the Palæolithic to the Neolithic periods.

The Palæolithic flint workshops on the Theban hills have been visited of late years by Mr. Seton-Karr, by Prof. Schweinfurth, Mr. Allen Sturge, and Dr. Blanckenhorn, by Mr. Portch, Mr. Ayrton, and Mr. Hall. The weapons illustrated here were found by Messrs. Hall and Ayrton, and are now preserved in the British Museum. Among these flints shown we notice two fine specimens of the pear-shaped type of St. Acheul, with curious adze-shaped implements of primitive type to left and right. Below, to the right, is a very primitive instrument of Chelléan type, being merely a sharpened pebble. Above, to left and right, are two specimens of the curious half-moon-shaped instruments which are characteristic of the Theban flint

Palæolithic Implements of the Quaternary Period.
From the desert plateau and slopes west of Thebes.

field, and are hardly known elsewhere. All have the beautiful brown patina, which only ages of sunburn can give. The " poignard " type to the left, at the bottom of the plate, is broken off short.

In the smaller illustration we see some remarkable types: two scrapers or knives with strongly marked "bulb of percussion" (the spot where the flint-knapper struck and from which the flakes flew off), a very regular *coup-de-poing* which looks almost like a large arrowhead, and on the right a much weathered and patinated scraper which must be of immemorial age. This came from the top plateau, not from the slopes (or subsidiary plateaus at the head of the *wadis*), as did the great St. Acheulian weapons. The circular object is very remarkable: it is the half of the ring of a " morpholith " (a round flinty accretion often found in the Theban limestone) which has been split, and the split (flat) side carefully bevelled. Several of these interesting objects have been found in conjunction with Palæolithic implements at Thebes. No doubt the flints lie on the actual surface where they were made.

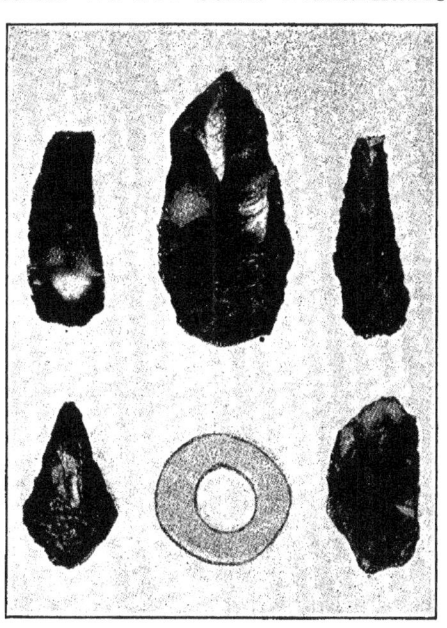

PALÆOLITHIC IMPLEMENTS.
From *Man*, March, 1905.

No later water action has swept them away and covered them with gravel, no later human habitation has hidden them with successive deposits of soil, no gradual deposit of dust and rubbish has buried them deep. They lie as they were left in the far-away Palæolithic Age, and they have lain there till taken away by the modern explorer.

But this is not the case with all the Palæolithic flints of Thebes. In the year 1882 Maj.-Gen. Pitt-Rivers discovered Palæolithic flints in the deposit of diluvial detritus which lies between the cultivation and the mountains on the west bank of the Nile opposite Luxor. Many of these are of the same type as those found on the surface of the mountain plateau which lies at the head of the great *wadi* of the Tombs of the Kings, while the diluvial deposit is at its mouth. The stuff of which the detritus is composed evidently came originally from the high plateau, and was washed down, with the flints, in ancient times.

This is quite conceivable, but how is it that the flints left behind on the plateau remain on the original ancient surface? How is it conceivable that if (on the old theory) these plateaus were in Palæolithic days clothed with forest, the Palæolithic flints could even in a single instance remain undisturbed from Palæolithic times to the present day, when the forest in which they were made and the forest soil on which they reposed have entirely disappeared? If there were woods and forests on the heights, it would seem impossible that we should find, as we do, Palæolithic implements lying *in situ* on the desert surface, around the actual manufactories where they were made. Yet if the constant rainfall and the vegetation of the Libyan desert area in Palæolithic days is all a myth (as it most probably is), how came the embedded palæoliths, found by Gen. Pitt-Rivers, in the bed of diluvial detritus which is apparently *débris* from the plateau brought down by the Palæolithic *wadi* streams?

Water erosion has certainly formed the Theban *wadis*. But this water erosion was probably not that which would be the result of perennial streams flowing down from wooded heights, but of torrents like those of to-day, which fill the *wadis* once in three years or so after heavy rain, but repeated at much closer intervals. We may in fact suppose just so much difference in meteorological conditions as would make it possible for sudden rain-storms to occur over the desert at far more frequent intervals than at present. That would account for the detritus bed at the mouth of the *wadi*, and its embedded flints, and at the same time maintain the general probability of the idea that the desert plateans were desert in Palæolithic days as now, and that early man only knapped his flints up there because he found the flint there. He himself lived on the slopes and nearer the marsh.

This new view seems to be much sounder and more probable than the old one, maintained by Flinders Petrie and Blanckenhorn, according to which the high plateau was the home of man in Palæolithic times, when " the rainfall, as shown by the valley erosion and waterfalls, must have caused an abundant vegetation on the plateau, where man could live and hunt his game."[1] Were this so, it is patent that the Palæolithic flints could not have been found on the desert surface as they are. Mr. H. J. L. Beadnell, of the Geological Survey of

UPPER DESERT PLATEAU, WHERE PALÆOLITHIC IMPLEMENTS ARE FOUND.
Thebes: 1,400 feet above the Nile.

Egypt, to whom we are indebted for the promulgation of the more modern and probable view, says: "Is it certain that the high plateau was then clothed with forests? What evidence is there to show that it differed in any important respect from its present aspect? And if, as I suggest, desert conditions obtained then as now,

[1] Petrie, *Nagada and Ballas*, p. 49.

and man merely worked his flints along the edges of the plateaus overlooking the Nile valley, I see no reason why flint implements, dating even from Palæolithic times, should not in favourable cases still be found in the spots where they were left, surrounded by the flakes struck off in manufacture. On the flat plateaus the occasional rains which fall—once in three or four years—can effect but little transport of material, and merely lower the general level by dissolving the underlying limestone, so that the plateau surface is left with a coating of nodules and blocks of insoluble flint and chert. Flint implements might thus be expected to remain in many localities for indefinite periods, but they would certainly become more or less ' patinated,' pitted on the surface, and rounded at the angles after long exposure to heat, cold, and blown sand." This is exactly the case of the Palæolithic flint tools from the desert plateau.

We do not know whether Palæolithic man in Egypt was contemporary with the cave-man of Europe. We have no means of gauging the age of the Palæolithic Egyptian weapons, as we have for the Neolithic period. The historical (dynastic) period of Egyptian annals began with the unification of the kingdom under one head somewhere about 4500 B.C. At that time copper as well as stone weapons were used, so that we may say that at the beginning of the historical age the Egyptians were living in the " Chalcolithic " period. We can trace the use of copper back for a considerable period anterior to the beginning of the Ist Dynasty, so that we shall probably not be far wrong if we do not bring down the close of the purely Neolithic Age in Egypt—the close of the Age of Stone, properly so called —later than + 5000 B. C. How far back in the remote ages the transition period between the Palæolithic and Neolithic Ages should be placed, it is utterly impossible to say. The use of stone for weapons and implements continued in Egypt as late as the time of the XIIth Dynasty, about 2500 - 2000 B. C. But these XIIth Dynasty stone implements show by their forms how late they are in the history of the Stone Age. The axe heads, for instance, are in form imitations of the copper and bronze axe heads usual at that period; they are stone imitations of metal, instead of the originals on whose model the metal weapons were formed. The flint implements of the XIIth Dynasty were a curious survival from long past ages. After the time of the XIIth Dynasty stone was no longer used for tools or weapons, except for the sacred rite of making the first incision in the dead bodies before beginning the operations of embalming; for this purpose, as Herodotus tells us, an "Ethiopian stone" was used. This was no doubt a knife of flint or chert, like those of the Neolithic ancestors of the Egyptians, and the continued use of a stone knife for this one purpose only is a very interesting instance of a ceremonial survival. We may compare the wigs of British judges.

We have no specimen of a flint knife which can definitely be asserted to have belonged to an embalmer, but of the archaistic flint weapons of the XIIth Dynasty

Flint Knife.
Photograph reproduced from M. de Morgan's *Récherches*.

we have several specimens. They were found by Prof. Petrie at the place named by him "Kahun," the site of a XIIth Dynasty town built near the pyramid of King Usertsen (or Senusret) II at Illahun, at the mouth of the canal leading from the Nile valley into the oasis-province of the Fayyûm. These Kahun flints, and others of probably the same period found by Mr. Seton-Karr at the very ancient flint works in the Wadi esh-Shêkh, are of very coarse and poor workmanship as compared with the stone-knapping triumphs of the late Neolithic and early Chalcolithic periods. The delicacy of the art had all been lost. But the best flint knives of the early period—dating to just a little before the time of the Ist Dynasty, when flint-working had attained its apogee, and copper had just begun to be used—are undoubtedly the most remarkable stone weapons ever made in the world. The grace and utility of the form, the delicacy of the fluted chipping on the side, and the minute care with which the tiny serrations of the cutting edge, serrations so small that often they can hardly be seen with the naked eye, are made, can certainly not be parallelled elsewhere. The art of flint-knapping reached its zenith in Ancient Egypt. The specimen illustrated has a handle covered with gold decorated with incised designs representing animals.

The prehistoric Egyptians may also fairly be said to have attained greater perfection than other peoples in the Neolithic stage of culture, in other arts besides the making of stone tools and weapons. Their pottery is of remarkable perfection. Now that the sites of the

Egyptian prehistoric settlements have been so thoroughly explored by competent archæologists (and, unhappily, as thoroughly pillaged by incompetent natives), this prehistoric Egyptian pottery has become extremely well known. In fact, it is so common that good specimens may be bought anywhere in Egypt for a few piastres. Most museums possess sets of this pottery, of which great quantities have been brought back from Egypt by Prof. Petrie and other explorers. It is of very great interest, artistically as well as historically. The potter's wheel was not yet invented, and all the vases, even those of the most perfect shape, were built up by hand. The perfection of form attained without the aid of the wheel is truly marvellous.

The commonest type of this pottery is a red polished ware vase with black top, due to its having been baked mouth downward in a fire, the ashes of which, according to Prof. Petrie, deoxidized the hæmatite burnishing, and so turned the red colour to black. "In good examples the hæmatite has not only been reduced to black magnetic oxide, but the black has the highest polish, as seen on fine Greek vases. This is probably due to the formation of carbonyl gas in the smothered fire. This gas acts as a solvent of magnetic oxide, and hence allows it to assume a new surface, like the glassy surface of some marbles subjected to solution in water." This black and red ware appears to be the most ancient prehistoric Egyptian pottery known. Later in date are a red ware and a black ware with rude geometrical incised designs, imitating basketwork, and with the incised lines filled in with white. Later again is a buff ware, either plain or decorated with wavy lines, concentric circles, and elaborate drawings of boats sailing on the Nile, ostriches, fish, men and women, and so on. These designs are in deep red. With this elaborate pottery the Neolithic ceramic art of Egypt reached its highest point; in the succeeding period (the beginning of the historic age) there was a decline in workmanship, exhibiting clumsy forms and bad colour, and it is not until the time of the IVth Dynasty that good pottery (a fine polished red) is once more found. Meanwhile the invention of *glazed* pottery, which was unknown to the prehis-

BUFF WARE VASE.

Predynastic period, before 4000 B.C. Photograph reproduced from M. de Morgan's *Recherches*, vol. i.

toric Egyptians, had been made (before the beginning of the Ist Dynasty). The unglazed ware of the first three dynasties was bad, but the new invention of light blue glazed *faïence* (not porcelain properly so called) seems to have made great progress, and we possess fine specimens at the beginning of the Ist Dynasty. The prehistoric Egyptians were also proficient in other arts.

They carved ivory and they worked gold, which is known to have been almost the first metal worked by man; certainly in Egypt it was utilized for ornament even before copper was used for work. We may refer to the illustration of a flint knife with gold handle, already given.[1]

The date of the actual introduction of copper for tools and weapons into Egypt is uncertain, but it seems probable that copper was occasionally used at a very early period. Copper weapons have been found in predynastic graves beside the finest buff pottery with elaborate red designs, so that we may say that when the flint-working and pottery of the Neolithic Egyptians had reached its zenith, the use of copper was already known, and copper weapons were occasionally employed. We can thus speak of the "Chalcolithic" period in Egypt as having already begun at that time, no doubt several centuries before the beginning of the historical or dynastic age. Strictly speaking, the Egyptians remained in the "Chalcolithic" period till the end of the XIIth Dynasty, but in practice it is best to speak of this period, when the word is used, as extending from the time of the finest flint weapons and pottery of the prehistoric age (when the "Neolithic" period may be said to close) till about the IId or IIId Dynasty. By that time the "Bronze," or, rather, "Copper," Age of Egypt had well begun, and already stone was not in common use.

The prehistoric pottery is of the greatest value to

[1] See illustration.

the archæologist, for with its help some idea may be obtained of the succession of periods within the late Neolithic-Chalcolithic Age. The enormous number of prehistoric graves which have been examined enables us to make an exhaustive comparison of the different kinds of pottery found in them, so that we can arrange them in order according to pottery they contained. By this means we obtain an idea of the development of different types of pottery, and the sequence of the types. Thus it is that we can say with some degree of confidence that the black and red ware is the most ancient form, and that the buff with red designs is one of the latest forms of prehistoric pottery. Other objects found in the graves can be classified as they occur with different pottery types.

With the help of the pottery we can thus gain a more or less reliable conspectus of the development of the late "Neolithic" culture of Egypt. This system of "sequence-dating" was introduced by Prof. Petrie, and is certainly very useful. It must not, however, be pressed too far or be regarded as an iron-bound system, with which all subsequent discoveries must be made to fit in by force. It is not to be supposed that all prehistoric pottery developed its series of types in an absolutely orderly manner without deviations or throwsback. The work of man's hands is variable and eccentric, and does not develop or evolve in an undeviating course as the work of nature does. It is a mistake, very often made by anthropologists and archæologists, who forget this elementary fact, to assume "curves of development," and so forth, or semi-savage culture, on absolutely even and regular lines. Human culture has not developed either evenly or regularly, as a matter of fact. Therefore we cannot always be sure that, because the Egyptian black and red pottery does not occur in graves with buff and red, it is for this reason absolutely earlier in date than the latter. Some of the development-sequences may in reality be contemporary with others instead of earlier, and allowance must always be made for aberrations and reversions to earlier types.

This caveat having been entered, however, we may provisionally accept Prof. Petrie's system of sequence-dating as giving the best classification of the prehistoric antiquities according to development. So it may fairly be said that, *as far as we know*, the black and red pottery ("sequence-date 30—") is the most ancient Neolithic Egyptian ware known; that the buff and red did not begin to be used till about "sequence-date 45;" that bone and ivory carvings were commonest in the earlier period ("sequence-dates 30-50"); that copper was almost unknown till "sequence-date 50," and so on. The arbitrary numbers used range from 30 to 80, in order to allow for possible earlier and later additions, which may be rendered necessary by the progress of discovery. The numbers are of course as purely arbitrary and relative as those of the different thermometrical systems, but they afford a convenient system of arrangement. The products of the prehistoric Egyptians are, so to speak, distributed on a conventional plan over a scale numbered from 30 to 80, 30 representing the beginning and 80 the close of the term, so far as its close has as yet been ascertained. It is probable that "sequence-date 80" more or less accurately marks the beginning of the dynastic or historical period.

This hypothetically chronological classification is, as has been said, due to Prof. Petrie, and has been adopted by Mr. Randall-MacIver and other students of prehistoric Egypt in their work.[1] To Prof. Petrie then is due the credit of systematizing the study of Egyptian prehistoric antiquities; but the further credit of having *discovered* these antiquities themselves and settled their date belongs not to him but to the distinguished French archæologist, M. J. de Morgan, who was for several years director of the museum at Giza, and is now chief of the French archæological delegation in Persia, which has made of late years so many important discoveries. The proof of the prehistoric date of this class of antiquities was given, not by Prof. Petrie after his excavations at Dendera in 1897-8, but by M. de Morgan in his volume, *Recherches sur les Origines de l'Égypte: l'Âge de la Pierre et les Métaux*, published in 1895-6. In this book the true chronological position of the prehistoric antiquities was pointed out, and the existence of an Egyptian Stone Age finally decided. M. de Morgan's work was based on careful study of the results of excavations carried on for several years by the Egyptian government in various parts of Egypt, in the course of which a large number of cemeteries of the

[1] *El Amra and Abydos*, Egypt Exploration Fund, 1902.

primitive type had been discovered. It was soon evident to M. de Morgan that these primitive graves, with their unusual pottery and flint implements, could be nothing less than the tombs of the prehistoric Egyptians, the Egyptians of the Stone Age.

Objects of the prehistoric period had been known to the museums for many years previously, but owing to the uncertainty of their provenance and the absence of knowledge of the existence of the primitive cemeteries, no scientific conclusions had been arrived at with regard to them; and it was not till the publication of M. de Morgan's book that they were recognized and classified as prehistoric. The necropoles investigated by M. de Morgan and his assistants extended from Kawâmil in the north, about twenty miles north of Abydos, to Edfu in the south. The chief cemeteries between these two points were those of Bêt Allam, Saghel el-Baglieh, el-'Amra, Nakâda, Tûkh, and Gebelên. All the burials were of simple type, analogous to those of the Neolithic races in the rest of the world. In a shallow, oval grave, excavated often but a few inches below the surface of the soil, lay the body, cramped up with the knees to the chin, sometimes in a rough box of pottery, more often with only a mat to cover it. Ready to the hand of the dead man were his flint weapons and tools, and the usual red and black, or buff and red, pots lay beside him; originally, no doubt, they had been filled with the funeral meats, to sustain the ghost in the next world. Occasionally a simple copper weapon was found. With the body were also buried slate palettes for grinding the green eye-paint which the Egyptians loved even at this early period. These are often carved to suggest the forms of animals, such as birds, bats, tortoises, goats, etc.; on others are fantastic creatures with two heads. Combs of bone, too, are found, ornamented in a similar way with birds' or goats' heads, often double. And most interesting of all are the small bone and ivory figures of men and women which are also found. These usually have little blue beads for eyes, and are of the quaintest and naïvest appearance conceivable. Here we have an elderly man with a long pointed beard, there two women with inane smiles upon their countenances, here another woman, of better work this time, with a child slung across her shoulder. This figure, which is in the British Museum, must be very late, as prehistoric Egyptian antiquities go. It is almost as good in style as the early Ist Dynasty objects. Such were the objects which the simple piety of the early Egyptian prompted him to bury with the bodies of his dead, in order that they might find solace and contentment in the other world.

All the prehistoric cemeteries are of this type, with the graves pressed closely together, so that they often impinge upon one another. The nearness of the graves to the surface is due to the exposed positions, at the entrances to *wadis*, in which the primitive cemeteries are usually found. The result is that they are always swept by the winds, which prevent the desert sand from accumulating over them, and so have preserved the original level of the ground. From their proximity to the surface they are often found disturbed, more often by the agency of jackals than that of man.

Contemporaneously with M. de Morgan's explorations, Prof. Flinders Petrie and Mr. J. Quibell had, in the winter of 1894-5, excavated in the districts of Tûkh and Nakâda, on the west bank of the Nile opposite Koptos, a series of extensive cemeteries of the primitive type, from which they obtained a large number of antiquities, published in their volume *Nagada and Ballas*. The plates giving representations of the antiquities found were of the highest interest, but the scientific value of the letter-press is vitiated by the fact that the true historical position of the antiquities was not perceived by their discoverers, who came to the conclusion that these remains were those of a "New Race" of Libyan invaders. This race, they supposed, had entered Egypt after the close of the flourishing period of the "Old Kingdom" at the end of the VIth Dynasty, and had occupied part of the Nile valley from that time till the period of the Xth Dynasty.

This conclusion was proved erroneous by M. de Morgan almost as soon as made, and the French archæologist's identification of the primitive remains as predynastic was at once generally accepted. It was obvious that a hypothesis of the settlement of a stone-using barbaric race in the midst of Egypt at so late a date as the period immediately preceding the XIIth Dynasty, a race which mixed in no way with the native Egyptians themselves, and left no trace of their influence upon the later Egyptians, was one which demanded greater faith than the simple explanation of M. de Morgan.

The error of the British explorers was at once admitted by Mr. Quibell, in his volume on the excavations of 1897 at el-Kab, published in 1898.[1] Mr. Quibell at once found full and adequate confirmation of M. de Morgan's discovery in his diggings at el-Kab. Prof. Petrie admitted the correctness of M. de Morgan's views in the preface to his volume *Diospolis Parva*, published three years later in 1901.[2] The preface to the first volume of M. de Morgan's book contained a generous recognition of the method and general accuracy of Prof. Petrie's excavations, which contrasted favourably, according to M. de Morgan, with the excavations of others, generally carried on without scientific control, and with the sole aim of obtaining antiquities or literary texts.[3] That M. de Morgan's own work was carried out as scientifically and as carefully is evident from the fact that his conclusions as to the chronological position of the prehistoric antiquities have been shown to be correct. To describe M. de Morgan's discovery as a "happy guess," as has been done, is therefore beside the mark.

Another most important British excavation was that carried on by Messrs. Randall-MacIver and Wilkin at el-'Amra. The imposing lion-headed promontory of el-'Amra stands out into the plain on the west bank

[1] *El-Kab.* Egyptian Research Account, 1897, p. 11.
[2] *Diospolis Parva.* Egypt Exploration Fund, 1901, p. 2.
[3] *Recherches: Age de la Pierre*, p. xiii.

of the Nile about five miles south of Abydos. At the foot of this hill M. de Morgan found a very extensive prehistoric necropolis, which he examined, but did not excavate to any great extent, and the work of thoroughly excavating it was performed by Messrs. Randall-MacIver and Wilkin for the Egypt Exploration Fund. The results have thrown very great light upon the prehistoric culture of Egypt, and burials of all prehistoric types, some of them previously unobserved, were found. Among the most interesting are burials in pots, which have also been found by Mr. Garstang in a predynastic necropolis at Ragagna, north of Abydos. One of the more remarkable observations made at el-'Amra was the progressive development of the tombs from the simplest pot-burial to a small brick chamber, the embryo of the brick tombs of the Ist Dynasty. Among the objects recovered from this site may be mentioned a pottery model of oxen, a box in the shape of a model hut, and a slate " palette " with what is perhaps the oldest Egyptian hieroglyph known, a representation of the fetish-sign of the god Min, in relief. All these are preserved in the British Museum. The skulls of the bodies found were carefully preserved for craniometric examination.

In 1901 an extensive prehistoric cemetery was being excavated by Messrs. Reisner and Lythgoe at Nag' ed-Dêr, opposite Girga, and at el-Ahaiwa, further north, another prehistoric necropolis has been excavated by these gentlemen, working for the University of California. The cemetery of Nag' ed-Dêr is of the usual prehistoric type, with its multitudes of small oval graves, excavated just a little way below the surface. Graves of this kind are the most primitive of all. Those at el-'Amra are usually more developed, often, as has been noted, rising to the height of regular brick tombs. They are evidently later, nearer to the time of the Ist

CAMP OF THE EXPEDITION OF THE UNIVERSITY OF CALIFORNIA AT NAG' ED-DÊR, 1901.

Dynasty. The position of the Nag' ed-Dêr cemetery is also characteristic. It lies on the usual low ridge at the entrance to a desert *wadi*, which is itself one of the most picturesque in this part of Egypt, with its chaos of great boulders and fallen rocks. An illustration of the camp of Mr. Reisner's expedition at Nag' ed-Dêr is given above. The excavations of the University of California are carried out with the greatest possible care and are financed with the greatest possible liberality. Mr. Reisner has therefore been able to keep an absolutely complete photographic record of everything, even down to the successive stages in the opening of a tomb, which will be of the greatest use to science when published.

For a detailed study of the antiquities of the prehistoric period the publications of Prof. Petrie, Mr. Quibell, and Mr. Randall-MacIver are more useful than that of M. de Morgan, who does not give enough details. Every atom of evidence is given in the publications of the British explorers, whereas it is a characteristic of French work to give brilliant conclusions, beautifully illustrated, without much of the evidence on which the conclusions are based. This kind of work does not appeal to the Anglo-Saxon mind, which takes nothing on trust, even from the most renowned experts, and always wants to know the why and wherefore. The complete publication of evidence which marks the British work will no doubt be met with, if possible in even more complete detail, in the American work of Messrs. Reisner, Lythgoe, and Mace (the last-named is an Englishman) for the University of California, when published. The question of speedy *versus* delayed publication is a very vexing one. Prof. Petrie prefers to publish as speedily as possible; six months after the season's work in Egypt is done, the full publication with photographs of everything appears. Mr. Reisner and the French explorers prefer to publish nothing until they have exhaustively studied the whole of the evidence, and can extract nothing more from it. This would be admirable if the French published their discoveries fully, but they do not. Even M. de Morgan has not approached the fulness of detail which characterizes British work and which will characterize Mr. Reisner's publication when it appears. The only drawback to this method is that general interest in the particular excavations described tends to pass away before the full description appears.

Prof. Petrie has explored other prehistoric sites at Abadiya, and Mr. Quibell at el-Kab. M. de Morgan and his assistants have examined a large number of sites, ranging from the Delta to el-Kab. Further research has shown that some of the sites identified by M. de Morgan as prehistoric are in reality of much later date, for example, Kahun, where the late flints of XIIth Dynasty date were found. He notes that "large numbers of Neolithic flint weapons are found in the desert on the borders of the Fayyûm, and at Helwân, south of Cairo," and that all the important necropoles and kitchen-middens of the predynastic people are to be found in the districts of Abydos and Thebes, from el-Kawâmil in the North to el-Kab in the South. It is of course too soon to assert with confidence that there are no prehistoric remains in any other part of Egypt, especially in the long tract between the Fayyûm and the district of Abydos, but up to the present time none have been found in this region.

This geographical distribution of the prehistoric

remains fits in curiously with the ancient legend concerning the origin of the ancestors of the Egyptians in Upper Egypt, and supports the much discussed theory that they came originally to the Nile valley from the shores of the Red Sea by way of the Wadi Hammamat, which debouches on to the Nile in the vicinity of Koptos and Kus, opposite Ballas and Tûkh. The supposition seems a very probable one, and it may well be that the earliest Egyptians entered the valley of the Nile by the route suggested and then spread northwards and southwards in the valley. The fact that their remains are not found north of el-Kawâmil nor south of el-Kab might perhaps be explained by the supposition that, when they had extended thus far north and south from their original place of arrival, they passed from the primitive Neolithic condition to the more highly developed copper-using culture of the period which immediately preceded the establishment of the monarchy. The Neolithic weapons of the Fayyûm and Helwân would then be the remains of a different people, which inhabited the Delta and Middle Egypt in very early times. This people may have been of Mediterranean stock, akin to the primitive inhabitants of Palestine, Greece, Italy, and Spain; and they no doubt were identical with the inhabitants of Lower Egypt who were overthrown and conquered by Kha-sekhem and the other Southern founders of the monarchy (who belonged to the race which had come from the Red Sea by the Wadi Hammamat), and so were the ancestors of the later natives of Lower Egypt. Whether the Southerners, whose primitive remains we find from el-Kawâmil to el-Kab, were of the same race as the Northerners whom they conquered, cannot be decided. The skull-form of the Southerners agrees with that of the Mediterranean races. But we have no necropoles of the Northerners to tell us much of their peculiarities. We have nothing but their flint arrowheads.

But it should be observed that, in spite of the present absence of all primitive remains (whether mere flints, or actual graves with bodies and relics) of the primeval population between the Fayyûm and el-Kawâmil, there is no proof that the primitive race of Upper Egypt was not coterminous and identical with that of the lower country. It might therefore be urged that the whole Neolithic population was "Mediterranean" by its skull-form and body-structure, and specifically "Nilotic" (indigenous Egyptian) in its culture-type. This is quite possible, but we have again to account for the legends of distant origin on the Red Sea coast, the probability that one element of the Egyptian population was of extraneous origin and came from the east into the Nile valley near Koptos, and finally the historical fact of an advance of the early dynastic Egyptians from the South to the conquest of the North. The latter fact might of course be explained as a civil war analogous to that between Thebes and Asyût in the time of the IXth Dynasty, but against this explanation is to be set the fact that the contemporary monuments of the Southerners exhibit the men of the North as of foreign and non-Egyptian ethnic type, resembling Libyans. It is possible that they were akin to the Libyans; and this would square very well with the first theory, but it may also be made to fit in with a development of the second, which has been generally accepted.

According to this view, the whole primitive Neolithic population of North and South was Nilotic, indigenous in origin, and akin to the "Mediterraneans" of Prof. Sergi and the other ethnologists. It was not this population, the stone-users whose necropoles have been found by Messrs. de Morgan, Petrie, and MacIver, that entered the Nile valley by the Wadi Hammamat. This was another race of different ethnic origin, which came from the Red Sea toward the end of the Neolithic period, and, being of higher civilization than the native Nilotes, assumed the lordship over them, gave a great impetus to the development of their culture, and started at once the institution of monarchy, the knowledge of letters, and the use of metals. The chiefs of this superior tribe founded the monarchy, conquered the North, unified the kingdom, and began Egyptian history. From many indications it would seem probable that these conquerors were of Babylonian origin, or that the culture they brought with them (possibly from Arabia) was ultimately of Babylonian origin. They themselves would seem to have been Semites, or rather proto-Semites, who came from Arabia to Africa by way of the straits of Bab el-Mandeb, and proceeded up the coast to about the neighbourhood of Kusêr, whence the Wadi Hammamat offered them an open road to the valley of the Nile. By this route they may have entered

Egypt, bringing with them a civilization, which, like that of the other Semites, had been profoundly influenced and modified by that of the Sumerian inhabitants of Babylonia. This Semitic-Sumerian culture, mingling with that of the Nilotes themselves, produced the civilization of Ancient Egypt as we know it.

This is a very plausible hypothesis, and has a great deal of evidence in its favour. It seems certain that in the early dynastic period two races lived in Egypt, which differed considerably in type, and also, apparently, in burial customs. The later Egyptians always buried the dead lying on their backs, extended at full length. During the period of the Middle Kingdom (XIth-XIIIth Dynasties) the head was usually turned over on to the left side, in order that the dead man might look through the two great eyes painted on that side of the coffin. Afterward the rigidly extended position was always adopted. The Neolithic Egyptians, however, buried the dead lying wholly on the left side and in a contracted position, with the knees drawn up to the chin. The bodies were not embalmed, and the extended position and mummification were never used. Under the IVth Dynasty we find in the necropolis of Mêdûm (north of the Fayyûm) the two positions used simultaneously, and the extended bodies are mummified. The contracted bodies are skeletons, as in the case of most of the predynastic bodies. When these are found with flesh, skin, and hair intact, their preservation is due to the dryness of the soil and the preservative salts it contains, not to intentional embalming, which was evidently introduced by those who employed the extended position in burial. The contracted position is found as late as the Vth Dynasty at Dashasha, south of the Fayyûm, but after that date it is no longer found.

The conclusion is obvious that the contracted position without mummification, which the Neolithic people used, was supplanted in the early dynastic period by the extended position with mummification, and by the time of the VIth Dynasty it was entirely superseded. This points to the supersession of the burial customs of the indigenous Neolithic race by those of another race which conquered and dominated the indigenes. And, since the extended burials of the IVth Dynasty are evidently those of the higher nobles, while the contracted ones are those of inferior people, it is probable that the customs of extended burial and embalming were introduced by a foreign race which founded the Egyptian monarchical state, with its hierarchy of nobles and officials, and in fact started Egyptian civilization on its way. The conquerors of the North were thus not the descendants of the Neolithic people of the South, but their conquerors; in fact, they dominated the indigenes both of North and South, who will then appear (since we find the custom of contracted burial in the North at Dashasha and Mêdûm) to have originally belonged to the same race.

The conquering race is that which is supposed to have been of Semitic or proto-Semitic origin, and to have brought elements of Sumerian culture to savage

Egypt. The reasons advanced for this supposition are the following:—

(1) Just as the Egyptian race was evidently compounded of two elements, of conquered " Mediterraneans " and conquering x, so the Egyptian language is evidently compounded of two elements, the one Nilotic, perhaps related in some degree to the Berber dialects of North Africa, the other not x, but evidently Semitic.

(2) Certain elements of the early dynastic civilization, which do not appear in that of the earlier predynastic period, resemble well-known elements of the civilization of Babylonia. We may instance the use of the cylinder-seal, which died out in Egypt in the time of the XVIIIth Dynasty, but was always used in Babylonia from the earliest to the latest times. The early Egyptian mace-head is of exactly the same type as the early Babylonian one. In the British Museum is an Egyptian mace-head of red breccia, which is identical in shape and size with one from Babylonia (also in the museum) bearing the name of Shargani-shar-ali (*i. e.* Sargon, King of Agade), one of the earliest Chaldæan monarchs, who must have lived about the same time as the Egyptian kings of the IId—IIId Dynasties, to which period the Egyptian mace-head may also be approximately assigned. The Egyptian art of the earliest dynasties bears again a remarkable resemblance to that of early Babylonia. It is not till the time of the IId Dynasty that Egyptian art begins to take upon itself the regular form which we know so well, and not till that of the IVth that this form was finally crystallized.

Under the Ist Dynasty we find the figure of man or, to take other instances, that of a lion, or a hawk, or a snake, often treated in a style very different from that in which we are accustomed to see a man, a lion, a hawk, or a snake depicted in works of the later period. And the striking thing is that these early representations, which differ so much from what we find in later Egyptian art, curiously resemble the works of early Babylonian art, of the time of the patesis of Shirpurla or the Kings Shargani-shar-ali and Narâm-Sin. One of the best known relics of the early art of Babylonia is the famous " Stele of Vultures " now in Paris. On this we see the enemies of Eannadu, one of the early rulers of Shirpurla, cast out to be devoured by the vultures. On an Egyptian relief of slate, evidently originally dedicated in a temple as a record of some historical event, and dating from the beginning of the Ist Dynasty (practically contemporary, according to our latest knowledge, with Eannadu), we have an almost exactly similar scene of captives being cast out into the desert, and devoured by lions and vultures. The two reliefs are curiously alike in their clumsy, naïve style of art. A further point is that the official represented on the stele, who appears to be thrusting one of the bound captives out to die, wears a long fringed garment of Babylonish cut, quite different from the clothes of the later Egyptians.

(3) There are evidently two distinct and different main strata in the fabric of Egyptian religion. On the one hand we find a mass of myth and religious belief of very primitive, almost savage, cast, combining a

worship of the actual dead in their tombs—which were supposed to communicate and thus form a veritable "underworld," or, rather, "under-Egypt"—with veneration of magic animals, such as jackals, cats, hawks, and crocodiles. On the other hand, we have a sun and sky worship of a more elevated nature, which does not seem to have amalgamated with the earlier fetishism and corpse-worship until a comparatively late period. The main seats of the sun-worship were at Heliopolis in the Delta and at Edfu in Upper Egypt. Heliopolis seems always to have been a centre of light and leading in Egypt, and it is, as is well known, the On of the Bible, at whose university the Jewish lawgiver Moses is related to have been educated "in all the wisdom of the Egyptians." The philosophical theories of the priests of the Sun-gods, Rā-Harmachis and Tum, at Heliopolis seem to have been the source from which sprang the monotheistic heresy of the Disk-Worshippers (in the time of the XVIIIth Dynasty), who, under the guidance of the reforming King Akhunaten, worshipped only the disk of the sun as the source of all life, the door in heaven, so to speak, through which the hidden One Deity poured forth heat and light, the origin of life upon the earth. Very early in Egyptian history the Heliopolitans gained the upper hand, and the Rā-worship (under the Vth Dynasty, the apogee of the Old Kingdom) came to the front, and for the first time the kings took the afterwards time-honoured royal title of "Son of the Sun." It appears then as a more or less foreign importation into the Nile valley, and bears most

Under the Ist Dynasty we find the figure of man or, to take other instances, that of a lion, or a hawk, or a snake, often treated in a style very different from that in which we are accustomed to see a man, a lion, a hawk, or a snake depicted in works of the later period. And the striking thing is that these early representations, which differ so much from what we find in later Egyptian art, curiously resemble the works of early Babylonian art, of the time of the patesis of Shirpurla or the Kings Shargani-shar-ali and Narâm-Sin. One of the best known relics of the early art of Babylonia is the famous " Stele of Vultures " now in Paris. On this we see the enemies of Eannadu, one of the early rulers of Shirpurla, cast out to be devoured by the vultures. On an Egyptian relief of slate, evidently originally dedicated in a temple as a record of some historical event, and dating from the beginning of the Ist Dynasty (practically contemporary, according to our latest knowledge, with Eannadu), we have an almost exactly similar scene of captives being cast out into the desert, and devoured by lions and vultures. The two reliefs are curiously alike in their clumsy, naïve style of art. A further point is that the official represented on the stele, who appears to be thrusting one of the bound captives out to die, wears a long fringed garment of Babylonish cut, quite different from the clothes of the later Egyptians.

(3) There are evidently two distinct and different main strata in the fabric of Egyptian religion. On the one hand we find a mass of myth and religious belief of very primitive, almost savage, cast, combining a

worship of the actual dead in their tombs—which were supposed to communicate and thus form a veritable " underworld," or, rather, " under-Egypt "—with veneration of magic animals, such as jackals, cats, hawks, and crocodiles. On the other hand, we have a sun and sky worship of a more elevated nature, which does not seem to have amalgamated with the earlier fetishism and corpse-worship until a comparatively late period. The main seats of the sun-worship were at Heliopolis in the Delta and at Edfu in Upper Egypt. Heliopolis seems always to have been a centre of light and leading in Egypt, and it is, as is well known, the On of the Bible, at whose university the Jewish lawgiver Moses is related to have been educated " in all the wisdom of the Egyptians." The philosophical theories of the priests of the Sun-gods, Rā-Harmachis and Tum, at Heliopolis seem to have been the source from which sprang the monotheistic heresy of the Disk-Worshippers (in the time of the XVIIIth Dynasty), who, under the guidance of the reforming King Akhunaten, worshipped only the disk of the sun as the source of all life, the door in heaven, so to speak, through which the hidden One Deity poured forth heat and light, the origin of life upon the earth. Very early in Egyptian history the Heliopolitans gained the upper hand, and the Rā-worship (under the Vth Dynasty, the apogee of the Old Kingdom) came to the front, and for the first time the kings took the afterwards time-honoured royal title of " Son of the Sun." It appears then as a more or less foreign importation into the Nile valley, and bears most undoubtedly a Semitic impress. Its two chief seats were situated, the one, Heliopolis, in the North on the eastern edge of the Delta,—just where an early Semitic settlement from over the desert might be expected to be found,—the other, Edfu, in the Upper Egyptian territory south of the Thebaïd, Koptos, and the Wadi Hammamat, and close to the chief settlement of the earliest kings and the most ancient capital of Upper Egypt.

(4) The custom of burying at full length was evidently introduced into Egypt by the second, or x race. The Neolithic Egyptians buried in the cramped position. The early Babylonians buried at full length, as far as we know. On the same "Stele of Vultures," which has already been mentioned, we see the burying at full length of dead warriors.[1] There is no trace of any *early* burial in Babylonia in the cramped position. The tombs at Warka (Erech) with cramped bodies in pottery coffins are of very late date. A further point arises with regard to embalming. The Neolithic Egyptians did not embalm the dead. Usually their cramped bodies are found as skeletons. When they are mummified, it is merely owing to the preservative action of the salt in the soil, not to any process of embalming. The second, or x race, however, evidently introduced the custom of embalming as well as that of burial at full length and the use of coffins. The Neolithic Egyptian used no box or coffin, the nearest approach to this being a pot, which was inverted over the coiled up body. Usually only a mat was put over the body. Now it is evident

[1] See illustration.

that Babylonians and Assyrians, who buried the dead at full length in chests, had some knowledge of embalming. An Assyrian king tells us how he buried his royal father:—

> "Within the grave, the secret place,
> In kingly oil, I gently laid him.
> The grave-stone marketh his resting-place.
> With mighty bronze I sealed its entrance,
> And I protected it with an incantation."

The "kingly oil" was evidently used with the idea of preserving the body from decay. Salt also was used to preserve the dead, and Herodotus says that the Babylonians buried in honey, which was also used by the Egyptians. No doubt the Babylonian method was less perfect than the Egyptian, but the comparison is an interesting one, when taken in connection with the other points of resemblance mentioned above.

We find, then, that an analysis of the Egyptian language reveals a Semitic element in it; that the early dynastic culture had certain characteristics which were unknown to the Neolithic Egyptians but are closely parallelled in early Babylonia; that there were two elements in the Egyptian religion, one of which seems to have originally belonged to the Neolithic people, while the other has a Semitic appearance; and that there were two sets of burial customs in early Egypt, one, that of the Neolithic people, the other evidently that of a conquering race, which eventually prevailed over the former; these later rites were analogous to those of the Babylonians and Assyrians, though differing from them in points of detail. The conclusion is that the x or conquering race was Semitic and brought to Egypt the Semitic elements in the Egyptian religion and a culture originally derived from that of the Sumerian inhabitants of Babylonia, the non-Semitic parent of all Semitic civilizations.

The question now arises, how did this Semitic people reach Egypt? We have the choice of two points of entry: First, Heliopolis in the North, where the Semitic sun-worship took root, and, second, the Wadi Hammamat in the South, north of Edfu, the southern centre of sun-worship, and Hierakonpolis (Nekheb-Nekhen), the capital of the Upper Egyptian kingdom which existed before the foundation of the monarchy. The legends which seem to bring the ancestors of the Egyptians from the Red Sea coast have already been mentioned. They are closely connected with the worship of the Sky and Sun god Horus of Edfu. Hathor, his nurse, the " House of Horus," the centre of whose worship was at Dendera, immediately opposite the mouth of the Wadi Hammamat, was said to have come from Ta-neter, " The Holy Land," *i. e.* Abyssinia or the Red Sea coast, with the company or *paut* of the gods. Now the Egyptians always seem to have had some idea that they were connected racially with the inhabitants of the Land of Punt or Puenet, the modern Abyssinia and Somaliland. In the time of the XVIIIth Dynasty they depicted the inhabitants of Punt as greatly resembling themselves in form, feature, and dress, and as wearing the little turned-up beard which was worn by the Egyptians of the earliest times, but even as early as the IVth Dynasty was reserved for the gods. Further, the word *Punt* is always written without the hieroglyph determinative of a foreign country, thus showing that the Egyptians did not regard the Punites as foreigners. This certainly looks as if the Punites were a portion of the great migration from Arabia, left behind on the African shore when the rest of the wandering people pressed on northwards to the Wadi Hammamat and the Nile. It may be that the modern Gallas and Abyssinians are descendants of these Punites.

Now the Sky-god of Edfu is in legend a conquering hero who advances down the Nile valley, with his *Mesniu*, or "Smiths," to overthrow the people of the North, whom he defeats in a great battle near Dendera. This may be a reminiscence of the first fights of the invaders with the Neolithic inhabitants. The other form of Horus, "Horus, son of Isis," has also a body of retainers, the *Shemsu-Heru*, or "Followers of Horus," who are spoken of in late texts as the rulers of Egypt before the monarchy. They evidently correspond to the dynasties of *Manes*, Νεκύες, or "Ghosts," of Manetho, and are probably intended for the early kings of Hierakonpolis.

The mention of the Followers of Horus as "Smiths" is very interesting, for it would appear to show that the Semitic conquerors were notable as metal-users, that, in fact, their conquest was that old story in the dawn of the world's history, the utter overthrow and subjection of the stone-users by the metal-users, the primeval tragedy of the supersession of flint by copper. This may be, but if the "Smiths" were the Semitic conquerors who founded the kingdom, it would appear that the use of copper was known in Egypt to some extent before their arrival, for we find it in the graves of the late Neolithic Egyptians, very sparsely from "sequence-date 30" to "45," but afterwards more commonly. It was evidently becoming known. The supposition, however, that the "Smiths" were the Semitic conquerors, and that they won their way by the aid of their superior weapons of metal, may be provisionally accepted.

In favour of the view which would bring the conquerors by way of the Wadi Hammamat, an interesting discovery may be quoted. Immediately opposite Dendera, where, according to the legend, the battle between the *Mesniu* and the aborigines took place, lies Koptos, at the mouth of the Wadi Hammamat. Here, in 1894, underneath the pavement of the ancient temple, Prof. Petrie found remains which he then diagnosed as belonging to the most ancient epoch of Egyptian history. Among them were some extremely archaic statues of the god Min, on which were curious scratched drawings of bears, *crioceras*-shells, elephants walking over hills, etc., of the most primitive description. With them were lions' heads and birds of a style then unknown, but which we now know to belong to the period of the beginning of the Ist Dynasty. But the statues of Min are older. The *crioceras*-shells belong to the Red Sea. Are we to see in these statues the holy images of the conquerors from the Red Sea who reached the Nile valley by way of the Wadi Hammamat, and set up the first memorials of their presence at Koptos? It may be so, or the Min statues may be older than the conquerors, and belong to the Neolithic race, since Min and his fetish (which we find on the slate palette from el-'Amra, already mentioned) seem to belong to the indigenous Nilotes. In any case we have in these statues, two of which are in the Ashmolean Museum at Oxford, probably the most ancient cult-images in the world.

This theory, which would make all the Neolithic inhabitants of Egypt one people, who were conquered by a Semitic race, bringing a culture of Sumerian origin to Egypt by way of the Wadi Hammamat, is that generally accepted at the present time. It may, however, eventually prove necessary to modify it. For reasons given above, it may well be that the Neolithic population was itself not indigenous, and that it reached the Nile valley by way of the Wadi Hammamat, spreading north and south from the mouth of the *wadi*. It may also be considered probable that a Semitic wave invaded Egypt by way of the Isthmus of Suez, where the early sun-cultus of Heliopolis probably marks a primeval Semitic settlement. In that case it would seem that the *Mesniu* or " Smiths," who introduced the use of metal, would have to be referred to the originally Neolithic pre-Semitic people, who certainly were acquainted with the use of copper, though not to any great extent. But this is not a necessary supposition. The *Mesniu* are closely connected with the Sky-god Horus, who was possibly of Semitic origin, and another Semitic wave, quite distinct from that which entered Egypt by way of the Isthmus, may very well also have reached Egypt by the Wadi Hammamat, or, equally possibly, from the far south, coming down to the Nile from the Abyssinian mountains. The legend of the coming of Hathor from Ta-neter may refer to some such wandering, and we know that the Egyptians of the Old Kingdom communicated with the Land of Punt, not by way of the Red Sea coast as Hatshepsut did, but by way of the Upper Nile. This would tally well with the march of the *Mesniu* northwards from Edfu to their battle with the forces of Set at Dendera.

In any case, at the dawn of connected Egyptian history, we find two main centres of civilization in Egypt, Heliopolis and Buto in the Delta in the North, and Edfu and Hierakonpolis in the South. Here were established at the beginning of the Chalcolithic stage of culture, we may say, two kingdoms, of Lower and Upper Egypt, which were eventually united by the superior arms of the kings of Upper Egypt, who imposed their rule upon the North but at the same time removed their capital thither. The dualism of Buto and Hierakonpolis really lasted throughout Egyptian history. The king was always called "Lord of the Two Lands," and wore the crowns of Upper and Lower Egypt; the snakes of Buto and Nekhebet (the goddess of Nekheb, opposite Nekhen or Hierakonpolis) always typified the united kingdom. This dualism of course often led to actual division and reversion to the predynastic order of things, as, for instance, in the time of the XXIst Dynasty.

It might well seem that both the impulses to culture development in the North and South came from Semitic inspiration, and that it was to the Semitic invaders in North and South that the founding of the two kingdoms was due. This may be true to some extent, but it is at the same time very probable that the first development of political culture at Hierakonpolis was really of pre-Semitic origin. The kingdom of Buto, since its capital is situated so near to the seacoast, may have owed its origin to oversea Mediterranean connections. There is much in the political constitution of later Egypt which seems to have been of indigenous and pre-Semitic origin. Especially does this seem to be so in the case of the division and organization of the country into nomes. It is obvious that so soon as agriculture began to be practised on a large scale, boundaries would be formed, and in the unique conditions of Egypt, where all boundaries disappear beneath the inundation every year, it is evident that the fixing of division-lines as permanently as possible by means of landmarks was early essayed. We can therefore with confidence assign the formation of the nomes to very early times. Now the names of the nomes and the symbols or emblems by which they were distinguished are of very great interest in this connection. They are nearly all figures of the magic animals of the primitive religion, and fetish-emblems of the older deities. The names are, in fact, those of the territories of the Neolithic Egyptian tribes, and their emblems are those of the protecting tribal demons. The political divisions of the country seem, then, to be of extremely ancient origin, and if the nomes go back to a time before the Semitic invasions, so may also the kingdoms of the South and North.

Of these predynastic kingdoms we know very little, except from legendary sources. The Northerners who were conquered by Aha, Narmer, and Khāsekhemui do not look very much like Egyptians, but rather resemble Semites or Libyans. On the "Stele of Palermo," a chronicle of early kings inscribed in the period of the Vth Dynasty, we have a list of early kings of the North, — Seka, Desau, Tiu, Tesh, Nihab, Uatjāntj, Mekhe. The names are primitive in form. We know nothing more about them. Last year Mr. C. T. Currelly attempted to excavate at Buto, in order to find traces of the predynastic kingdom, but owing to the infiltration of water his efforts were unsuccessful. It is improbable that anything is now left of the most ancient period at that site, as the conditions in the Delta are so very different from those obtaining in Upper Egypt. There, at Hierakonpolis, and at el-Kab on the opposite bank of the Nile, the sites of the ancient cities Nekhen and Nekheb, the excavators have been very successful. The work was carried out by Messrs. Quibell and Green, in the years 1891-9. Prehistoric burials were found on the hills near by, but the larger portion of the antiquities were recovered from the temple-ruins, and date back to the beginning of the Ist Dynasty, exactly the time when the kings of Hierakonpolis first conquered the kingdom of Buto and founded the united Egyptian monarchy.

The ancient temple, which was probably one of the earliest seats of Egyptian civilization, was situated on a mound, now known as *el-Kom el-ahmar*, "the Red Hill," from its colour. The chief feature of the most ancient temple seems to have been a circular mound, revetted by a wall of sandstone blocks, which was apparently erected about the end of the predynastic period. Upon this a shrine was probably erected. This was the ancient shrine of Nekhen, the cradle of the Egyptian monarchy. Close by it were found some of the most valuable relics of the earliest Pharaonic age, the great ceremonial mace-heads and vases of Narmer and " the Scorpion," the shields or " palettes " of the same Narmer, the vases and stelæ of Khāsekhemui, and, of later date, the splendid copper colossal group of King Pepi I and his son, which is now at Cairo. Most of the Ist Dynasty objects are preserved in the Ashmolean Museum at Oxford, which is one of the best centres for the study of early Egyptian antiquities. Narmer and Khāsekhemui are, as we shall see, two of the first monarchs of all Egypt. These sculptured and inscribed mace-heads, shields, etc., are monuments dedicated by them in the ancestral shrine at Hierakonpolis as records of their deeds. Both kings seem to have waged war against the Northerners, the *Anu* of Heliopolis and the Delta, and on these votive monuments from Hierakonpolis we find hieroglyphed records of the defeat of the *Anu*, who have very definitely Semitic physiognomies.

On one shield or palette we see Narmer clubbing a man of Semitic appearance, who is called the " Only One of the Marsh " (Delta), while below two other Semites fly, seeking " fortress-protection." Above is a figure of a hawk, symbolizing the Upper Egyptian king, holding a rope which is passed through the nose of a Semitic head, while behind is a sign which may be read as " the North," so that the whole symbolizes the leading away of the North into captivity by the king of the South. It is significant, in view of what has been said above with regard to the probable Semitic origin of the Heliopolitan Northerners, to find the people typical of the North-land represented by the Southerners as Semites. Equally Semitic is the overthrown Northerner on the other side of this well-known monument which we are describing; he is being trampled under the hoofs and gored by the horns of â bull, who, like the hawk, symbolizes the king. The royal bull has broken down the wall of a fortified enclosure, in which is the hut or tent of the Semite, and the bricks lie about promiscuously.

In connection with the Semitic origin of the Northerners, the form of the fortified enclosures on both sides of this monument (that to whose protection the two Semites on one side fly, and that out of which the kingly bull has dragged the chief on the other) is noticeable. As usual in Egyptian writing, the hieroglyph of these buildings takes the form of a plan. The plan shows a crenelated enclosure, resembling the walls of a great Babylonian palace or temple, such as have been found at Telloh, Warka, or Mukayyar. The same design is found in Egypt at the Shuret ez-Zebib, an Old Kingdom fortress at Abydos, in the tomb of King Aha at Nakâda, and in many walls of mastaba-tombs of the early time. This is another argument in favour of an early connection between Egypt and Babylonia. We illustrate a fragment of another votive shield or palette of the same kind, now in the museum of the Louvre, which probably came originally from Hierakonpolis. It is of exactly similar workmanship to that of Narmer, and is no doubt a fragment of another monument of that king. On it we see the same subject of the overthrowing of a Northerner (of Semitic aspect) by the royal bull. On one side, below, is a fortified enclosure with crenelated walls of the type we have described, and within it a lion and a vase; below this another fort, and a bird within it. These signs may express the names of the two forts, but, owing to the fact that at this early period Egyptian orthography was not yet fixed, we cannot read them. On the other side we see a row of animated nome-standards of Upper Egypt, with the symbols of the god Min of Koptos, the hawk of Horus of Edfu, the ibis of Thot of Eshmunên, and the jackals of Anubis of Abydos, which drag a rope; had we the rest of the monument, we should see, bound at the end of the rope, some prisoner, king, or animal symbolic of the North.

On another slate shield, which we also reproduce,

we see a symbolical representation of the capture of seven Northern cities, whose names seem to mean the "Two Men," the "Heron," the "Owl," the "Palm," and the "Ghost" Cities. "Ghost City" is attacked by a lion, "Owl City" by a hawk, "Palm City" by two hawk nome-standards, and another, whose name we cannot guess at, is being opened up by a scorpion. The operating animals evidently represent nomes and tribes of the Upper Egyptians. Here again we see the same crenelated walls of the Northern towns, and there is no doubt that this slate fragment also, which is preserved in the Cairo Museum, is a monument of the conquests of Narmer. It is executed in the same archaic style as those from Hierakonpolis. The animals on the other side no doubt represent part of the spoil of the North.

OBVERSE OF A SLATE RELIEF.

With symbolical representation of the King of Upper Egypt, in the form of a bull, overthrowing a Northern enemy. Below are representations of fortresses with archaic hieroglyphs giving their names. Reproduced from de Morgan, *Recherches*, vol. i.

Returning to the great shield or palette found by

Mr. Quibell, we see the king coming out, followed by his sandal-bearer, the *Hen-neter* or "God's Servant,"[1] to view the dead bodies of the slain Northerners which lie arranged in rows, decapitated, and with their heads between their feet. The king is preceded by a procession of nome-standards. Above the dead men are symbolic representations of a hawk perched on a harpoon over a boat, and a hawk and a door, which doubtless again refer to the fights of the royal hawk of Upper Egypt on the Nile and at the gate of the North. The designs on the mace-heads refer to the same conquest of the North.

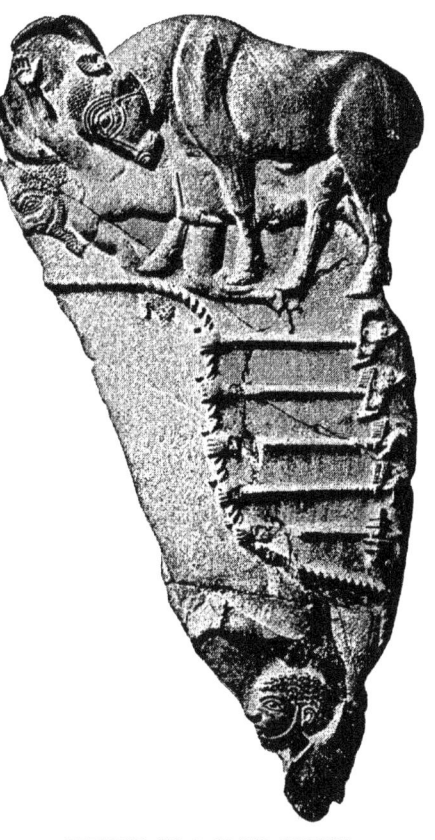

REVERSE OF A SLATE RELIEF.

With the same symbolical representation. 1st Dynasty. Reproduced from de Morgan, *Recherches*, vol. i.

The monuments of Khāsekhemui, a later king, show us that he conquered the North also and slew 47,209 "Northern Enemies." The contorted attitudes of the dead North-

---

[1] In his commentary (*Hierakonpolis*, i. p. 9) on this scene, Prof. Petrie supposes that the seven-pointed star sign means "king," and compares the eight-pointed star "used for king in Babylonia." The eight-pointed star of the

erners were greatly admired and sketched at the time, and were reproduced on the pedestal of the king's statue found by Mr. Quibell, which is now at Oxford. It was an age of cheerful savage energy, like most

OBVERSE OF A SLATE RELIEF.
With symbolical representations of the Egyptian nomes. Reproduced from de Morgan, *Recherches*, vol. i.

times when kingdoms and peoples are in the making. About 4000 B. C. is the date of these various monuments.

Khāsekhemui probably lived later than Narmer, and we may suppose that his conquest was in reality a

cuneiform script does not mean "king," but "god." The star then ought to mean "god," and the title "servant of a god," and this supposition may be correct. *Hen-neter*, "god's servant," was the appellation of a peculiar kind of priest in later days, and was then spelt with the ordinary sign for a god, the picture of an axe. But in the archaic period, with which we are dealing, a star like the Babylonian sign may very well have been used for "god," and the title of Narmer's sandal-bearer may read *Hen-neter*. He was the slave of the living god Narmer. All Egyptian kings were regarded as deities, more or less.

KHĀSEKHEMUI AND NARMER 53

re-conquest. He may have lived as late as the time of the IId Dynasty, whereas Narmer must be placed at the beginning of the Ist, and his conquest was probably that which first united the two kingdoms of the South and North. As we shall see in the next chapter, he is probably one of the originals of the legendary " Mena," who was regarded from the time of the XVIIIth Dy-

REVERSE OF A SLATE RELIEF, REPRESENTING ANIMALS.
Ist Dynasty. Reproduced from de Morgan, *Recherches*, vol. i.

nasty onwards as the founder of the kingdom, and was first made known to Europe by Herodotus, under the name of " Menes." Narmer is therefore the last of the ancient kings of Hierakonpolis, the last of Manetho's " Spirits." We may possibly have recovered the names of one or two of the kings anterior to Narmer in the excavations at Abydos (see Chapter II), but this is uncertain. To all intents and purposes we have only

54   THE DISCOVERY OF PREHISTORIC EGYPT

legendary knowledge of the Southern kingdom until its close, when Narmer the mighty went forth to strike down the Anu of the North, an exploit which he recorded in votive monuments at Hierakonpolis, and which was commemorated ' henceforward throughout Egyptian history in the yearly "Feast of the Smiting of the Anu." Then was Egypt for the first time united, and the fortress of the "White Wall," the "Good Abode" of Memphis, was built to dominate the lower country. The Ist Dynasty was founded and Egyptian history began.

CHAPTER II

ABYDOS AND THE FIRST THREE DYNASTIES

UNTIL the recent discoveries had been made, which have thrown so much light upon the early history of Egypt, the traditional order and names of the kings of the first three Egyptian dynasties were, in default of more accurate information, retained by all writers on the history of the period. The names were taken from the official lists of kings at Abydos and elsewhere, and were divided into dynasties according to the system of Manetho, whose names agree more or less with those of the lists and were evidently derived from them ultimately. With regard to the fourth and later dynasties it was clear that the king-lists were correct, as their evidence agreed entirely with that of the contemporary monuments. But no means existed of checking the lists of the first three dynasties, as no contemporary monuments other than a IVth Dynasty mention of a IId Dynasty king, Send, had been found. The lists dated from the time of the XVIIIth and XIXth Dynasties, so that it was very possible that with regard to the earliest dynasties they might not be very correct. This conclusion gained additional weight from the fact that no monuments of these earliest kings were ever discovered; it therefore seemed probable that they were purely legendary figures, in whose time (if they ever did exist) Egypt was still a semi-barbarous nation. The jejune stories told about them by Manetho seemed to confirm this idea. Mena, the reputed founder of the monarchy, was generally regarded as a historical figure, owing to the persistence of his name in all ancient literary accounts of the beginnings of Egyptian history; for it was but natural to suppose that the name of the man who unified Egypt and founded Memphis would endure in the mouths of the people. But with regard to his successors no such supposition seemed probable, until the time of Sneferu and the pyramid-builders.

This was the critical view. Another school of historians accepted all the kings of the lists as historical *en bloc*, simply because the Egyptians had registered their names as kings. To them Teta, Ateth, and Ata were as historical as Mena.

Modern discovery has altered our view, and truth is seen to lie between the opposing schools, as usual. The kings after Mena do not seem to be such entirely unhistorical figures as the extreme critics thought; the names of several of them, *e.g.* Merpeba, of the Ist Dynasty, are correctly given in the later lists, and those of others were simply misread, *e.g.* that of Semti of the same dynasty, misread "Hesepti" by the list-makers. On the other hand, Mena himself has become a somewhat doubtful quantity. The real names of most of the early monarchs of Egypt have been recovered for us by the latest excavations, and we can now see when the list-makers of the XIXth Dynasty were right and when they were wrong, and can distinguish what is legendary in their work from what is really historical. It is true that they very often appear to have been wrong, but, on the other hand, they were sometimes unexpectedly near the mark, and the general number and arrangement of their kings seems correct; so that we can still go to them for assistance in the arrangement of the names which are communicated to us by the newly discovered monuments. Manetho's help, too, need never be despised because he was a copyist of copyists; we can still use him to direct our investigations, and his arrangement of dynasties must still remain the framework of our chronological scheme, though he does not seem to have been always correct as to the places in which the dynasties originated.

More than the names of the kings have the new discoveries communicated to us. They have shed a flood of light on the beginnings of Egyptian civilization and art, supplementing the recently ascertained facts concerning the prehistoric age which have been described in the preceding chapter. The impulse to these discoveries was given by the work of M. de Morgan, who excavated sites of the early dynastic as well as of the predynastic age. Among these was a great mastaba-tomb at Nakâda, which proved to be that of a very early king who bore the name of **Aha**, " the Fighter." The walls of this tomb are crenelated like those of the early Babylonian palaces and the forts of the Northerners, already referred to. M. de Morgan early perceived the difference between the Neolithic antiquities and those of the later archaic period of Egyptian civilization, to which the tomb at Nakâda belonged. In the second volume of his great work on the primitive antiquities of Egypt (*L'Âge des Métaux et le Tombeau Royale de Négadeh*), he described the antiquities of the Ist Dynasty which had been found at the time he wrote. Antiquities of the same primitive period and even of an earlier date had been discovered by Prof. Flinders Petrie, as has already been said, at Koptos, at the mouth of the Wadi Hammamat. But though Prof. Petrie correctly diagnosed the age of the great statues of the god Min which he found, he was led, by his misdating of the "New Race" antiquities from Ballas and Tûkh, also to misdate several of the primitive antiquities,—the lions and hawks, for instance, found at Koptos, he placed in the period between the VIIth and Xth Dynasties; whereas they can now, in the light of further discoveries at Abydos, be seen to date to the earlier part of the Ist Dynasty, the time of Narmer and Aha.

It is these discoveries at Abydos, coupled with those (already described) of Mr. Quibell at Hierakonpolis, which have told us most of what we know with regard to the history of the first three dynasties. At Abydos Prof. Petrie was not himself the first in the field, the site having already been partially explored by a

French Egyptologist, M. Amélineau. The excavations of M. Amélineau were, however, perhaps not conducted strictly on scientific lines, and his results have been insufficiently published with very few photographs, so that with the best will in the world we are unable to give M. Amélineau the full credit which is, no doubt, due to him for his work. The system of Prof. Petrie's publications has been often, and with justice, criticized, but he at least tells us every year what he has been doing, and gives us photographs of everything he has found. For this reason the epoch-making discoveries at Abydos have been coupled chiefly with the name of Prof. Petrie, while that of M. Amélineau is rarely heard in connection with them. As a matter of fact, however, M. Amélineau first excavated the necropolis of the early kings at Abydos, and discovered most of the tombs afterwards worked over by Prof. Petrie and Mr. Mace. Yet most of the important scientific results are due to the later explorers, who were the first to attempt a classification of them, though we must add that this classification has not been entirely accepted by the scientific world.

The necropolis of the earliest kings of Egypt is situated in the great bay in the hills which lies behind Abydos, to the southwest of the main necropolis. Here, at holy Abydos, where every pious Egyptian wished to rest after death, the bodies of the most ancient kings were buried. It is said by Manetho that the original seat of their dominion was This, a town in the vicinity of Abydos, now represented by the modern Girga, which lies a few miles distant from its site (el-Birba). This may be a fact, but we have as yet obtained no confirmation of it. It may well be that the attribution of a Thinite origin to the Ist and IId Dynasties was due simply to the fact that the kings of these dynasties were buried at Abydos, which lay within the Thinite nome. Manetho knew that they were buried at Abydos, and so jumped to the conclusion that they lived there

PROF. PETRIE'S CAMP AT ABYDOS, 1901.

also, and called them "Thinites." Their real place of origin must have been Hierakonpolis, where the predynastic kingdom of the South had its seat. The IIId Dynasty was no doubt of Memphite origin, as Manetho says. It is certain that the seat of the government of the IVth Dynasty was at Memphis, where the pyramid-building kings were buried, and we know that the sepulchres of two IIId Dynasty kings, at least, were situated in the necropolis of Memphis (Sakkâra-Mêdûm). So that probably the seat of government was transferred from Hierakonpolis to Memphis by the first king of the IIId Dynasty. Thenceforward the kings were buried in the Memphite necropolis.

The two great necropoles of Memphis and Abydos were originally the seats of the worship of the two Egyptian gods of the dead, Seker and Khentamenti, both of whom were afterwards identified with the Busirite god Osiris. Abydos was also the centre of the worship of Anubis, an animal-deity of the dead, the jackal who prowls round the tombs at night. Anubis and Osiris-Khentamenti, "He who is in the West," were associated in the minds of the Egyptians as the protecting deities of Abydos. The worship of these gods as the chief Southern deities of the dead, and the pre-eminence of the necropolis of Abydos in the South, no doubt date back before the time of the Ist Dynasty, so that it would not surprise us were burials of kings of the predynastic Hierakonpolite kingdom discovered at Abydos. Prof. Petrie indeed claims to have discovered actual royal relics of that period at Abydos, but this seems to be one of the least certain of his conclusions. We cannot definitely state that the names "Ro," "Ka," and "Sma" (if they are names at all, which is doubtful) belong to early kings of Hierakonpolis who were buried at Abydos. It may be so, but further confirmation is desirable before we accept it as a fact; and as yet such confirmation has not been forthcoming. The oldest kings, who were certainly buried at Abydos, seem to have been the first rulers of the united kingdom of the North and South, Aha and his successors. Narmer is not represented. It may be that he was not buried at Abydos, but in the necropolis of Hierakonpolis. This would point to the kings of the South not having been buried at Abydos until after the unification of the kingdom.

That Aha possessed a tomb at Abydos as well as another at Nakâda seems peculiar, but it is a phenomenon not unknown in Egypt. Several kings, whose bodies were actually buried elsewhere, had second tombs at Abydos, in order that they might *possess* last resting-places near the tomb of Osiris, although they might not prefer to *use* them. Usertsen (or Senusret) III is a case in point. He was really buried in a pyramid at Illahun, up in the North, but he had a great rock tomb cut for him in the cliffs at Abydos, which he never occupied, and probably had never intended to occupy. We find exactly the same thing far back at the beginning of Egyptian history, when Aha possessed not only a great mastaba-tomb at Nakâda, but also a tomb-chamber in the great necropolis of Abydos. It may be that other kings of the earliest period also had second sepulchres elsewhere. It is noteworthy that in none of the early tombs at Abydos were found any bodies which might be considered those of the kings themselves. M. Amélineau discovered bodies of attendants or slaves (who were in all probability purposely strangled and buried around the royal chamber in order that they should attend the king in the next world), but no royalties. Prof. Petrie found the arm of a female mummy, who may have been of royal blood, though there is nothing to show that she was. And the quaint plait and fringe of false hair, which were also found, need not have belonged to a royal mummy. It is therefore quite possible that these tombs at Abydos were not the actual last resting-places of the earliest kings, who may really have been buried at Hierakonpolis or elsewhere, as Aha was. Messrs. Newberry and Garstang, in their *Short History of Egypt*, suppose that Aha was actually buried at Abydos, and that the great tomb with objects bearing his name, found by M. de Morgan at Nakâda, is really not his, but belonged to a royal princess named Neit-hetep, whose name is found in conjunction with his at Abydos and Nakâda. But the argument is equally valid turned round the other way: the Nakâda tomb might just as well be Aha's and the Abydos one Neit-hetep's. Neit-hetep, who is supposed by Messrs. Newberry and Garstang to have been Narmer's daughter and Aha's wife, was evidently closely connected with Aha, and she may have been buried with him at Nakâda and commemorated with him at Abydos.[1] It is probable that the XIXth Dynasty list-makers and Manetho considered the Abydos tombs to have been the real graves of the kings, but it is by no means impossible that they were wrong.

This view of the royal tombs at Abydos tallies to a great extent with that of M. Naville, who has energetically maintained the view that M. Amélineau and Prof. Petrie have not discovered the real tombs of the

[1] A princess named Bener-ab ("Sweet-heart"), who may have been Aha's daughter, was actually buried beside his tomb at Abydos.

early kings, but only their contemporary commemorative "tombs" at Abydos. The only real tomb of the Ist Dynasty, therefore, as yet discovered is that of Aha at Nakâda, found by M. de Morgan. The fact that attendant slaves were buried around the Abydos tombs is no bar to the view that the tombs were only the monuments, not the real graves, of the kings. The royal ghosts would naturally visit their commemorative chambers at Abydos, in order to be in the company of the great Osiris, and ghostly servants would be as necessary to their Majesties at Abydos as elsewhere.

It must not be thought that this revised opinion of the Abydos tombs detracts in the slightest degree from the importance of the discovery of M. Amélineau and its subsequent and more detailed investigation by Prof. Petrie. These monuments are as valuable for historical purposes as the real tombs themselves. The actual bodies of these primeval kings themselves we are never likely to find. The tomb of Aha at Nakâda had been completely rifled in ancient times.

The commemorative tombs of the kings of the Ist and IId Dynasties at Abydos lie southwest of the great necropolis, far within the bay in the hills. Their present aspect is that of a wilderness of sand hillocks, covered with masses of fragments of red pottery, from which the site has obtained the modern Arab name of *Umm el-Ga'ab*, "Mother of Pots." It is impossible to move a step in any direction without crushing some of these potsherds under the heel. They are chiefly the remains of the countless little vases of rough red pottery, which were dedicated here as *ex-votos* by the pious, between the XIXth and XXVIth Dynasties, to the memory of the ancient kings and of the great god Osiris, whose tomb, as we shall see, was supposed to have been situated here also. Intermingled with these later fragments are pieces of the original Ist Dynasty vases, which were filled with wine and provisions and were placed in the tombs, for the refreshment and delectation of the royal ghosts when they should visit their houses at Abydos. These were thrown out and broken when the tombs were violated. Here and there one sees a dip

THE TOMB OF KING DEN AT ABYDOS.
About 4000 B. C.

in the sand, out of which rise four walls of great bricks, forming a rectangular chamber, half-filled with sand. This is one of the royal tomb-chambers of the Ist Dynasty. That of King Den is illustrated above. A straight staircase descends into it from the ground-level above. In several of the tombs the original flooring of wooden beams is still preserved. Den's is the most magnificent of all, for it has a floor of granite blocks; we know of no other instance of stone being used for building in this early age. Almost every tomb has been burnt at some period unknown. The brick walls are burnt red, and many of the alabaster vases are almost calcined. This was probably the work of some unknown enemy.

The wide complicated tombs have around the main chamber a series of smaller rooms, which were used to store what was considered necessary for the use of the royal ghost. Of these necessaries the most interesting to us are the slaves, who were, as there is little reason to doubt, purposely killed and buried round the royal chamber so that their spirits should be on the spot when the dead king came to Abydos; thus they would be always ready to serve him with the food and other things which had been stored in the tomb with them and placed under their charge. There were stacks of great vases of wine, corn, and other food; these were covered up with masses of fat to preserve the contents, and they were corked with a pottery stopper, which was protected by a conical clay sealing, stamped with the impress of the royal cylinder-seal. There were bins of corn, joints of oxen, pottery dishes, copper pans, and other things which might be useful for the ghostly cuisine of the tomb. There were numberless small objects, used, no doubt, by the dead monarch during life, which he would be pleased to see again in the next world,—carved ivory boxes, little slabs for grinding eye-paint, golden buttons, model tools, model vases with gold tops, ivory and pottery figurines, and other *objets d'art;* the golden royal seal of judgment of King Den in its ivory casket, and so forth. There were memorials of the royal victories in peace and war, little ivory plaques with inscriptions commemorating the founding of new buildings, the institution of new religious festivals in honour of the gods,

CONICAL VASE - STOPPERS.
From Abydos. Ist Dynasty: about 4000 B. C.   Photograph reproduced from M. de Morgan's *Recherches*, vol. i.

the bringing of the captives of the royal bow and spear to the palace, the discomfiture of the peoples of the North-land. All these things, which have done so much to reconstitute for us the history of the earliest period of the Egyptian monarchy, were placed under the care of the dead slaves whose bodies were buried round the empty tomb-chamber of their royal master in Abydos.

The killing and entombment of the royal servants is of the highest anthropological interest, for it throws a vivid light upon the manners of the time. It shows the primeval Egyptians as a semi-barbaric people of childishly simple ways of thought. The king was dead. For all his kingship he was a man, and no man was immortal in this world. But yet how could one really die? Shadows, dreams, all kinds of phenomena which the primitive mind could not explain, induced the belief that, though the outer man might rot, there was an inner man which could not die and still lived on. The idea of total death was unthinkable. And where should this inner man still live on but in the tomb to which the outer man was consigned? And here, doubtless it was believed, in the house to which the body was consigned, the ghost lived on. And as each ghost had his house with the body, so no doubt all ghosts could communicate with one another from tomb to tomb; and so there grew up the belief in a tomb-world, a subterranean Egypt of tombs, in which the dead Egyptians still lived and had their being. Later on the boat of the sun, in which the god of light crossed the heavens by day, was thought to pass through this dead world between his setting and his rising, accompanied by the souls of the righteous. But of this belief we find no trace yet in the ideas of the Ist Dynasty. All we can see is that the *sahus*, or bodies of the dead, were supposed to reside in awful majesty in the tomb, while the ghosts could pass from tomb to tomb through the mazes of the underworld. Over this dread realm of dead men presided a dead god, Osiris of Abydos; and so the necropolis of Abydos was the necropolis of the underworld, to which all ghosts who were not its rightful citizens would come from afar to pay their court to their ruler. Thus the man of substance would have a monumental tablet put up to himself in this necropolis as a sort of *pied-à-terre*, even if he could not be buried there; for the king, who, for reasons chiefly connected with local patriotism, was buried near the city of his earthly abode, a second tomb would be erected, a stately mansion in the city of Osiris, in which his ghost could reside when it pleased him to come to Abydos.

Now none could live without food, and men living under the earth needed it as much as men living on the earth. The royal tomb was thus provided with an enormous amount of earthly food for the use of the royal ghost, and with other things as well, as we have seen. The same provision had also to be made for the royal resting-place at Abydos. And in both cases royal slaves were needed to take care of all this provision, and to serve the ghost of the king, whether in his real tomb at Nakâda, or elsewhere, or in his second tomb at Abydos. Ghosts only could serve ghosts, so that of the slaves ghosts had to be made. That was easily done; they died when their master died and followed him to the tomb. No doubt it seemed perfectly natural to all concerned, to the slaves as much as to anybody else. But it shows the child's idea of the value of life. An animate thing was hardly distinguished at this period from an inanimate thing. The most ancient Egyptians buried slaves with their kings as naturally as they buried jars of wine and bins of corn with them. Both were buried with a definite object. The slaves had to die before they were buried, but then so had the king himself. They all had to die sometime or other. And the actual killing of them was no worse than killing a dog, no worse even than " killing " golden buttons and ivory boxes. For, when the buttons and boxes were buried with the king, they were just as much dead as the slaves. Of the sanctity of *human* life as distinct from other life, there was probably no idea at all. The royal ghost needed ghostly servants, and they were provided as a matter of course.

But as civilization progressed, the ideas of the Egyptians changed on these points, and in the later ages of the ancient world they were probably the most humane of the peoples, far more so than the Greeks, in fact. The cultured Hellenes murdered their prisoners of war without hesitation. Who has not been troubled in mind by the execution of Nikias and Demosthenes after the surrender of the Athenian army at Syracuse? When we compare this with Grant's refusal even to take Lee's sword at Appomattox, we see how we have progressed in these matters; while Gylippus and the Syracusans were as much children as the Ist Dynasty Egyptians. But the Egyptians of Gylippus's time had probably advanced much further than the Greeks in the direction of rational manhood. When Amasis had his rival Apries in his power, he did not put him to death, but kept him as his coadjutor on the throne. Apries fled from him, allied himself with Greek pirates, and advanced against his generous rival. After his defeat and murder at Momemphis, Amasis gave him a splendid burial. When we compare this generosity to a beaten foe with the savagery of the Assyrians, for instance, we see how far the later Egyptians had progressed in the paths of humanity.

The ancient custom of killing slaves was first discontinued at the death of the lesser chieftains, but we find a possible survival of it in the case of a king, even as late as the time of the XIth Dynasty; for at Thebes, in the precinct of the funerary temple of King Nebhapet-Rā Mentuhetep and round the central pyramid which commemorated his memory, were buried a number of the ladies of his *harîm*. They were all buried at one and the same time, and there can be little doubt that they were all killed and buried round the king, in order to be with him in the next world. Now with each of these ladies, who had been turned into ghosts, was buried a little waxen human figure placed in a little model coffin. This was to replace her own slave. She who went to accompany the king in the next world had to have her own attendant also. But, not being royal, a real slave was not killed for her; she only took with her a waxen figure, which by means of charms and incantations would, when she called upon it, turn into a real slave, and say, " Here am I," and do whatever work might be required of her. The actual killing and burial of the slaves had in all cases except that of the king been long " commuted," so to speak, into a burial with the dead person of *ushabtis*, or " Answerers," little figures like those described above, made more usually of stone, and inscribed with the name of the deceased. They were called " Answerers " because they answered the call of their dead master or mistress, and by magic power became ghostly servants. Later on they were made of wood and-glazed *faïence*, as well as stone. By this means the greater humanity of a later age sought a relief from the primitive disregard of the death of others.

Anthropologically interesting as are the results of the excavations at Umm el-Ga'ab, they are no less historically important. There is no need here to weary the reader with the details of scientific controversy; it will suffice to set before him as succinctly and clearly as possible the net results of the work which has been done.

Messrs. Amélineau and Petrie have found the secondary tombs and have identified the names of the following primeval kings of Egypt. We arrange them in their apparent historical order.

1. Aha Men (?).
2. Narmer (or Betjumer) Sma (?).
3. Tjer (or Khent).
4. Tja Ati.
5. Den Semti.
6. Atjab Merpeba.
7. Semerkha Nekht.
8. Qā Sen.
9. Khāsekhem (Khāsekhemui) Besh.
10. Hetepsekhemui.
11. Rāneb.
12. Neneter.
13. Sekhemab Perabsen.

Two or three other names are ascribed by Prof. Petrie to the Hierakonpolite dynasty of Upper Egypt, which, as it occurs before the time of Mena and the Ist Dynasty, he calls "Dynasty O." Dynasty O, however, is no dynasty, and in any case we should prefer to call the "predynastic" dynasty "Dynasty —I." The names of "Dynasty minus One," however, remain problematical, and for the present it would seem safer to suspend judgment as to the place of the supposed royal names "Ro" and "Ka" (Men-ka?), which Prof. Petrie supposes to have been those of two of the kings of Upper Egypt who reigned before Mena. The king "Sma" ("Uniter") is possibly identical with Aha or Narmer, more probably the latter. It is not necessary to detail the process by which Egyptologists have sought to identify these thirteen kings with the successors of Mena in the lists of kings and the Ist and IId Dynasties of Manetho. The work has been very successful, though not perhaps quite so completely accomplished as Prof. Petrie himself inclines to believe. The first identification was made by Prof. Sethe, of Göttingen, who pointed out that the names Semti and Merpeba on a vase-fragment found by M. Amélineau were in reality those of the kings Hesepti and Merbap of the lists, the Ousaphaïs and Miebis of Manetho. The perfectly certain identifications are these:—

5. Den Semti = Hesepti, *Ousaphaïs*, Ist Dynasty.
6. Atjab Merpeba = Merbap, *Miebis*, Ist Dynasty.
7. Semerkha Nekht = Shemsu or Semsem (?), *Semempres*, Ist Dynasty.
8. Qā Sen = Qebh, *Bienekhes*, Ist Dynasty.

9. Khāsekhemui Besh = Betju-mer (?), *Boethos*, IId Dynasty.
12 Neneter = Bineneter, *Binothris*, IId Dynasty.

Six of the Abydos kings have thus been identified with names in the lists and in Manetho; that is to say, we now know the real names of six of the earliest Egyptian monarchs, whose appellations are given us under mutilated forms by the later list-makers. Prof. Petrie further identifies (4) Tja Ati with Ateth, (3) Tjer with Teta, and (1) Aha with Mena. Mena, Teta, Ateth, Ata, Hesepti, Merbap, Shemsu (?), and Qebh are the names of the Ist Dynasty as given in the lists. The equivalent of Ata Prof. Petrie finds in the name " Merneit," which is found at Umm el-Ga'ab. But there is no proof whatever that Merneit was a king; he was much more probably a prince or other great personage of the reign of Den, who was buried with the kings. Prof. Petrie accepts the identification of the personal name of Aha as " Men," and so makes him the only equivalent of Mena. But this reading of the name is still doubtful. Arguing that Aha must be Mena, and having all the rest of the kings of the Ist Dynasty identified with the names in the lists, Prof. Petrie is compelled to exclude Narmer from the dynasty, and to relegate him to " Dynasty O," before the time of Mena. It is quite possible, however, that Narmer was the successor, not the predecessor, of Mena. He was certainly either the one or the other, as the style of art in his time was exactly the same as that in the time of Aha. The " Scorpion," too, whose name is found at Hierakonpolis, certainly dates to the same time as Narmer and Aha, for the style of his work is the same. And it may well be that he is not to be counted as a separate king, belonging to " Dynasty O " (or " Dynasty —I ") at all, but as identical with Narmer, just as " Sma " may also be. We thus find that the two kings who left the most developed remains at Hierakonpolis are the two whose monuments at Abydos are the oldest of all on that site. That is to say, the kings whose monuments record the conquest of the North belong to the period of transition from the old Hierakonpolite dominion of Upper Egypt to the new kingdom of all Egypt. They, in fact, represent the " Mena " or Menes of tradition. It may be that Aha bore the personal name of *Men*, which would thus be the original of Mena, but this is uncertain. In any case both Aha and Narmer must be assigned to the Ist Dynasty, with the result that we know of more kings belonging to the dynasty than appear in the lists.

Nor is this improbable. Manetho's list is evidently based upon old Egyptian lists derived from the authorities upon which the king-lists of Abydos and Sakkâra were based. These old lists were made under the XIXth Dynasty, when an interest in the oldest kings seems to have been awakened, and the ruling monarchs erected temples at Abydos in their honour. This phenomenon can only have been due to a discovery of Umm el-Ga'ab and its treasures, the tombs of which were recognized as the burial-places (real or secondary) of the kings before the pyramid-builders. Seti I. and his son Ramses then worshipped the kings of Umm el-Ga'ab, with their names set before them in the order, number, and spelling in which the scribes considered they ought to be inscribed. It is highly probable that the number known at that time was not quite correct. We know that the spelling of the names was very much garbled (to take one example only, the signs for *Sen* were read as one sign *Qebh*), so that one or two kings may have been omitted or displaced. This may be the case with Narmer, or, as his name ought possibly to be read, *Betjumer*. His monuments show by their style that he belongs to the very beginning of the Ist Dynasty. No name in the Ist Dynasty list corresponds to his. But one of the lists gives for the first king of the IId Dynasty (the successor of " Qebh " = Sen) a name which may also be read Betjumer, spelt syllabically this time, not ideographically. On this account Prof. Naville wishes to regard the Hierakonpolite monuments of Narmer as belonging to the IId Dynasty, but, as we have seen, they are among the most archaic known, and certainly must belong to the beginning of the Ist Dynasty. It is therefore probable that Khāsekhemui Besh and Narmer (Betjumer?) were confused by this list-maker, and the name Betjumer was given to the first king of the IId Dynasty, who was probably in reality Khāsekhemui. The resemblance of *Betju* to *Besh* may have contributed to this confusion.

So Narmer (or Betjumer) found his way out of his proper place at the beginning of the Ist Dynasty. Whether Aha was also called " Men " or not, it seems evident that he and Narmer were jointly the originals of the legendary Mena. Narmer, who possibly also bore the name of Sma, "the Uniter," conquered the North. Aha, "the Fighter," also ruled both South and North at the same period. Khāsekhemui, too, conquered the North, but the style of his monuments shows such an advance upon that of the days of Aha and Narmer that it seems best to make him the successor of Sen (or "Qebh"), and, explaining the transference of the name Betjumer to the beginning of the IId Dynasty as due to a confusion with Khāsekhemui's personal name Besh, to make Khāsekhemui the founder of the IId Dynasty. The beginning of a new dynasty may well have been marked by a reassertion of the new royal power over Lower Egypt, which may have lapsed somewhat under the rule of the later kings of the Ist Dynasty.

Semti is certainly the "Hesepti" of the lists, and Tja Ati is probably "Ateth." "Ata" is thus unidentified. Prof. Petrie makes him = Merneit, but, as has already been said, there is no proof that the tomb of Merneit is that of a king. "Teta" may be Tjer or Khent, but of this there is no proof. It is most probable that the names "Teta," "Ateth," and "Ata" are all founded on Ati, the personal name of Tja. The king Tjer is then not represented in the lists, and "Mena" is a compound of the two oldest Abydos kings, Narmer (Betjumer) Sma (?) and Aha Men (?).

These are the bare historical results that have been attained with regard to the names, identity, and order of the kings. The smaller memorials that have been found with them, especially the ivory plaques, have told us of events that took place during their reigns; but, with the exception of the constantly recurring references to the conquest of the North, there is little that can be considered of historical interest or importance. We will take one as an example. This is the tablet No. 32,650 of the British Museum, illustrated by Prof. Petrie, *Royal Tombs* i (Egypt Exploration Fund), pl. xi, 14, xv, 16. This is the record of a single year, the first in the reign of Semti, King of Upper and Lower Egypt. On it we see a picture of a king performing a religious dance before the god Osiris, who is seated in a shrine placed on a daïs. This religious dance was performed by all the kings in later times. Below we find hieroglyphic (ideographic) records of a river expedition to fight the Northerners and of the capture of a fortified town called Ān. The capture of the town is indicated by a broken line of fortification, half-encircling the name, and the hoe with which the emblematic hawks on the slate reliefs already described [1] are armed; this signifies the opening and breaking down of the wall.

On the other half of the tablet we find the viceroy of Lower Egypt, Hemaka, mentioned; also " the Hawk (*i. e.* the king) seizes the seat of the Libyans," and some unintelligible record of a jeweller of the palace and a king's carpenter. On a similar tablet (of Sen) we find the words " the king's carpenter made this record." All these little tablets are then the records of single years of a king's life, and others like them, preserved no doubt in royal archives, formed the base of regular

[1] See p. 51.

annals, which were occasionally carved upon stone. We have an example of one of these in the "Stele of Palermo," a fragment of black granite, inscribed with the annals of the kings up to the time of the Vth Dynasty, when the monument itself was made. It is a matter for intense regret that the greater portion of this priceless historical monument has disappeared, leaving us but a piece out of the centre, with part of the records of only six kings before Snefru. Of these six the name of only one, Neneter, of the IId Dynasty, whose name is also found at Abydos, is mentioned. The only important historical event of Neneter's reign seems to have occurred in his thirteenth year, when the towns or palaces of *Ha* ("North") and *Shem-Rā* ("The Sun proceeds") were founded. Nothing but the institution and celebration of religious festivals is recorded in the sixteen yearly entries preserved to us out of a reign of thirty-five years. The annual height of the Nile is given, and the occasions of numbering the people are recorded (every second year): nothing else. Manetho tells us that in the reign of Binothris, who is Neneter, it was decreed that women could hold royal honours and privileges. This first concession of women's rights is not mentioned on the strictly official "Palermo Stele."

More regrettable than aught else is the absence from the "Palermo Stele" of that part of the original monument which gave the annals of the earliest kings. At any rate, in the lines of annals which still exist above that which contains the chronicle of the reign of Neneter no entry can be definitely identified as belonging to the reigns of Aha or Narmer. In a line below there is a mention of the "birth of Khāsekhemui," apparently a festival in honour of the birth of that king celebrated in the same way as the reputed birthday of a god. This shows the great honour in which Khāsekhemui was held, and perhaps it was he who really finally settled the question of the unification of North and South and consolidated the work of the earlier kings.

As far as we can tell, then, Aha and Narmer were the first conquerors of the North, the unifiers of the kingdom, and the originals of the legendary Mena. In their time the kingdom's centre of gravity was still in the South, and Narmer (who is probably identical with "the Scorpion") dedicated the memorials of his deeds in the temple of Hierakonpolis. It may be that the legend of the founding of Memphis in the time of "Menes" is nearly correct (as we shall see, historically, the foundation may have been due to Merpeba), but we have the authority of Manetho for the fact that the first two dynasties were "Thinite" (that is, Upper Egyptian), and that Memphis did not become the capital till the time of the IIId Dynasty. With this statement the evidence of the monuments fully agrees. The earliest royal tombs in the pyramid-field of Memphis date from the time of the IIId Dynasty, so that it is evident that the kings had then taken up their abode in the Northern capital. We find that soon after the time of Khāsekhemui the king Perabsen was especially connected with Lower Egypt. His personal name is unknown to us (though he may be the "Uatjnes" of the lists), but we do know that he had two banner-names, Sekhem-ab and Perabsen. The first is his hawk or Horus-name, the second his Set-name; that is to say, while he bore the first name as King of Upper Egypt under the special patronage of Horus, the hawk-god of the Upper Country, he bore the second as King of Lower Egypt, under the patronage of Set, the deity of the Delta, whose fetish animal appears above this name instead of the hawk. This shows how definitely Perabsen wished to appear as legitimate King of Lower as well as Upper Egypt. In later times the Theban kings of the XIIth Dynasty, when they devoted themselves to winning the allegiance of the Northerners by living near Memphis rather than at Thebes, seem to have been imitating the successors of Khāsekhemui.

Moreover, we now find various evidences of increasing connection with the North. A princess named Ne-maat-hap, who seems to have been the mother of Sa-nekht, the first king of the IIId Dynasty, bears the name of the sacred Apis of Memphis, her name signifying " Possessing the right of Apis." According to Manetho, the kings of the IIId Dynasty are the first Memphites, and this seems to be quite correct. With Ne-maat-hap the royal right seems to have been transferred to a Memphite house. But the Memphites still had associations with Upper Egypt: two of them, Tjeser Khet-neter and Sa-nekht, were buried near Abydos, in the desert at Bêt Khallâf, where their tombs were discovered and excavated by Mr. Garstang in 1900. The tomb of Tjeser, which is illustrated on page 82, is a great brick-built mastaba, forty feet high and measuring 300 feet by 150 feet. The actual tomb-chambers are excavated in the rock, twenty feet below the ground-level and sixty feet below the top of the mastaba. They had been violated in ancient times, but a number of clay jar-sealings, alabaster vases, and bowls belonging to the tomb furniture were found by the discoverer. Sa-nekht's tomb is similar. In it was found the preserved

THE TOMB OF KING TJESER AT BÊT KHALLÂF.
About 3700 B. C.

skeleton of its owner, who was a giant seven feet high. It is remarkable that Manetho chronicles among the kings of the early period a king named Sesokhris, who was five cubits high. This may have been Sa-nekht.

Tjeser had two tombs, one, the above-mentioned, near Abydos, the other at Sakkâra, in the Memphite pyramid-field. This is the famous Step-Pyramid. Since Sa-nekht seems really to have been buried at Bêt Khallâf, probably Tjeser was, too, and the Step-Pyramid may have been his secondary or sham tomb, erected in the necropolis of Memphis as a compliment to Seker, the

Northern god of the dead, just as Aha had his secondary tomb at Abydos in compliment to Khentamenti. Sneferu, also, the last king of the IIId Dynasty, seems to have had two tombs. One of these was the great Pyramid of Mêdûm, which was explored by Prof. Petrie in 1891, the other was at Dashûr. Near by was the interesting necropolis already mentioned, in which was discovered evidence of the continuance of the cramped position of burial and of the absence of mummification among a certain section of the population even as late as the time of the IVth Dynasty. This has been taken to imply that the fusion of the primitive Neolithic and invading sub-Semitic races had not been effected at that time.

With the IVth Dynasty the connection of the royal house with the South seems to have finally ceased. The governmental centre of gravity was finally transferred to Memphis, and the kings were thenceforth for several centuries buried in the great pyramids which still stand in serried order along the western desert border of Egypt, from the Delta to the province of the Fayyûm. With the latest discoveries in this Memphite pyramid-field we shall deal in the next chapter.

The transference of the royal power to Memphis under the IIId Dynasty naturally led to a great increase of Egyptian activity in the Northern lands. We read in Manetho of a great Libyan war in the reign of Necherophes, and both Sa-nekht and Tjeser seem to have finally established Egyptian authority in the Sinaitic peninsula, where their rock-inscriptions have been found.

portcullises which were intended to bar the way to possible plunderers through the passages of the tomb. The Step-Pyramid at Sakkâra is, so to speak, a series of mastabas of stone, imposed one above the other; it never had the continuous casing of stone which is the mark of a true pyramid. The pyramid of Snefru at Mêdûm is more developed. It also originated in a mastaba, enlarged, and with another mastaba-like erection on the top of it; but it was given a continuous sloping casing of fine limestone from bottom to top, and so is a true pyramid. A discussion of recent theories as to the building of the later pyramids of the IVth Dynasty will be found in the next chapter.

In the time of the Ist Dynasty the royal tomb was known by the name of "Protection-around-the-Hawk, *i.e.* the king" (*Sa-ha-heru*); but under the IIId and IVth Dynasties regular names, such as "the Firm," "the Glorious," "the Appearing," etc., were given to each pyramid.

We must not omit to note an interesting point in connection with the royal tombs at Abydos. In that of King Khent or Tjer (the reading of the ideograph is doubtful) M. Amélineau found a large bed or bier of granite, with a figure of the god Osiris lying in state sculptured in high relief upon it. This led him to jump to the conclusion that he had found the tomb of the god Osiris himself, and that a skull he found close by was the veritable cranium of the primeval folk-hero, who, according to the euhemerist theory, was the deified original of the god. The true explanation is given by Dr.

False Door of the Tomb of Teta.
An official of the IVth Dynasty; about 3600 B.C. From Gîza. British Museum. Photograph by Messrs. Mansell & Co.

Wallis Budge in his *History of Egypt*, i, p. 19. It is a fact that the tomb of Tjer was regarded by the Egyptians of the XIXth Dynasty as the veritable tomb of Osiris. They thought they had discovered it, just as M. Amélineau did. When the ancient royal tombs of Umm el-Ga'ab were rediscovered and identified at the beginning of the XIXth Dynasty, and Seti I built the great temple of Abydos to the divine ancestors in honour of the discovery, embellishing it with a relief of himself and his son Ramses making offerings to the names of his predecessors (the " Tablet of Abydos "), the name of King Khent or Tjer (which is perhaps the really correct original form) was read by the royal scribes as " Khent " and hastily identified with the first part of the name of the god *Khent*-amenti Osiris, the lord of Abydos. The tomb was thus regarded as the tomb of Osiris himself, and it was furnished with a great stone figure of the god lying on his bier, attended by the two hawks of Isis and Nephthys; ever after the site was visited by crowds of pilgrims, who left at Umm el-Ga'ab the thousands of little votive vases whose fragments have given the place its name of the " Mother of Pots."[1] This is the explanation of the discovery of the " Tomb of Osiris." We have not found what M. Amélineau seems rather naïvely to have thought possible, a confirmation of the ancient view that Osiris was originally a man who ruled over Egypt and was deified after his death; but we have found that the Egyptians themselves were more or less euhemerists, and did think so.

[1] See p. 64.

It may seem remarkable that all this new knowledge of ancient Egypt is derived from tombs and has to do with the resting-places of the kings when dead, rather than with their palaces or temples when living. Of temples at this early period we have no trace. The oldest temple in Egypt is perhaps the little chapel in front of the pyramid of Snefru at Mêdûm. We first hear of temples to the gods under the IVth Dynasty, but of the actual buildings of that period we have recovered nothing but one or two inscribed blocks of stone. Prof. Petrie has traced out the plan of the oldest temple of Osiris at Abydos, which may be of the time of Khufu, from scanty evidences which give us but little information. It is certain, however, that this temple, which is clearly one of the oldest in Egypt, goes back at least to his time. Its site is the mound called *Kom es-Sultan*, "The Mound of the King," close to the village of el-Kherba, and on the borders of the cultivation northeast of the royal tombs at Umm el-Ga'ab.

Of royal palaces we have more definite information. North of the Kom es-Sultan are two great fortress-enclosures of brick: the one is known as *Shûnet ez-Zebîb*, "the Storehouse of Dried Grapes;" the other is occupied by the Coptic monastery of Dêr Anba Musâs. Both are certainly fortress-palaces of the earliest period of the Egyptian monarchy. We know from the small record-plaques of this period that the kings were constantly founding or repairing places of this kind, which were always great rectangular enclosures with crenelated brick walls like those of early Babylonian buildings.

We have seen that the Northern Egyptian possessed similar fortress-cities which were captured by Narmer.[1] These were the seats of the royal residence in various parts of the country. Behind their walls was the king's house, and no doubt also a town of nobles and retainers, while the peasants lived on the arable land without. The Shûnet ez-Zebib and its companion fortress were

THE SHÛNET EZ-ZEBÎB: THE FORTRESS-TOWN OF THE SECOND DYNASTY AT ABYDOS.
About 3900 B. C.

evidently the royal cities of the Ist and IId Dynasties at Abydos. The former has been excavated by Mr. E. R. Ayrton for the Egypt Exploration Fund, under the supervision of Prof. Petrie. He found jar-sealings of Khāsekhemui and Perabsen. In later times the place was utilized as a burial-place for ibis-mummies (it had already been abandoned as a city before the time of the XIIth Dynasty), and from this fact it received the name of *Shenet deb-hib*, or "Storehouse of Ibis Burials." The Arab invaders adapted this name to their own language

[1] See p. 50.

in the nearest form which would have any meaning, as *Shûnet ez-Zebîb*, "the Storehouse of Dried Grapes." The Arab word *shûna* ("Barn" or "Storehouse") was, it should be noted, taken over from the Coptic *sheune*, which is the old-Egyptian *shenet*. The identity of *sheune* or *shûna* with the German "Scheune" is a quaint and curious coincidence. In the illustration of the Shûnet ez-Zebib the curved line of crenelated wall, following the contour of the hill, should be noted, as it is a remarkable example of the building of this early period.

It will have been seen from the foregoing description of what far-reaching importance the discoveries at Abydos have been. A new chapter of the history of the human race has been opened, which contains information previously undreamt of, information which Egyptologists had never dared to hope would be recovered. The sand of Egypt indeed conceals inexhaustible treasures, and no one knows what the morrow's work may bring forth.

Ex Africâ semper aliquid novi!

CHAPTER III

MEMPHIS AND THE PYRAMIDS

MEMPHIS, the "beautiful abode," the "City of the White Wall," is said to have been founded by the legendary Menes, who in order to build it diverted the stream of the Nile by means of a great dyke constructed near the modern village of Koshêsh, south of the village of Mitrahêna, which marks the central point of the ancient metropolis of Northern Egypt. It may be that the city was founded by Aha or Narmer, the historical originals of Mena or Menes; but we have another theory with regard to its foundation, that it was originally built by King Merpeba Atjab, whose tomb was also discovered at Abydos near those of Aha and Narmer. Merpeba is the oldest king whose name is absolutely identified with one occurring in the XIXth Dynasty king-lists and in Manetho. He is certainly the "Merbap" or "Merbepa" ("Merbapen") of the lists and the *Miebis* of Manetho. In both the lists and in Manetho he stands fifth in order from Mena, and he was therefore the sixth king of the Ist Dynasty. The lists, Manetho, and the small monuments in his own tomb agree in making him the immediate successor of Semti Den (Ousaphaïs), and from the style of these latter it is evident that he comes after Tja, Tjer, Narmer, and Aha. That is to say, the contemporary evidence makes him the fifth king from Aha, the first original of "Menes."

Now after the piety of Seti I had led him to erect a great temple at Abydos in memory of the ancient kings, whose sepulchres had probably been brought to light shortly before, and to compile and set up in the temple a list of his predecessors, a certain pious snobbery or snobbish piety impelled a worthy named Tunure, who lived at Memphis, to put up in his own tomb at Sakkâra a tablet of kings like the royal one at Abydos. If Osiris-Khentamenti at Abydos had his tablet of kings, so should Osiris-Seker at Sakkâra. But Tunure does not begin his list with Mena; his initial king is Merpeba. For him Merpeba was the first monarch to be commemorated at Sakkâra. Does not this look very much as if the strictly historical Merpeba, not the rather legendary and confused Mena, was regarded as the first Memphite king? It may well be that it was in the reign of Merpeba, not in that of Aha or Narmer, that Memphis was founded.

The XIXth Dynasty lists of course say nothing about Mena or Merpeba having founded Memphis; they only give the names of the kings, nothing more. The earliest authority for the ascription of Memphis to "Menes" is Herodotus, who was followed in this ascription, as in many other matters, by Manetho; but it must be remembered that Manetho was writing for the edification of a Greek king (Ptolemy Philadelphus) and his Greek court at Alexandria, and had therefore to evince a respect for the great Greek classic which he may not always have really felt. Herodotus is not, of course, accused of any wilful misstatement in this or in any other matter in which his accuracy is suspected. He merely wrote down what he was told by the Egyptians themselves, and Merpeba was sufficiently near in time to Aha to be easily confounded with him by the scribes of the Persian period, who no doubt ascribed everything to " Mena " that was done by the kings of the Ist and IId Dynasties. Therefore it may be considered quite probable that the " Menes " who founded Memphis was Merpeba, the fifth or sixth king of the Ist Dynasty, whom Tunure, a thousand years before the time of Herodotus and his informants, placed at the head of the Memphite " List of Sakkâra."

The reconquest of the North by Khāsekhemui doubtless led to a further strengthening of Memphis; and it is quite possible that the deeds of this king also contributed to make up the sum total of those ascribed to the Herodotean and Manethonian Menes.

It may be that a town of the Northerners existed here before the time of the Southern Conquest, for Phtah, the local god of Memphis, has a very marked character of his own, quite different from that of Khentamenti, the Osiris of Abydos. He is always represented as a little bow-legged hydrocephalous dwarf very like the Phœnician *Kabeiroi*. It may be that here is another connection between the Northern Egyptians and the Semites. The name "Phtah," the "Opener," is definitely Semitic. We may then regard the dwarf Phtah as originally a non-Egyptian god of the Northerners, probably Semitic in origin, and his town also as antedating the conquest. But it evidently was to the Southerners that Memphis owed its importance and its eventual promotion to the position of capital of the united kingdom. Then the dwarf Phtah saw himself rivalled by another Phtah of Southern Egyptian origin, who had been installed at Memphis by the Southerners. This Phtah was a sort of modified edition of Osiris, in mummy-form and holding crook and whip, but with a refined edition of the Kabeiric head of the indigenous Phtah. The actual god of "the White Wall" was undoubtedly confused with the dead god of the necropolis, whose name was Seker or Sekri (Sokari), "the Coffined." The original form of this deity was a mummied hawk upon a coffin, and it is very probable that he was imported from the South, like the second Phtah, at the time of the conquest, when the great Northern necropolis began to grow up as a duplicate of that at Abydos. Later on we find Seker confused with the ancient dwarf-god, and it is the latter who was afterwards chiefly revered as Phtah-Socharis-Osiris, the protector of the necropolis, the mummied Phtah being the generally recognized ruler of the City of the White Wall.

It is from the name of Seker that the modern Sakkâra takes its title. Sakkâra marks the central point of the great Memphite necropolis, as it is the nearest point of the western desert to Memphis. Northwards the necropolis extended to Giza and Abû Roâsh, southwards, to Dashûr; even the necropoles of Lisht and Mêdûm may be regarded as appanages of Sakkâra. At Sakkâra itself Tjeser of the IIId Dynasty had a pyramid, which, as we have seen, was probably not his real tomb (which was the great mastaba at Bêt Khallâf), but a secondary or sham tomb corresponding to the "tombs" of the earliest kings at Umm el-Ga'ab in the necropolis of Abydos. Many later kings, however, especially of the VIth Dynasty, were actually buried at Sakkâra. Their tombs have all been thoroughly described by their discoverer, Prof. Maspero, in his history. The last king of the IIId Dynasty, Snefru, was buried away down south at Mêdûm, in splendid isolation, but he may also have had a second pyramid at Sakkâra or Abû Roash.

The kings of the IVth Dynasty were the greatest of the pyramid builders, and to them belong the huge edifices of Giza. The Vth Dynasty favoured Abusîr, between Giza and Sakkâra; the VIth, as we have said, preferred Sakkâra itself. With them the end of the Old Kingdom and of Memphite dominion was reached; the sceptre fell from the hands of the Memphite kings and was taken up by the princes of Herakleopolis (Ahnasyet el-Medina, near Beni Suêf, south of the Fayyûm) and Thebes. Where the Herakleopolite kings were buried we do not know; probably somewhere in the local necropolis of the Gebel es-Sedment, between Ahnasya and the Fayyûm. The first Thebans (the XIth Dynasty) were certainly buried at Thebes, but when the Herakleopolites had finally disappeared, and all Egypt was again united under one strong sceptre, the Theban kings seem to have been drawn northwards. They removed to the seat of the dominion of those whom they had supplanted, and they settled in the neighbourhood of Herakleopolis, near the fertile province of the Fayyûm, and between it and Memphis. Here, in the royal fortress-palace of Itht-taui, "Controlling the Two Lands," the kings of the XIIth Dynasty lived, and they were buried in the necropoles of Dashûr, Lisht, and Illahun (Hawara), in pyramids like those of the old Memphite kings. These facts, of the situation of Itht-taui, of their burial in the southern annex of the old necropolis of Memphis, and of the form of their tombs (the true Upper Egyptian and Theban form was a rock-cut gallery and chamber driven deep into the hill), show how solicitous were the Amenemhats and Senusrets of the suffrages of Lower Egypt, how anxious they were to conciliate the ancient royal pride of Memphis.

Where the kings of the XIIIth Dynasty and the Hyksos or "Shepherds" were buried, we do not know. The kings of the restored Theban empire were all interred at Thebes. There are, in fact, no known royal sepulchres between the Fayyûm and Abydos. The great kings were mostly buried in the neighbourhood of Memphis, Abydos, and Thebes. The sepulchres of the "Middle Empire"—the XIth to XIIIth Dynasties—in the neighbourhood of the Fayyûm may fairly be grouped with those of the same period at Dashûr, which belongs to the necropolis of Memphis, since it is only a mile or two south of Sakkâra.

It is chiefly with regard to the sepulchres of the kings that the most momentous discoveries of recent years have been made—at Thebes, and at Sakkâra, Abusîr, Dashûr, and Lisht, as at Abydos. For this reason we deal in succession with the finds in the necropoles of Abydos, Memphis, and Thebes respectively. And with the sepulchres of the "Old Kingdom," in the Memphite necropolis proper, we have naturally grouped those of the "Middle Kingdom" at Dashûr, Lisht, Illahun, and Hawara.

Some of these modern discoveries have been commented on and illustrated by Prof. Maspero in his great history. But the discoveries that have been made since this publication have been very important,—those at Abusîr, indeed, of first-rate importance, though not so momentous as those of the tombs of the Ist and IId Dynasties at Abydos, already described. At Abû Roash and at Giza, at the northern end of the Memphite necropolis, several expeditions have had considerable success, notably those of the American Dr. Reisner, assisted by Mr. Mace, who excavated the royal tombs at Umm el-Ga'ab for Prof. Petrie, those of the German Drs. Steindorff and Borchardt,—the latter working for the *Deutsch-Orient Gesellschaft*,—and those of other American excavators. Until the full publication of the results of these excavations appears, very little can be said about them. Many mastaba-tombs have, it is understood, been found, with interesting remains. Nothing of great historical importance seems to have been discovered, however. It is otherwise when we come to the discoveries of Messrs. Borchardt and Schäfer at Abusîr, south of Gîza and north of Sakkâra. At this place results of first-rate historical importance have been attained.

The main group of pyramids at Abusîr consists of the tombs of the kings Sahurā, Neferarikarā, and Ne-user-Rā, of the Vth Dynasty. The pyramids themselves are smaller than those of Gîza, but larger than those of Sakkâra. In general appearance and effect they resemble those of Gîza, but they are not so imposing, as the desert here is low. Those of Gîza, Sakkâra, and Dashûr owe much of their impressiveness to the fact that they are placed at some height above the cultivated land. The excavation and planning of these pyramids were carried out by Messrs. Borchardt and Schäfer at the expense of Baron von Bissing, the well-known Egyptologist of Munich, and of the *Deutsch-Orient Gesellschaft* of Berlin. The antiquities found have been divided between the museums of Berlin and Cairo.

One of the most noteworthy discoveries was that of the funerary temple of Ne-user-Rā, which stood at the base of his pyramid. The plan is interesting, and the granite lotus-bud columns found are the most ancient yet discovered in Egypt. Much of the paving and the wainscoting of the walls was of fine black marble, beautifully polished. An interesting find was a basin and drain with lion's-head mouth, to carry away the blood of the sacrifices. Some sculptures in relief were discovered, including a gigantic representation of the king and the goddess Isis, which shows that in the early days of the Vth Dynasty the king and the gods were already depicted in exactly the same costume as they wore in the days of the Ramses and the Ptolemies. The hieratic art of Egypt had, in fact, now taken on itself the final outward appearance which it retained to the very end. There is no more of the archaism and absence of conventionality, which marks the art of the earliest dynasties.

We can trace by successive steps the swift development of Egyptian art from the rude archaism of the Ist Dynasty to its final consummation under the Vth, when the conventions became fixed. In the time of Khāsekhemui, at the beginning of the IId Dynasty, the archaic character of the art has already begun to wear off. Under the same dynasty we still have styles of unconventional naïveté, such as the famous Statue " No. 1 " of the Cairo Museum,[1] bearing the names of Kings Hetepahaui, Neb-rā, and Neneter. But with the IVth Dynasty we no longer look for unconventionality. Prof. Petrie discovered at Abydos a small ivory statuette of Khufu or Cheops, the builder of the Great Pyramid of Giza. The portrait is a good one and carefully executed. It was not till the time of the XVIIIth Dynasty, indeed, that the Egyptians ceased to portray their kings as they really were, and gave them a purely conventional type of face. This convention, against which the heretical King Amenhetep IV (Akhunaten) rebelled,

[1] See illustration, p. 100.

in order to have himself portrayed in all his real ungainliness and ugliness, did not exist till long after the time of the IVth and Vth Dynasties. The kings of the XIIth

STATUE NO. 1 OF THE CAIRO MUSEUM.
About 3900 B.C. Photograph reproduced from M. de Morgan's *Recherches*, vol 1.

Dynasty especially were most careful that their statues should be accurate portraits; indeed, the portraits of Usertsen (Senusret) III vary from a young face to an old one, showing that the king was faithfully depicted at different periods of his life.

But the general conventions of dress and deportment were finally fixed under the Vth Dynasty. After this time we no longer have such absolutely faithful and original presentments as the other little ivory statuette found by Prof. Petrie at Abydos (now in the British Museum), which shows us an aged monarch of the Ist Dynasty. It is obvious that the features are absolutely true to life, and the figure wears an unconventionally party-coloured and bordered robe of a kind which kings of a later day may have worn in actual life, but which they would assuredly never be depicted as wearing by the artists of their day. To the end of Egyptian history, the kings, even the Roman emperors, were represented on the monuments clothed in the official costume of their ancestors of the IVth and Vth Dynasties, in the same manner as we see Khufu wearing his robe in the little figure from Abydos, and Ne-user-Rā on the great relief from Abusîr. There are one or two exceptions, such as the representations of the original genius Akhunaten at Tell el-Amarna and the beautiful statue of Ramses II at Turin, in which we see these kings wearing the real costume of their time, but such exceptions are very rare.

The art of Abusîr is therefore of great interest, since it marks the end of the development of the priestly art. Secular art might develop as it liked, though the crystallizing influence of the ecclesiastical canon is always evident here also. But henceforward it was an impiety, which only an Akhunaten could commit, to depict a king or a god on the walls of a temple otherwise (except so far as the portrait was concerned) than as he had been depicted in the time of the Vth Dynasty.

Other buildings have been excavated by the Germans at Abusîr, notably the usual town of mastaba-tombs belonging to the chief dignitaries of the reign, which is always found at the foot of a royal pyramid of this period. Another building of the highest interest, belonging to the same age, was also excavated, and its true character was determined. This is a building at a place called er-Righa or Abû Ghuraib, "Father of Crows," between Abusîr and Giza. It was formerly supposed to be a pyramid, but the German excavations have shown that it is really a temple of the Sun-god Rā of Heliopolis, specially venerated by the kings of the Vth Dynasty, who were of Heliopolitan origin. The great pyramid-builders of the IVth Dynasty seem to have been the last true Memphites. At the end of the reign of Shepseskaf, the last monarch of the dynasty, the sceptre passed to a Heliopolitan family. The following VIth Dynasty may again have been Memphite, but this is uncertain. The capital continued to be Memphis, and from the beginning of the IIId Dynasty to the end of the Old Kingdom and the rise of Herakleopolis and Thebes, Memphis remained the chief city of Egypt.

The Heliopolitans were naturally the servants of the Sun-god above all other gods, and they were the first to call themselves "Sons of the Sun," a title retained by the Pharaohs throughout all subsequent history. It was Ne-user-Rā who built the Sun-temple of

Abû Ghuraib, on the edge of the desert, north of his pyramid and those of his two immediate predecessors at Abusîr. As now laid bare by the excavations of 1900, it is seen to consist of an artificial mound, with a great court in front to the eastward. On the mound was erected a truncated obelisk, the stone emblem of the Sun-god. The worshippers in the court below looked towards the Sun's stone erected upon its mound in the west, the quarter of the sun's setting; for the Sun-god of Heliopolis was primarily the setting sun, Tum-Rā, not Rā Harmachis, the rising sun, whose emblem is the Great Sphinx at Gîza, which looks towards the east. The sacred emblem of the Heliopolitan Sun-god reminds us forcibly of the Semitic *bethels* or *baetyli*, the sacred stones of Palestine, and may give yet another hint of the Semitic origin of the Heliopolitan cult. In the court of the temple is a huge circular altar of fine alabaster, several feet across, on which slain oxen were offered to the Sun, and behind this, at the eastern end of the court, are six great basins of the same stone, over which the beasts were slain, with drains running out of them by which their blood was carried away. This temple is a most interesting monument of the civilization of the " Old Kingdom " at the time of the Vth Dynasty.

At Sakkâra itself, which lies a short distance south of Abusîr, no new royal tombs have, as has been said, been discovered of late years. But a great deal of work has been done among the private mastaba-tombs by the officers of the *Service des Antiquités*, which reserves to itself the right of excavation here and at Dashûr. The mastaba of the sage and writer Kagemna (or rather Gemnika, "I-have-found-a-ghost," which sounds very like an American Indian appellation) is very fine. "I-have-found-a-ghost" lived in the reign of the king Tātkarā Assa, the "Tancheres" of Manetho, and he wrote maxims like his great contemporary Phtahhetep ("Offered to Phtah"), who was also buried at Sakkâra. The officials of the *Service des Antiquités* who cleaned the tomb unluckily misread his name *Ka-bi-n* (an impossible form which could only mean, literally translated, "Ghost-soul-of" or "Ghost-soul-to-me"), and they have placed it in this form over the entrance to his tomb. This mastaba, like those, already known, of Mereruka (sometimes misnamed "Mera") and the famous Ti, both also at Sakkâra, contains a large number of chambers, ornamented with reliefs. In the vicinity M. Grébaut, then Director of the Service of Antiquities, discovered a very interesting Street of Tombs, a regular Via Sacra, with rows of tombs of the dignitaries of the VIth Dynasty on either side of it. They are generally very much like one another; the workmanship of the reliefs is fine, and the portrait of the owner of the tomb is always in evidence.

Several of the smaller mastabas have lately been disposed of to the various museums, as they are liable to damage if they remain where they stand; moreover, they are not of great value to the Museum of Cairo, but are of considerable value to various museums which do not already possess complete specimens of this class of tombs. A fine one, belonging to the chief Uerarina, is now exhibited in the Assyrian Basement of the British Museum; another is in the Museum of Leyden; a third at Berlin, and so on. Most of these are simple tombs of one chamber. In the centre of the rear wall we always see the *stele* or gravestone proper, built into the fabric of the tomb. Before this stood the low table of offerings with a bowl for oblations, and on either side a tall incense-altar. From the altar the divine smoke (*senetr*) arose when the *hen-ka*, or priest of the ghost (literally, " Ghost's Servant "), performed his duty of venerating the spirits of the deceased, while the *Kher-heb*, or cantor, enveloped in the mystic folds of the leopard-skin and with bronze incense-burner in hand, sang the holy litanies and spells which should propitiate the ghost and enable him to win his way to ultimate perfection in the next world.

The stele is always in the form of a door with pyloniform cornice. On either side is a figure of the deceased, and at the sides are carved prayers to Anubis, and at a later date to Osiris, who are implored to give the funerary meats and " everything good and pure on which the god there (as the dead man in the tomb has been constituted) lives; " often we find that the biography and list of honorary titles and dignities of the deceased have been added.

Sakkâra was used as a place of burial in the latest as well as in the earliest time. The Egyptians of the XXVIth Dynasty, wearied of the long decadence and devastating wars which had followed the glorious epoch of the conquering Pharaohs of the XVIIIth and XIXth

Dynasties, turned for a new and refreshing inspiration to the works of the most ancient kings, when Egypt was a simple self-contained country, holding no intercourse with outside lands, bearing no outside burdens for the sake of pomp and glory, and knowing nothing of the decay and decadence which follows in the train of earthly power and grandeur. They deliberately turned their backs on the worn-out and discredited imperial trappings of the Thothmes and Ramses, and they took the supposed primitive simplicity of the Snefrus, the Khufus, and the Ne-user-Rās for a model and ensampler to their lives. It was an age of conscious and intended archaism, and in pursuit of the archaistic ideal the Memphites of the Saïte age had themselves buried in the ancient necropolis of Sakkâra, side by side with their ancestors of the time of the Vth and VIth Dynasties. Several of these tombs have lately been discovered and opened, and fitted with modern improvements. One or two of them, of the Persian period, have wells (leading to the sepulchral chamber) of enormous depth, down which the modern tourist is enabled to descend by a spiral iron staircase. The Serapeum itself is lit with electricity, and in the Tombs of the Kings at Thebes nothing disturbs the silence but the steady thumping pulsation of the dynamo-engine which lights the ancient sepulchres of the Pharaohs. Thus do modern ideas and inventions help us to see and so to understand better the works of ancient Egypt. But it is perhaps a little too much like the Yankee at the Court of King Arthur.

The interiors of the later tombs are often decorated

with reliefs which imitate those of the early period, but with a kind of delicate grace which at once marks them for what they are, so that it is impossible to confound them with the genuine ancient originals from which they were adapted.

Riding from Sakkâra southwards to Dashûr, we pass on the way the gigantic stone mastaba known as the *Mastabat el-Fara'ûn*, "Pharaoh's Bench." This was considered to be the tomb of the Vth Dynasty king, Unas, until his pyramid was found by Prof. Maspero at Sakkâra. From its form it might be thought to belong to a monarch of the IIId Dynasty, but the great size of the stone blocks of which it is built seems to point rather to the XIIth. All attempts to penetrate its secret by actual excavation have been unavailing.

Further south across the desert we see from the Mastabat el-Fara'ûn four distinct pyramids, symmetrically arranged in two lines, two in each line. The two to the right are great stone erections of the usual type, like those of Gîza and Abusîr, and the southernmost of them has a peculiar broken-backed appearance, due to the alteration of the angle of inclination of its sides during construction. Further, it is covered almost to the ground by the original casing of polished white limestone blocks, so that it gives a very good idea of the original appearance of the other pyramids, which have lost their casing. These two pyramids very probably belong to kings of the IIId Dynasty, as does the Step-Pyramid of Sakkâra. They strongly resemble the Gîza type, and the northernmost of the two looks very like an understudy of the Great Pyramid. It seems to mark the step in the development of the royal pyramid which was immediately followed by the Great Pyramid. But no excavations have yet proved the accuracy of this view. Both pyramids have been entered, but nothing has been found in them. It is very probable that one of them is the second pyramid of Snefru.

The other two pyramids, those nearest the cultivation, are of very different appearance. They are half-ruined, they are black in colour, and their whole effect is quite different from that of the stone pyramids. For they are built of brick, not of stone. They are pyramids, it is true, but of a different material and of a different date from those which we have been describing. They are built above the sepulchres of kings of the XIIth Dynasty, the Theban house which transferred its residence northwards to the neighbourhood of the ancient Northern capital. We have, in fact, reached the end of the Old Kingdom at Sakkâra; at Dashûr begin the sepulchres of the Middle Kingdom. Pyramids are still built, but they are not always of stone; brick is used, usually with stone in the interior. The general effect of these brick pyramids, when new, must have been indistinguishable from that of the stone ones, and even now, when it has become half-ruined, such a great brick pyramid as that of Usertsen (Senusret) III at Dashûr is not without impressiveness. After all, there is no reason why a brick building should be less admirable than a stone one. And in its own way the construction of such colossal masses of bricks as the two eastern pyramids of Dashûr must have been as arduous, even as difficult, as that of building a moderate-sized stone pyramid. The photograph of the brick pyramids of Dashûr on this page shows well the great size of these

EXTERIOR OF THE SOUTHERN BRICK PYRAMID OF DASHÛR: XIITH DYNASTY.

Excavated by M. de Morgan, 1895. This is the secondary tomb of Amenemhat III; about 2200 B. C.

masses of brickwork, which are as impressive as any of the great brick structures of Babylonia and Assyria. The XIIth Dynasty use of brick for the royal tombs was a return to the custom of earlier days, for from the time of Aha to that Tjeser, from the Ist Dynasty to the IIId, brick had been used for the building of the royal mastaba-tombs, out of which the pyramids had developed.

At this point, where we take leave of the great pyramids of the Old Kingdom, we may notice the latest theory as to the building of these monuments, which has of late years been enunciated by Dr. Borchardt, and is now generally accepted. The great Prussian explorer Lepsius, when he examined the pyramids in the 'forties, came to the conclusion that each king, when he ascended the throne, planned a small pyramid for himself. This was built in a few years' time, and if his reign were short, or if he were unable to enlarge the pyramid for other reasons, it sufficed for his tomb. If, however, his reign seemed likely to be one of some length, after the first plan was completed he enlarged his pyramid by building another and a larger one around it and over it. Then again, when this addition was finished, and the king still reigned and was in possession of great resources, yet another coating, so to speak, was put on to the pyramid, and so on till colossal structures like the First and Second Pyramid of Giza, which, we know, belonged to kings who were unusually long-lived, were completed. And finally the aged monarch died, and was buried in the huge tomb which his long life and his great power had enabled him to erect. This view appeared eminently reasonable at the time, and it seemed almost as though we ought to be able to tell whether a king had reigned long or not by the size of his pyramid, and even to obtain a rough idea of the length of his reign by counting the successive coats or accretions which it had received, much as we tell the age of a tree by the rings in its bole. A pyramid seemed to have been constructed something after the manner of an onion or a Chinese puzzle-box.

Prof. Petrie, however, who examined the Giza pyramids in 1881, and carefully measured them all up and finally settled their trigonometrical relation, came to the conclusion that Lepsius's theory was entirely erroneous, and that every pyramid was built and now stands as it was originally planned. Dr. Borchardt, however, who is an architect by profession, has examined the pyramids again, and has come to the conclusion that Prof. Petrie's statement is not correct, and that there is an element of truth in Lepsius's hypothesis. He has shown that several of the pyramids, notably the First and Second at Giza, show unmistakable signs of a modified, altered, and enlarged plan; in fact, long-lived kings like Khufu seem to have added considerably to their pyramids and even to have entirely remodelled them on a larger scale. This has certainly been the case with the Great Pyramid. We can, then, accept Lepsius's theory as modified by Dr. Borchardt.

THE PYRAMIDS OF GÎZA DURING THE INUNDATION.

Another interesting point has arisen in connection

with the Great Pyramid. Considerable difference of opinion has always existed between Egyptologists and the professors of European archæology with regard to the antiquity of the knowledge of iron in Egypt. The majority of the Egyptologists have always maintained, on the authority of the inscriptions, that iron was known to the ancient Egyptians from the earliest period. They argued that the word for a certain metal in old Egyptian was the same as the Coptic word for "iron." They stated that in the most ancient religious texts the Egyptians spoke of the firmament of heaven as made of this metal, and they came to the conclusion that it was because this metal was blue in colour, the hue of iron or steel; and they further pointed out that some of the weapons in the tomb-paintings were painted blue and others red, some being of iron, that is to say, others of copper or bronze. Finally they brought forward as incontrovertible evidence an actual fragment of worked iron, which had been found between two of the inner blocks, down one of the air-shafts, in the Great Pyramid. Here was an actual piece of iron of the time of the IVth Dynasty, about 3500 B. C.

This conclusion was never accepted by the students of the development of the use of metal in prehistoric Europe, when they came to know of it. No doubt their incredulity was partly due to want of appreciation of the Egyptological evidence, partly to disinclination to accept a conclusion which did not at all agree with the knowledge they had derived from their own study of prehistoric Europe. In Southern Europe it was quite certain that iron did not come into use till about 1000 B.C.; in Central Europe, where the discoveries at Hallstatt in the Salzkammergut exhibit the transition from the Age of Bronze to that of Iron, about 800 B.C. The exclusively Iron Age culture of La Tène cannot be dated earlier than the eighth century, if as early as that. How then was it possible that, if iron had been known to the Egyptians as early as 3500 B.C., its knowledge should not have been communicated to the Europeans until over two thousand years later? No; iron could not have been really known to the Egyptians much before 1000 B.C., and the Egyptological evidence was all wrong. This line of argument was taken by the distinguished Swedish archæologist, Prof. Oscar Montelius, of Upsala, whose previous experience in dealing with the antiquities of Northern Europe, great as it was, was hardly sufficient to enable him to pronounce with authority on a point affecting far-away African Egypt. And when dealing with Greek prehistoric antiquities Prof. Montelius's views have hardly met with that ready agreement which all acknowledge to be his due when he is giving us the results of his ripe knowledge of Northern antiquities. He has, in fact, forgotten, as most " prehistoric " archæologists do forget, that the antiquities of Scandinavia, Greece, Egypt, the Semites, the bronze-workers of Benin, the miners of Zimbabwe, and the Ohio mound-builders are not to be treated all together as a whole, and that hard and fast lines of development cannot be laid down for them, based on the experience of Scandinavia.

We may perhaps trace this misleading habit of thought to the influence of the professors of natural science over the students of Stone Age and Bronze Age antiquities. Because nature moves by steady progression and develops on even lines—*nihil facit per saltum*—it seems to have been assumed that the works of man's hands have developed in the same way, in a regular and even scheme all over the world. On this supposition it would be impossible for the great discovery of the use of iron to have been known in Egypt as early as 3500 B.C., for this knowledge to have remained dormant there for two thousand years, and then to have been suddenly communicated about 1000 B.C. to Greece, spreading with lightning-like rapidity over Europe and displacing the use of bronze everywhere. Yet, as a matter of fact, the work of man does develop in exactly this haphazard way, by fits and starts and sudden leaps of progress after millennia of stagnation. Throwsback to barbarism are just as frequent. The analogy of natural evolution is completely inapplicable and misleading.

Prof. Montelius, however, following the "evolutionary" line of thought, believed that because iron was not known in Europe till about 1000 B.C. it could not have been known in Egypt much earlier; and in an important article which appeared in the Swedish ethnological journal *Ymer* in 1883, entitled *Brönsaldern i Egypten* ("The Bronze Age in Egypt"), he essayed to prove the contrary arguments of the Egyptologists wrong. His main points were that the colour of the weapons in the frescoes was of no importance, as it was purely conventional and arbitrary, and that the evidence of the piece of iron from the Great Pyramid was insufficiently authenticated, and therefore valueless, in the absence of other definite archæological evidence in the shape of iron of supposed early date. To this article the Swedish Egyptologist, Dr. Piehl, replied in the same periodical, in an article entitled *Bronsaldern i Egypten*, in which he traversed Prof. Montelius's conclusions from the Egyptological point of view, and adduced other instances of the use of iron in Egypt, all, it is true, later than the time of the IVth Dynasty. But this protest received little notice, owing to the fact that it remained buried in a Swedish periodical, while Prof. Montelius's original article was translated into French, and so became well-known.

For the time Prof. Montelius's conclusions were generally accepted, and when the discoveries of the prehistoric antiquities were made by M. de Morgan, it seemed more probable than ever that Egypt had gone through a regular progressive development from the Age of Stone through those of copper and bronze to that of iron, which was reached about 1100 or 1000 B. C. The evidence of the iron fragment from the Great Pyramid was put on one side, in spite of the circumstantial account of its discovery which had been given by its finders. Even Prof. Petrie, who in 1881 had accepted the pyramid fragment as undoubtedly contemporary with that building, and had gone so far as to adduce additional evidence for its authenticity, gave way, and accepted Montelius's view, which held its own until in 1902 it was directly controverted by a discovery of Prof. Petrie at Abydos. This discovery consisted of an undoubted fragment of iron found in conjunction with bronze tools of VIth Dynasty date; and it settled the matter.[1] The VIth Dynasty date of this piece of iron, which was more probably worked than not (since it was buried with tools), was held to be undoubted by its discoverer and by everybody else, and, if this were undoubted, the IVth Dynasty date of the Great Pyramid fragment was also fully established. The discoverers of the earlier fragment had no doubt whatever as to its being contemporary with the pyramid, and were supported in this by Prof. Petrie in 1881. Therefore it is now known to be the fact that iron was used by the Egyptians as early as 3500 B. C.[2]

It would thus appear that though the Egyptians cannot be said to have used iron generally and so to have entered the " Iron Age " before about 1300 B. C. (reign of Ramses II), yet iron was well known to them and had been used more than occasionally by them for tools and building purposes as early as the time of the IVth Dynasty, about 3500 B. C. Certainly dated examples of its use occur under the IVth, VIth, and XIIIth Dynasties. Why this knowledge was not communicated to

[1] See H. R. Hall's note on "The Early Use of Iron in Egypt," in *Man* (the organ of the Anthropological Society of London), iii (1903), No. 86.

[2] Prof. Montelius objected to these conclusions in a review of the British Museum " Guide to the Antiquities of the Bronze Age," which was published in *Man*, 1905 (Jan.), No 7. For an answer to these objections, see Hall, *ibid.*, No. 40.

Europe before about 1000 B. C. we cannot say, nor are Egyptologists called upon to find the reason. So the Great Pyramid has played an interesting part in the settlement of a very important question.

It was supposed by Prof. Petrie that the piece of iron from the Great Pyramid had been part of some arrangement employed for raising the stones into position. Herodotus speaks of the machines, which were used to raise the stones, as made of little pieces of wood. The generally accepted explanation of his meaning used to be that a small crane or similar wooden machine was used for hoisting the stone by means of pulley and rope; but M. Legrain, the director of the works of restoration in the Great Temple of Karnak, has explained it differently. Among the "foundation deposits" of the XVIIIth Dynasty at Dêr el-Bahari and elsewhere, beside the little plaques with the king's name and the model hoes and vases, was usually found an enigmatic wooden object like a small cradle, with two sides made of semicircular pieces of wood, joined along the curved portion by round wooden bars. M. Legrain has now explained this as a model of the machine used to raise heavy stones from tier to tier of a pyramid or other building, and illustrations of the method of its use may be found in Choisy's *Art de Bâtir chez les anciens Egyptiens*. There is little doubt that this primitive machine is that to which Herodotus refers as having been used in the erection of the pyramids.

The later historian, Diodorus, also tells us that great mounds or ramps of earth were used as well, and that the stones were dragged up these to the requisite height. There is no doubt that this statement also is correct. We know that the Egyptians did build in this very way, and the system has been revived by M. Legrain for his work at Karnak, where still exist the remains of the actual mounds and ramps by which the great western pylon was erected in Ptolemaïc times. Work carried on in this way is slow and expensive, but it is eminently suited to the country and understood by the people. If they wish to put a great stone architrave weighing many tons across the top of two columns, they do not hoist it up into position; they rear a great ramp or embankment of earth against the two pillars, half-burying them in the process, then drag the architrave up the ramp by means of ropes and men, and put it into position. Then the ramp is cleared away. This is the ancient system which is now followed at Karnak, and it is the system by which, with the further aid of the wooden machines, the Great Pyramid and its compeers were erected in the days of the IVth Dynasty. *Plus cela change, plus c'est la même chose.*

The brick pyramids of the XIIth Dynasty were erected in the same way, for the Egyptians had no knowledge of the modern combination of wooden scaffolding and ladders. There was originally a small stone pyramid of the same dynasty at Dashûr, half-way between the two brick ones, but this has now almost disappeared. It belonged to the king Amenemhat II, while the others belonged, the northern to Usertsen (Senusret) III, the southern to Amenemhat III. Both these latter monarchs had other tombs elsewhere,—Usertsen a great rock-cut gallery and chamber in the cliff at Abydos, Amenemhat a pyramid not very far to the south, at Hawara, close to the Fayyûm. It is uncertain whether the Hawara pyramid or that of Dashûr was the real burial-place of the king, as at neither place is his name found alone. At Hawara it is found in cônjunction with that of his daughter, the queen-regnant Sebekneferurā (Skemiophris), at Dashûr with that of a king Auabrā Hor, who was buried in a small tomb near that of the king, and adjoining the tombs of the king's children. Who King Hor was we do not quite know. His name is not given in the lists, and was unknown until M. de Morgan's discoveries at Dashûr. It is most probable that he was a prince who was given royal honours during the lifetime of Amenemhat III, whom he predeceased.[1] In the beautiful wooden statue of him found in his tomb, which is now in the Cairo Museum, he is represented as quite a youth. Amenemhat III was certainly succeeded by Amenemhat IV, and it is impossible to intercalate Hor between them.

The identification of the owners of the three western pyramids of Dashûr is due to M. de Morgan and his assistants, Messrs. Legrain and Jéquier, who excavated them from 1894 till 1896. The northern pyramid, that of Usertsen (Senusret) III, is not so well preserved as the southern. It is more worn away, and does not present so imposing an appearance. In both pyramids the outer casing of white stone has entirely disap-

[1] See below, p. 121. Possibly he was a son of Amenemhat III.

peared, leaving only the bare black bricks. Each stood in the midst of a great necropolis of dignitaries of the period, as was usually the case. Many of the mastabas were excavated by M. de Morgan. Some are of older periods than the XIIth Dynasty, one belonging to a priest of King Snefru, Aha-f-ka ("Ghost-fighter"), who bore the additional titles of "director of prophets and general of infantry." There were pluralists even in those days. And the distinction between the privy councillor (Geheimrat) and real privy councillor (Wirklicher-Geheimrat) was quite familiar; for we find it actually made, many an old Egyptian officially priding himself in his tomb on having been a *real* privy councillor! The Egyptian bureaucracy was already ancient and had its survivals and its anomalies even as early as the time of the pyramid-builders.

In front of the pyramid of Usertsen (Senusret) III at one time stood the usual funerary temple, but it has been totally destroyed. By the side of the pyramid were buried some of the princesses of the royal family, in a series of tombs opening out of a subterranean gallery, and in this gallery were found the wonderful jewels of the princesses Sit-hathor and Merit, which are among the greatest treasures of the Cairo Museum. Those who have not seen them can obtain a perfect idea of their appearance from the beautiful watercolour paintings of them by M. Legrain, which are published in M. de Morgan's work on the "Fouilles â Dahchour" (Vienna, 1895). Altogether one hundred and seven objects were recovered, consisting of all kinds of jewelry in gold and coloured stones. Among the most beautiful are the great " pectorals," or breast-ornaments, in the shape of pylons, with the names of Usertsen II, Usertsen III, and Amenemhat III; the names are surrounded by hawks standing on the sign for gold, gryphons, figures of the king striking down enemies, etc., all in *cloisonné* work, with beautiful stones such as lapis lazuli, green felspar, and carnelian taking the place of coloured enamels. The massive chains of golden beads and cowries are also very remarkable. These treasures had been buried in boxes in the floor of the subterranean gallery, and had luckily escaped the notice of plunderers, and so by a fortunate chance have survived to tell us what the Egyptian jewellers could do in the days of the XIIth Dynasty. Here also were found two great Nile barges, full-sized boats, with their oars and other gear complete. They also may be seen in the Museum of Cairo. It can only be supposed that they had served as the biers of the royal mummies, and had been brought up in state on sledges. The actual royal chamber was not found, although a subterranean gallery was driven beneath the centre of the pyramid.

The southern brick pyramid was constructed in the same way as the northern one. At the side of it were also found the tombs of members of the royal house, including that of the king Hor, already mentioned, with its interesting contents. The remains of the mummy of this ephemeral monarch, known only from his tomb, were also found. The entrails of the king were placed in the usual "canopic jars," which were sealed with the seal of Amenemhat III; it is thus that we know that Hor died before him. In many of the inscriptions of this king, on his coffin and stelæ, a peculiarly affected manner of writing the hieroglyphs is found,—the birds are without their legs, the snake has no tail, the bee no head. Birds are found without their legs in other inscriptions of this period; it was a temporary fashion and soon discarded.

In the tomb of a princess named Nubhetep, near at hand, were found more jewels of the same style as those of Sit-hathor and Merit. The pyramid itself contained the usual passages and chambers, which were reached with much difficulty and considerable tunnelling by M. de Morgan. In fact, the search for the royal death-chambers lasted from December 5, 1894, till March 17, 1895, when the excavators' gallery finally struck one of the ancient passages, which were found to be unusually extensive, contrasting in this respect with the northern pyramid. The royal tomb-chamber had, of course, been emptied of what it contained. It must be remembered that, in any case, it is probable that the king was not actually buried here, but in the pyramid of Hawara.

The pyramid of Amenemhat II, which lies between the two brick pyramids, was built entirely of stone. Nothing of it remains above ground, but the investigation of the subterranean portions showed that it was remarkable for the massiveness of its stones and the care with which the masonry was executed. The same characteristics are found in the dependent tombs of the princesses Ha and Khnumet, in which more jewelry was found. This splendid stonework is characteristic of the Middle Kingdom; we find it also in the temple of Mentuhetep III at Thebes.

Some distance south of Dashûr is Mêdûm, where the pyramid of Sneferu reigns in solitude, and beyond this again is Lisht, where in the years 1894-6 MM. Gautier and Jéquier excavated the pyramid of Usertsen (Senusret) I. The most remarkable find was a cache of the seated statues of the king in white limestone, in absolutely perfect condition. They were found lying on their sides, just as they had been hidden. Six figures of the king in the form of Osiris, with the face painted red, were also found. Such figures seem to have been regularly set up in front of a royal sepulchre; several were found in front of the funerary temple of Mentuhetep III, Thebes, which we shall describe later. A fine altar of gray granite, with representations in relief of the nomes bringing offerings, was also recovered. The pyramid of Lisht itself is not built of bricks, like those of Dashûr, but of stone. It was not, however, erected in so solid a fashion as those of earlier days at Giza or Abusîr, and nothing is left of it now but a heap of débris. The XIIth Dynasty architects built walls of magnificent masonry, as we have seen, and there is no doubt that the stone casing of their pyramids was originally very fine, but the interior is of brick or rubble; the wonderful system of building employed by kings of the IVth Dynasty at Giza was not practised.

South of Lisht is Illahun, and at the entrance to the province of the Fayyûm, and west of this, nearer the Fayyûm, is Hawara, where Prof. Petrie excavated the pyramids of Usertsen (Senusret) II and Amenemhat III. His discoveries have already been described by Prof. Maspero in his history, so that it will suffice here merely to compare them with the results of M. de Morgan's later work at Dashûr and that of MM. Gautier and Jéquier at Lisht, to note recent conclusions in connection with them, and to describe the newest discoveries in the same region.

Both pyramids are of brick, lined with stone, like those of Dashûr, with some differences of internal construction, since stone walls exist in the interior. The central chambers and passages leading to them were discovered; and in both cases the passages are peculiarly complex, with dumb chambers, great stone portcullises, etc., in order to mislead and block the way to possible plunderers. The extraordinary sepulchral chamber of the Hawara pyramid, which, though it is over twenty-two feet long by ten feet wide over all, is hewn out of one solid block of hard yellow quartzite, gives some idea of the remarkable facility of dealing with huge stones and the love of utilizing them which is especially characteristic of the XIIth Dynasty. The pyramid of Hawara was provided with a funerary temple the like of which had never been known in Egypt before and was never known afterwards. It was a huge building far larger than the pyramid itself, and built of fine limestone and crystalline white quartzite, in a style eminently characteristic of the XIIth Dynasty. In actual superficies this temple covered an extent of ground within which the temples of Karnak, Luxor, and the Ramesseum, at Thebes, could have stood, but has now almost entirely disappeared, having been used as a quarry for two thousand years. In Roman times this destroying process had already begun, but even then the building was still magnificent, and had been noted with wonder by all the Greek visitors to Egypt from the time of Herodotus downwards. Even before his day it had received the name of the "Labyrinth," on account of its supposed resemblance to the original labyrinth in Crete.

That the Hawara temple was the Egyptian labyrinth was pointed out by Lepsius in the 'forties of the last century. Within the last two or three years attention has again been drawn to it by Mr. Arthur Evans's discovery of the Cretan labyrinth itself in the shape of the Minoan or early Mycenæan palace of Knossos, near Candia in Crete. It is impossible to enter here into all the arguments by which it has been proved that the Knossian palace is the veritable labyrinth of the Minotaur legend, nor would it be strictly germane to our subject were we to do so; but it may suffice to say here that the word λαβύρινθος has been proved to be of Greek—or rather of pre-Hellenic—origin, and would mean in Karian "Place of the Double-Axe," like Labraunda in Karia, where Zeus was depicted with a double axe (*labrys*) in his hand. The non-Aryan, "Asianic," group of languages, to which certainly

Lycian and probably Karian belong, has been shown by the German philologer Kretschmer to have spread over Greece into Italy in the period before the Aryan Greeks entered Hellas, and to have left undoubted traces of its presence in Greek place-names and in the Greek language itself. Before the true Hellenes reached Crete, an Asianic dialect must have been spoken there, and to this language the word "labyrinth" must originally have belonged. The classical labyrinth was "in the Knossian territory." The palace of Knossos was emphatically the chief seat of the worship of a god whose emblem was the double-axe; it was the Knossian "Place of the Double-Axe," the Cretan "Labyrinth."

It used to be supposed that the Cretan labyrinth had taken its name from the Egyptian one, and the word itself was supposed to be of Egyptian origin. An Egyptian etymology was found for it as "*Ro-pi-ro-henet*," "Temple-mouth-canal," which might be interpreted, with some violence to Egyptian construction, as "The temple at the mouth of the canal," *i. e.* the Bahr Yusuf, which enters the Fayyûm at Hawara. But unluckily this word would have been pronounced by the natives of the vicinity as "Elphilahune," which is not very much like λαβύρινθος. "*Ro-pi-ro-henet*" is, in fact, a mere figment of the philological imagination, and cannot be proved ever to have existed. The element *Ro-henet*, "canal-mouth" (according to the local pronunciation of the Fayyûm and Middle Egypt, called *La-hune*), is genuine; it is the origin of the modern

Illahun (*el-Lahûn*), which is situated at the "canal-mouth." However, now that we know that the word labyrinth can be explained satisfactorily with the help of Karian, as evidently of Greek (pre-Aryan) origin, and as evidently the original name of the Knossian labyrinth, it is obvious that there is no need to seek a far-fetched explanation of the word in Egypt, and to suppose that the Greeks called the Cretan labyrinth after the Egyptian one.

The contrary is evidently the case. Greek visitors to Egypt found a resemblance between the great Egyptian building, with its numerous halls and corridors, vast in extent, and the Knossian palace. Even if very little of the latter was visible in the classical period, as seems possible, yet the site seems always to have been kept holy and free from later building till Roman times, and we know that the tradition of the mazy halls and corridors of the labyrinth was always clear, and was evidently based on a vivid reminiscence. Actually, one of the most prominent characteristics of the Knossian palace is its mazy and labyrinthine system of passages and chambers. The parallel between the two buildings, which originally caused the Greek visitors to give the pyramid-temple of Hawara the name of "labyrinth," has been traced still further. The white limestone walls and the shining portals of "Parian marble," described by Strabo as characteristic of the Egyptian labyrinth, have been compared with the shining white selenite or gypsum used at Knossos, and certain general resemblances between the Greek architecture of the Minoan age and the almost contemporary Egyptian architecture of the XIIth Dynasty have been pointed out.[1] Such resemblances may go to swell the amount of evidence already known, which tells us that there was a close connection between Egyptian and Minoan art and civilization, established at least as early as 2500 B. C.

For it must be remembered that within the last few years we have learned from the excavations in Crete a new chapter of ancient history, which, it might almost seem, shows us Greece and Egypt in regular communication from nearly the beginnings of Egyptian history. As the excavations which have told us this were carried on in Crete, not in Egypt, to describe them does not lie within the scope of this book, though a short sketch of their results, so far as they affect Egyptian history in later days, is given in Chapter VII. Here it may suffice to say that, as far as the early period is concerned, Egypt and Crete were certainly in communication in the time of the XIIth Dynasty, and quite possibly in that of the VIth or still earlier. We have IIId Dynasty Egyptian vases from Knossos, which were certainly not imported in later days, for no ancient nation had antiquarian tastes till the time of the Saïtes in Egypt and of the Romans still later. In fact, this communication seems to go so far back in time that we are gradually being led to perceive the possibility that the Minoan culture of Greece was in its origin an offshoot from that

---

[1] See H. R. Hall, *Journal of Hellenic Studies*, 1905 (Pt. ii). The Temple of the Sphinx at Gîza may also be compared with those of Hawara and Knossos. It seems most probable that the Temple of the Sphinx is a XIIth Dynasty building.

of primeval Egypt, probably in early Neolithic times. That is to say, the Neolithic Greeks and Neolithic Egyptians were both members of the same "Mediterranean" stock, which quite possibly may have had its origin in Africa, and a portion of which may have crossed the sea to Europe in very early times, taking with it the seeds of culture which in Egypt developed in the Egyptian way, in Greece in the Greek way. Actual communication and connection may not have been maintained at first, and probably they were not. Prof. Petrie thinks otherwise, and would see in the boats painted on the predynastic Egyptian vases (see Chapter I) the identical galleys by which, in late Neolithic times, commerce between Crete and Egypt was carried on across the Mediterranean. It is certain, however, that these boats are ordinary little river craft, the usual Nile *felûkas* and *gyassas* of the time; they are depicted together with emblems of the desert and cultivated land,—ostriches, antelopes, hills, and palm-trees,—and the thoroughly inland and Upper Egyptian character of the whole design springs to the eye. There can be no doubt whatever that the predynastic boats were not seagoing galleys.

It was probably not till the time of the pyramid-builders that connection between the Greek Mediterraneans and the Nilotes was re-established. Thenceforward it increased, and in the time of the XIIth Dynasty, when the labyrinth of Amenemhat III was built, there seems to have been some kind of more or less regular communication between the two countries.

It is certain that artistic ideas were exchanged between them at this period. How communication was carried on we do not know, but it was probably rather by way of Cyprus and the Syrian coast than directly across the open sea. We shall revert to this point when we come to describe the connection between Crete and Egypt in the time of the XVIIIth Dynasty, when Cretan ambassadors visited the Egyptian court and were depicted in tomb paintings at Thebes. Between the time of the XIIth Dynasty and that of the XVIIIth this connection seems to have been very considerably strengthened; for at Knossos have been found an Egyptian statuette of an Egyptian named Abnub, who from his name must have lived about the end of the XIIIth Dynasty, and the top of an alabastron with the royal name of Khian, one of the Hyksos kings.

Quite close to Hawara, at Illahun, in the ruins of the town which was built by Usertsen's workmen when they were building his pyramid, Prof. Petrie found fragments of pottery of types which we now know well from excavations in Crete and Cyprus, though they were then unknown. They are fragments of the polychrome Cretan ware called, after the name of the place where it was first found in Crete, Kamáres ware, and of a black ware ornamented with small punctures, which are often filled up with white. This latter ware has been found elsewhere associated with XIIIth Dynasty antiquities. The former is known to belong in Crete to the "early Minoan" period, long anterior to the "late Minoan" or "Palace" period, which was contemporary with the

Egyptian XVIIIth Dynasty. We have here another interesting proof of a connection between XIIth Dynasty Egypt and early Minoan Crete. The later connection, under the XVIIIth and following dynasties, is also illustrated in the same reign by Prof. Petrie's finds of late Mycenæan objects and foreign graves at Medinet Gurob.[1]

These excavations at Hawara, Illahun, Kahun, and Gurob were carried out in the years 1887 - 9. Since then Prof. Petrie and his co-workers have revisited the same district, and Gurob has been re-examined (in 1904) by Messrs. Loat and Ayrton, who discovered there a shrine devoted to the worship of fish. This work was carried on at the same time as Prof. Petrie's main excavation for the Egypt Exploration Fund at Ahnas, or Ahnasyet el-Medina, the site of the ancient Henensu, the Herakleopolis of the Greeks. Prof. Naville had excavated there for the Egypt Exploration Fund in 1892, but had not completely cleared the temple. This work was now taken up by Prof. Petrie, who laid the whole building bare. It is dedicated to Hershefi, the local deity of Herakleopolis. This god, who was called Arsaphes by the Greeks, and identified with Herakles, was in fact a form of Horus with the head of a ram; his name means "Terrible-Face." The greater part of the temple dates to the time of the XIXth Dynasty, and nothing of the early period is left. We know, however,

---

[1] One man who was buried here bore the name An-Tursha, "Pillar of the Tursha." The Tursha were a people of the Mediterranean, possibly Tylissians of Crete.

that the Middle Kingdom was the flourishing period of the city of Hershefi. For a comparatively brief period, between the age of Memphite hegemony and that of Theban dominion, Herakleopolis was the capital city of Egypt. The kings of the IXth and Xth Dynasties were Herakleopolites, though we know little of them. One, Kheti, is said to have been a great tyrant. Another, Nebkaurā, is known only as a figure in the "Legend of the Eloquent Peasant," a classical story much in vogue in later days. Another, Merikarā, is a more real personage, for we have contemporary records of his days in the inscriptions of the tombs at Asyût, from which we see that the princes of Thebes were already wearing down the Northerners, in spite of the resistance of the adherents of Herakleopolis, among whom the most valiant were the chiefs of Asyût. The civil war eventuated in favour of Thebes, and the Theban XIth Dynasty assumed the double crown. The sceptre passed from Memphis and the North, and Thebes enters upon the scene of Egyptian history.

With this event the Nile-land also entered upon a new era of development. The metropolis of the kingdom was once more shifted to the South, and, although the kings of the XIIth Dynasty actually resided in the North, their Theban origin was never forgotten, and Thebes was regarded as the chief city of the country. The XIth Dynasty kings actually reigned at Thebes, and there the later kings of the XIIIth Dynasty retired after the conquest of the Hyksos. The fact that with Thebes were associated all the heroic traditions of the struggle against the Hyksos ensured the final stability of the capital there when the hated Semites were finally driven out, and the national kingdom was re-established in its full extent from north to south. But for occasional intervals, as when Akhunaten held his court at Tell el-Amarna and Ramses II at Tanis, Thebes remained the national capital for six hundred years, till the time of the XXIId Dynasty.

Another great change which differentiates the Middle Kingdom (XIth-XIIIth Dynasties) from the Old Kingdom was caused by Egypt's coming into contact with other outside nations at this period. During the whole history of the Old Kingdom, Egyptian relations with the outer world had been nil. We have some inkling of occasional connection with the Mediterranean peoples, the *Ha-nebu* or Northerners; we have accounts of wars with the people of Sinai and other Bedawin and negroes; and expeditions were also sent to the land of Punt (Somaliland) by way of the Upper Nile. But we have not the slightest hint of any connection with, or even knowledge of, the great nations of the Euphrates valley or the peoples of Palestine. The Babylonian king Narâm-Sin invaded the Sinaitic peninsula (the land of Magan) as early as 3750 B. C., about the time of the IIId Egyptian Dynasty. The great King Tjeser, of that dynasty, also invaded Sinai, and so did Snefru, the last king of the dynasty. But we have no hint of any collision between Babylonians and Egyptians at that time, nor do either of them betray the slightest knowledge of one another's existence. It can hardly be that the two civilized peoples of the world in those days were really absolutely ignorant of each other, but we have no trace of any connection between them, other than the possible one before the founding of the Egyptian monarchy.

This early connection, however, is very problematical. We have seen that there seems to be in early Egyptian civilization an element ultimately of Babylonian origin, and that there are two theories as to how it reached Egypt. One supposes that it was brought by a Semitic people of Arab affinities (represented by the modern Gallas), who crossed the Straits of Bab el-Mandeb and reached Egypt either by way of the Wadi Hammamat or by the Upper Nile. The other would bring it across the Isthmus of Suez to the Delta, where, at Heliopolis, there certainly seems to have been a settlement of a Semitic type of very ancient culture. In both cases we should have Semites bringing Babylonian culture to Egypt. This, as we may remind the reader, was not itself of Semitic origin, but was a development due to a non-Semitic people, the Sumerians as they are called, who, so far as we know, were the aboriginal inhabitants of Babylonia. The Sumerian language was of agglutinative type, radically distinct both from the pure Semitic idioms and from Egyptian. The Babylonian elements of culture which the early Semitic invaders brought with them to Egypt were, then, ultimately of Sumerian origin. Sumerian civilization had profoundly influenced the Semitic tribes for centuries before the Semitic conquest of Babylonia, and when the

Sumerians became more and more a conquered race, finally amalgamating with their conquerors and losing their racial and linguistic individuality, they were conquered by an alien race but not by an alien culture. For the culture of the Semites was Sumerian, the Semitic races owing their civilization to the Sumerians. That is as much as to say that a great deal of what we call Semitic culture is fundamentally non-Semitic.

In the earliest days, then, Egypt received elements of Sumerian culture through a Semitic medium, which introduced Semitic elements into the language of the people, and a Semitic racial strain. It is possible that both theories as to the routes of these primeval conquerors are true, and that two waves of Semites entered the Nile valley towards the close of the Neolithic period, one by way of the Upper Nile or Wadi Hammamat, the other by way of Heliopolis.

After the reconsolidation of the Egyptian people, with perhaps an autocratic class of Semitic origin and a populace of indigenous Nilotic race, we have no trace of further connection with the far-away centre of Semitic culture in Babylonia till the time of the Theban hegemony. Under the XIIth Dynasty we see Egyptians in friendly relations with the Bedawin of Idumæa and Southern Palestine. Thus Sanehat, the younger son of Amenemhat I, when the death of his royal father was announced, fled from the new king Usertsen (Senusret) into Palestine, and there married the daughter of the chief Ammuanshi and became a Syrian chief himself, only finally returning to Egypt as an old man on the assurance of the royal pardon and favour. We have in the reign of Usertsen (Senusret) II the famous visit of the Arab chief Abisha (Abêshu') with his following to the court of Khnumhetep, the prince of the Oryx nome in Middle Egypt, as we see it depicted on the walls of Khnumhetep's tomb at Beni Hasan. We see Usertsen (Senusret) III invading Palestine to chastise the land of Sekmem and the vile Syrians.[1]

The arm of Egypt was growing longer, and its weight was being felt in regions where it had previously been entirely unknown. Eventually the collision came. Egypt collided with an Asiatic power, and got the worst of the encounter. So much the worse that the Theban monarchy of the Middle Kingdom was overthrown, and Northern Egypt was actually conquered by the Asiatic foreigners and ruled by a foreign house for several centuries. Who these conquering Hyksos, or Shepherd Kings, were no recent discovery has told us. An old idea was that they were Mongols. It was supposed that the remarkable faces of the sphinxes of Tanis, now in the Cairo Museum, which bore the names of Hyksos kings, were of Mongolian type, as also those of two colossal royal heads discovered by M. Naville at Bu-

[1] We know of this campaign from the interesting historical stele of the general Sebek-khu (who took part in it), which was found during Mr. Garstang's excavations at Abydos, not previously referred to above. They were carried out in 1900, and resulted in the complete clearance of a part of the great cemetery which had been created during the XIIth Dynasty. The group of objects from the tombs of this cemetery, and those of XVIIIth Dynasty tombs also found, is especially valuable as showing the styles of objects in use at these two periods (see Garstang, *el-Arábah*, 1901).

bastis. But M. Golénischeff has now shown that these heads are really those of XIIth Dynasty kings, and not of Hyksos at all. Messrs. Newberry and Garstang have lately endeavoured to show that this type was foreign, and probably connected with that of the Kheta, or Hittites, of Northern Syria, who came into prominence as enemies of Egypt at a later period. They think that the type was introduced into the Egyptian royal family by Nefret, the queen of Usertsen (Senusret) II, whom they suppose to have been a Hittite princess. At the same time they think it probable that the type was also that of the Hyksos, whom they consider to have been practically Hittites. They therefore revive the theory of de Cara, which connects the Hyksos with the Hittites and these with the Pelasgi and Tyrseni.

This is a very interesting theory, which, when carried out to its logical conclusion, would connect the Hyksos and Hittites racially with the pre-Hellenic " Minoans " or Mycenæans of Greece, as well as with the Etruscans of Italy. But there is little of certainty in it. It is by no means impossible that we may eventually come to know that the Hittites (*Kheta*, the *Khattê* of the Assyrians) and other tribes of Asia Minor were racially akin to the " Minoans " of Greece, but the connection between the Hyksos and the Hittites is to seek. The countenances of the Kheta on the Egyptian monuments of Ramses II's time have an angular cast, and so have those of the Tanis sphinxes, of Queen Nefret, of the Bubastis statues, and the statues of Usertsen (Senusret) III and Amenemhat III. We might then suppose, with Messrs. Newberry and Garstang, that Nefret was a Kheta princess, who gave her peculiar racial traits to her son Usertsen (Senusret) III and his son Amenemhat, were it not far more probable that the resemblance between this peculiar XIIth Dynasty type and the Kheta face is purely fortuitous.

There is really no reason to suppose that the type of face presented by Nefret, Usertsen, and Amenemhat is not purely Egyptian. It may be seen in many a modern fellah, and the truth probably is that the sculptors have in the case of these rulers very faithfully and carefully depicted their portraits, and that their faces happen to have been of a rather hard and forbidding type. But, if we grant the contention of Messrs. Newberry and Garstang for the moment, where is the connection between these XIIth Dynasty kings and the Hyksos? All the Tanite monuments with this peculiar facial type which would be considered Hyksos are certainly of the XIIth Dynasty. The only statue of a Hyksos king, which was undoubtedly originally made for him and is not one of the XIIth Dynasty usurped, is the small one of Khian at Cairo, discovered by M. Naville at Bubastis, and this has no head. So that we have not the slightest idea of what a Hyksos looked like. Moreover, the evidence of the Hyksos names which are known to us points in quite a different direction. The Kheta, or Hittites, were certainly not Semites, yet the Hyksos names are definitely Semitic. In fact it is most probable that the Hyksos, or Shepherd Kings, were, as the classical authorities say they were, and as their name (*hiku-semut* or *hiku-shasu*, " princes of the deserts " or " princes of the Bedawin ") also testifies, purely and simply Arabs.

Now it is not a little curious that almost at the same time that a nomad Arab race conquered Lower Egypt and settled in it as rulers (just as 'Amr and the followers of Islam did over two thousand years later), another Arab race may have imposed its rule upon Babylonia. Yet this may have been the case; for the First Dynasty of Babylon, to which the famous Hammurabi belonged, was very probably of Arab origin, to judge by the forms of some of the royal names. It is by no means impossible that there was some connection between these two conquests, and that both Babylonia and Egypt fell, in the period before the year 2000 B. C., before some great migratory movement from Arabia, which overran Babylonia, Palestine, and even the Egyptian Delta.

In this manner Egypt and Babylonia may have been brought together in common subjection to the Arab. We do not know whether any regular communication between Egypt, under Semitic rule, and Babylonia was now established; but we do know that during the Hyksos period there were considerable relations between Egypt and over-sea Crete, and relations with Mesopotamia may possibly have been established. At any rate, when the war of liberation, which was directed by the princes of Thebes, was finally brought to a successful conclusion and the Arabs were expelled, we find the Egyptians a much changed nation. They had adopted for war the use of horse and chariot, which they learnt from their Semitic conquerors, whose victory was in all probability largely gained by their use, and, generally speaking, they had become much more like the Western Asiatic nations. Egypt was no longer isolated, for she had been forcibly brought into contact with the foreign world, and had learned much. She was no longer self-contained within her own borders. If the Semites could conquer her, so could she conquer the Semites. Armed with horse and chariot, the Egyptians went forth to battle, and their revenge was complete. All Palestine and Syria were Egyptian domains for five hundred years after the conquest by Thothmes I and III, and Ashur and Babel sent tribute to the Pharaoh of Egypt.

The reaction came, and Egypt was thrown prostrate beneath the feet of Assyria; but her claim to dominion over the Western Asiatics was never abandoned, and was revived in all its pomp by Ptolemy Euergetes, who brought back in triumph to Egypt the images of the gods which had been removed by Assyrians and Babylonians centuries before. This claim was never allowed by the Asiatics, it is true, and their kings wrote to the proudest Pharaoh as to an absolute equal. Even the King of Cyprus calls the King of Egypt his brother. But Palestine was admitted to be an Egyptian possession, and the Phœnicians were always energetic supporters of the Egyptian régime against the lawless Bedawin tribes, who were constantly intriguing with the Kheta or Hittite power to the north against Egypt.

The existence of this extra-Egyptian imperial possession meant that the eyes of the Egyptians were now permanently turned in the direction of Western Asia, with which they were henceforth in constant and intimate communication. The first Theban period and the Hyksos invasion, therefore, mark a turning-point in Egyptian history, at which we may fitly leave it for a time in order to turn our attention to those peoples of Western Asia with whom the Egyptians had now come into permanent contact.

Just as new discoveries have been made in Egypt, which have modified our previous conception of her history, so also have the excavators of the ancient sites in the Mesopotamian valley made, during the last few years, far-reaching discoveries, which have enabled us to add to and revise much of our knowledge of the history of Babylonia and Assyria. In Palestine and the Sinaitic peninsula also the spade has been used with effect, but a detailed account of work in Sinai and Palestine falls within the limits of a description of Biblical discoveries rather than of this book. The following chapters will therefore deal chiefly with modern discoveries which have told us new facts with regard to the history of the ancient Sumerians themselves, and of the Babylonians, Elamites, Kassites, and Assyrians, the inheritors of the ancient Sumerian civilization, which was older than that of Egypt, and which, as we have seen, probably contributed somewhat to its formation. These were the two primal civilizations of the ancient world. For two thousand years each marched

142 MEMPHIS AND THE PYRAMIDS

upon a solitary road, without meeting the other. Eventually the two roads converged. We have hitherto dealt with the road of the Egyptians; we now describe that of the Mesopotamians, up to the point of convergence.

CHAPTER IV

RECENT EXCAVATIONS IN WESTERN ASIA AND THE DAWN OF CHALDÆAN HISTORY

IN the preceding pages it has been shown how recent excavations in Egypt have revealed an entirely new chapter in the history of that country, and how, in consequence, our theories with regard to the origin of Egyptian civilization have been entirely remodelled. Excavations have been and are being carried out in Mesopotamia and the adjacent countries with no less enthusiasm and energy than in Egypt itself, and, although it cannot be said that they have resulted in any sweeping modification of our conceptions with regard to the origin and kinship of the early races of Western Asia, yet they have lately added considerably to our knowledge of the ancient history of the countries in that region of the world. This is particularly the case in respect of the Sumerians, who, so far as we know at present, were the earliest inhabitants of the fertile plains of Mesopotamia. The beginnings of this ancient people stretch back into the remote past, and their origin is still shrouded in the mists of antiquity. When first we come across them they have already attained a high level of civilization. They have built temples and palaces and houses of burnt and unburnt brick, and they have reduced their system of agriculture to a science, intersecting their country with canals for purposes of irrigation and to ensure a good supply of water to their cities. Their sculpture and pottery furnish abundant evidence that they have already attained a comparatively high level in the practice of the arts, and finally they have evolved a complicated system of writing which originally had its origin in picture-characters, but afterwards had been developed along phonetic lines. To have attained to this pitch of culture argues long periods of previous development, and we must conclude that they had been settled in Southern Babylonia many centuries before the period to which we must assign the earliest of their remains at present discovered.

That this people were not indigenous to Babylonia is highly probable, but we have little data by which to determine the region from which they originally came. From the fact that they built their ziggurats, or temple towers, of huge masses of unburnt brick which rose high above the surrounding plain, and that their ideal was to make each "like a mountain," it has been argued that they were a mountain race, and the home from which they sprang has been sought in Central Asia. Other scholars have detected signs of their origin in their language and system of writing, and, from the fact that they spoke an agglutinative tongue and at the earliest period arranged the characters of their script in vertical lines like the Chinese, it has been urged that they were of Mongol extraction.

Though a case may be made out for this hypothesis, it would be rash to dogmatize for or against it, and it is wiser to await the discovery of further material on which a more certain decision may be based. But whatever their origin, it is certain that the Sumerians exercised an extraordinary influence on all races with which, either directly or indirectly, they came in contact. The ancient inhabitants of Elam at a very early period adopted in principle their method of writing, and afterwards, living in isolation in the mountainous districts of Persia, developed it on lines of their own.[1] On their invasion of Babylonia the Semites fell absolutely under Sumerian influence, and, although they eventually conquered and absorbed the Sumerians, their civilization remained Sumerian to the core. Moreover, by means of the Semitic inhabitants of Babylonia Sumerian culture continued to exert its influence on other and more distant races. We have already seen how a Babylonian element probably enters into Egyptian civilization through Semitic infiltration across the Straits of Bab el-Mandeb or by way of the Isthmus of Suez, and it was Sumerian culture which these Semites brought with them. In like manner, through the Semitic Babylonians, the Assyrians, the Kassites, and the inhabitants of Palestine and Syria, and of some parts of Asia Minor, Armenia, and Kurdistan, all in turn

[1] See Chap. V, p. 232 and note.

experienced indirectly the influence of Sumerian civilization and continued in a greater or less degree to reproduce elements of this early culture.

It will be seen that the influence of the Sumerians furnishes us with a key to much that would otherwise prove puzzling in the history of the early races of Western Asia. It is therefore all the more striking to recall the fact that but a few years ago the very existence of this ancient people was called in question. At that time the excavations in Mesopotamia had not revealed many traces of the race itself, and its previous existence had been mainly inferred from a number of Sumerian compositions inscribed upon Assyrian tablets found in the library of Ashur-bani-pal at Nineveh. These compositions were furnished with Assyrian translations upon the tablets on which they were inscribed, and it was correctly argued by the late Sir Henry Rawlinson, the late M. Oppert, Prof. Schrader, Prof. Sayce, and other scholars that they were written in the language of the earlier inhabitants of the country whom the Semitic Babylonians had displaced. But M. Halévy started a theory to the effect that Sumerian was not a language at all, in the proper sense of the term, but was a cabalistic method of writing invented by the Semitic Babylonian priests. The argument on which the upholders of this theory mainly relied was that many of the phonetic values of the Sumerian signs were obviously derived from Semitic equivalents, and they hastily jumped to the conclusion that the whole language was similarly derived from Semitic Babylonian, and was, in fact, a purely arbitrary invention of the Babylonian priests. This theory ignored all questions of inherent probability, and did not attempt to explain

LIST OF ARCHAIC CUNEIFORM SIGNS.
Drawn up by an Assyrian scribe to assist him in his studies of early texts. Photograph by Messrs. Mansell & Co.

why the Babylonian priests should have troubled themselves to make such an invention and afterwards have stultified themselves by carefully appending Assyrian translations to the majority of the Sumerian compositions which they copied out. Moreover, the nature of these compositions is not such as we should expect to find recorded in a cabalistic method of writing. They contain no secret lore of the Babylonian priests, but are merely hymns and prayers and religious compositions similar to those employed by the Babylonians and Assyrians themselves.

But in spite of its inherent improbabilities, M. Halévy succeeded in making many converts to his theory, including Prof. Friedrich Delitzsch and a number of the younger school of German Assyriologists. More conservative scholars, such as Sir Henry Rawlinson, M. Oppert, and Prof. Schrader, stoutly opposed the theory, maintaining that Sumerian was a real language and had been spoken by an earlier race whom the Semitic Babylonians had conquered; and they explained the resemblance of some of the Sumerian values to Semitic roots by supposing that Sumerian had not been suddenly superseded by the language of the Semitic invaders of Babylonia, but that the two tongues had been spoken for long periods side by side and that each had been strongly influenced by the other. This very probable and sane explanation has been fully corroborated by subsequent excavations, particularly those that were carried out at Telloh in Southern Babylonia by the late M. de Sarzec. In these mounds, which mark the site of the ancient Sumerian city of Shirpurla, were found thousands of clay tablets inscribed in archaic characters and in the Sumerian language, proving that it had actually been the language of the early inhabitants of Babylonia; while the examples of their art and the representations of their form and features, which were also afforded by the diggings at Telloh, proved once for all that the Sumerians were a race of strongly marked characteristics and could not be ascribed to a Semitic stock.

The system of writing invented by the ancient Sumerians was adopted by the Semitic Babylonians, who modified it to suit their own language. Moreover, the archaic forms of the characters, many of which under the Sumerians still retained resemblances to the pictures of objects from which they were descended, were considerably changed. The lines, of which they were originally composed, gave way to wedges, and the number of the wedges of which each sign consisted was gradually diminished, so that in the time of the Assyrians and the later Babylonians many of the characters bore small resemblance to the ancient Sumerian forms from which they had been derived. The reading of Sumerian and early Babylonian inscriptions by the late Assyrian scribes was therefore an accomplishment only to be acquired as the result of long study, and it is interesting to note that as an assistance to the reading of these early texts the scribes compiled lists of archaic signs. Sometimes opposite each archaic character they drew a picture of the object from which they imagined it was derived. This fact is significant as proving that the Assyrian scribes recognized the pictorial origin of cuneiform writing, but the pictures they drew opposite the signs are rather fanciful, and it cannot be said that their guesses were very successful. That we are able to criticize the theories of the Assyrians as to the origin and forms of the early characters is in the main due to M. de Sarzec's labours, from whose excavations many thousands of inscriptions of the Sumerians have been recovered.

FRAGMENT OF A LIST OF ARCHAIC CUNEIFORM SIGNS.
Opposite each the scribe has drawn a picture of the object from which he imagined it was derived. Photograph by Messrs. Mansell & Co.

The main results of M. de Sarzec's diggings at Telloh have already been described by M. Maspero in his history, and therefore we need not go over them again, but will here confine ourselves to the results which have been obtained from recent excavations at Telloh and at other sites in Western Asia. With the death of M. de Sarzec, which occurred in his sixty-fifth year, on May 31, 1901, the wonderfully successful series of excavations which he had carried out at Telloh was brought to an end. In consequence it was feared at the time that the French diggings on this site might be interrupted for a considerable period. Such an event would have been regretted by all those who are interested in the early history of the East, for, in spite of the treasures found by M. de Sarzec in the course of his various campaigns, it was obvious that the site was far from being exhausted, and that the *tells* as yet unexplored contained inscriptions and antiquities extending back to the very earliest periods of Sumerian history. The announcement which was made in 1902, that the French government had appointed Capt. Gaston Cros as the late M. de Sarzec's successor, was therefore received with general satisfaction. The fact that Capt. Cros had already successfully carried out several difficult topographical missions in the region of the Sahara was a sufficient guarantee that the new diggings would be conducted on a systematic and exhaustive scale.

The new director of the French mission in Chaldæa arrived at Telloh in January, 1903, and one of his first acts was to shift the site of the mission's settlement from the bank of the Shatt el-Hai, where it had always been established in the time of M. de Sarzec, to the mounds where the actual digging took place. The Shatt el-Hai had been previously chosen as the site of the settlement to ensure a constant supply of water, and as it was more easily protected against attack by night. But the fact that it was an hour's ride from the diggings caused an unnecessary loss of time, and rendered the strict supervision of the diggers a matter of considerable difficulty. During the first season's work rough huts of reeds, surrounded by a wall of earth and a ditch, served the new expedition for its encampment among the mounds of Telloh, but last year these makeshift arrangements were superseded by a regular house built out of the burnt bricks which are found in abundance on the site. A reservoir has also been built, and caravans of asses bring water in skins from the Shatt el-Hai to keep it filled with a constant supply of water, while the excellent relations which Capt. Cros has established with the Karagul Arabs, who occupy Telloh and its neighbourhood, have proved to be the best kind of protection for the mission engaged in scientific work upon the site.

The group of mounds and hillocks, known as Telloh, which marks the site of the ancient Sumerian city of Shirpurla, is easily distinguished from the flat surrounding desert. The mounds extend in a rough oval formation running north and south, about two and a half miles long and one and a quarter broad. In the early spring, when the desert is covered with a light green verdure, the ruins are clearly marked out as a yellow spot in the surrounding green, for vegetation does not grow upon them. In the centre of this oval, which approximately marks the limits of the ancient city and its suburbs, are four large tells or mounds running, roughly, north and south, their sides descending steeply on the east, but with their western slopes rising by easier undulations from the plain. These four principal tells are known as the "Palace Tell," the "Tell of the Fruit-house," the "Tell of the Tablets," and the "Great Tell," and, rising as they do in the centre of the site, they mark the position of the temples and the other principal buildings of the city.

An indication of the richness of the site in antiquities was afforded to the new mission before it had started regular excavation and while it was yet engaged in levelling its encampment and surrounding it with a wall and ditch. The spot selected for the camp was a small mound to the south of the site of Telloh, and here, in the course of preparing the site for the encampment and digging the ditch, objects were found at a depth of less than a foot beneath the surface of the soil. These included daggers, copper vases, seal-cylinders, rings of lapis and cornelian, and pottery. M. de Sarzec had carried out his latest diggings in the Tell of the Tablets, and here Capt. Cros continued the excavations and came upon the remains of buildings and recovered numerous objects, dating principally from the period of Gudea and the kings of Ur. The finds included small terra-cotta figures, a boundary-stone of Gamil-Sin, and a new statue of Gudea, to which we will refer again presently.

In the Tell of the Fruit-house M. de Sarzec had already discovered numbers of monuments dating from the earlier periods of Sumerian history before the conquest and consolidation of Babylonia under Sargon of Agade, and had excavated a primitive terrace built by the early king Ur-Nina. Both on and around this large mound Capt. Cros cut an extensive series of trenches, and in digging to the north of the mound he found a number of objects, including an alabaster tablet of Entemena which had been blackened by fire. At the foot of the tell he found a copper helmet like those represented on the famous Stele of Vultures discovered by M. de Sarzec, and among the tablets here recovered was one with an inscription of the time of Urukagina, which records the complete destruction of the city of Shirpurla during his reign, and will be described in greater detail later on in this chapter. On the mound itself a considerable area was uncovered with remains of buildings still in place, the use of which appears to have been of an industrial character. They included flights of steps, canals with raised banks, and basins for storing water. Not far off are the previously discovered wells of Eannadu, so that it is legitimate to suppose that Capt. Cros has here come upon part of the works which were erected at a very early period of Sumerian history for the distribution of water to this portion of the city.

In the Palace Tell Capt. Cros has sunk a series of deep shafts to determine precisely the relations which the buildings of Ur-Bau and Gudea, found already on this part of the site, bear to each other, and to the building of Adad-nadin-akhê, which had been erected there at a much later period. From this slight sketch of the work carried out during the last two years at Telloh it will have been seen that the French mission in Chaldæa is at present engaged in excavations of a most important character, which are being conducted in

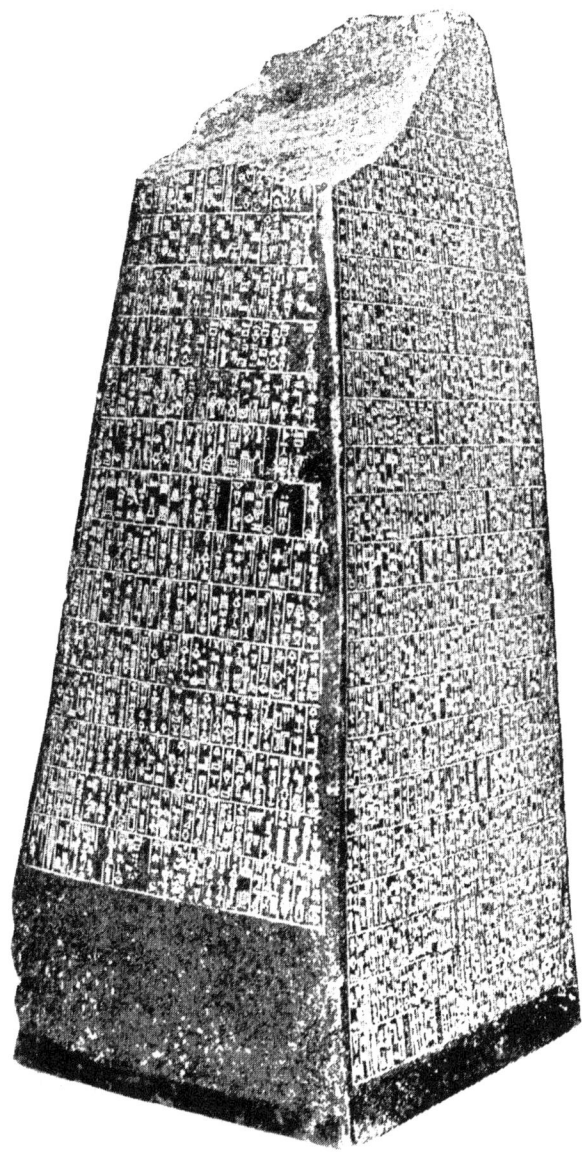

Obelisk of Manishtusu.

An early Semitic king of the city of Kish in Babylonia. The photograph is taken from M. de Morgan's *Délégation en Perse, Mém.*, t. 1, pl. ix.

a regular and scientific manner. As the area of the excavations marks the site of the chief city of the Sumerians, the diggings there have yielded and are yielding material of the greatest interest and value for the reconstruction of the early history of Chaldæa. After briefly describing the character and results of other recent excavations in Mesopotamia and the neighbouring lands, we will return to the discoveries at Telloh and sketch the new information they supply on the history of the earliest inhabitants of the country.

Another French mission that is carrying out work of the very greatest interest to the student of early Babylonian history is that which is excavating at Susa in Persia, under the direction of M. J. de Morgan, whose work on the prehistoric and early dynastic sites in Egypt has already been described. M. de Morgan's first season's digging at Susa was carried out in the years 1897-8, and the success with which he met from the very first, when cutting trenches in the mound which marks the acropolis of the ancient city, has led him to concentrate his main efforts in this part of the ruins ever since. Provisional trenches cut in the part of the ruins called "the Royal City," and in others of the mounds at Susa, indicate that many remains may eventually be found there dating from the period of the Achæmenian Kings of Persia. But it is in the mound of the acropolis at Susa that M. de Morgan has found monuments of the greatest historical interest and value, not only in the history of ancient Elam, but also in that of the earliest rulers of Chaldæa.

In the diggings carried out during the first season's work on the site, an obelisk was found inscribed on four sides with a long text of some sixty-nine columns, written in Semitic Babylonian by the orders of Manishtusu, a very early Semitic king of the city of Kish in Babylonia.[1] The text records the purchase by the King of Kish of immense tracts of land situated at Kish and in its neighbourhood, and its length is explained by the fact that it enumerates full details of the size and position of each estate, and the numbers and some of the names of the dwellers on the estates who were engaged in their cultivation. After details have been given of a number of estates situated in the same neighbourhood, a summary is appended referring to the whole neighbourhood, and the fact is recorded that the district dealt with in the preceding catalogue and summary had been duly acquired by purchase by Manishtusu, King of Kish. The long text upon the obelisk is entirely taken up with details of the purchase of the territory, and therefore its subject has not any great historical value. Mention is made in it of two personages, one of whom may possibly be identified with a Babylonian ruler whose name is known from other sources. If the proposed identification should prove to be correct, it would enable us to assign a more precise date to Manishtusu than has hitherto been possible. One of the personages in question was a certain Urukagina, the son of Engilsa, patesi of Shirpurla, and it has been suggested that he is the same Urukagina who is known to have occupied the

[1] See illustration.

throne of Shirpurla, though this identification would bring Manishtusu down somewhat later than is probable from the general character of his inscriptions. The other personage mentioned in the text is the son of Manishtusu, named Mesalim, and there is more to be said for the identification of this prince with Mesilim, the early King of Kish, who reigned at a period anterior to that of Eannadu, patesi of Shirpurla.

The mere fact of so large and important an obelisk, inscribed with a Semitic text by an early Babylonian king, being found at Susa was an indication that other monuments of even greater interest might be forthcoming from the same spot; and this impression was intensified when a stele of victory was found bearing an inscription of Narâm-Sin, the early Semitic King of Agade, who reigned about 3750 B.C. One face of this stele is sculptured with a representation of the king conquering his enemies in a mountainous country.[1] The king himself wears a helmet adorned with the horns of a bull, and he carries his battle-axe and his bow and an arrow. He is nearly at the summit of a high mountain, and up its steep sides, along paths through the trees which clothe the mountain, climb his allies and warriors bearing standards and weapons. The king's enemies are represented suing for mercy as they turn to fly before him. One grasps a broken spear, while another, crouching before the king, has been smitten in the throat by an arrow from the king's bow. On the plain surface of the stele above the king's head may

[1] See illustration.

be seen traces of an inscription of Narâm-Sin engraved in three columns in the archaic characters of his period. From the few signs of the text that remain, we gather that Narâm-Sin had conducted a campaign with the assistance of certain allied princes, including the Princes of Sidur, Saluni, and Lulubi, and it is not improbable that they are to be identified with the warriors represented on the stele as climbing the mountain behind Narâm-Sin.

In reference to this most interesting stele of Narâm-Sin we may here mention another inscription of this king, found quite recently at Susa and published only this year, which throws additional light on Narâm-Sin's allies and on the empire which he and his father Sargon founded. The new inscription was engraved on the base of a diorite statue, which had been broken to pieces so that only the base with a portion of the text remained. From this inscription we learn that Narâm-Sin was the head of a confederation of nine chief allies, or vassal princes, and waged war on his enemies with their assistance. Among these nine allies of course the Princes of Sidur, Saluni, and Lulubi are to be included. The new text further records that Narâm-Sin made an expedition against Magan (the Sinaitic peninsula), and defeated Manium, the lord of that region, and that he cut blocks of stone in the mountains there and transported them to his city of Agade, where from one of them he made the statue on the base of which the text was inscribed. It was already known from the so-called " Omens of Sargon and Narâm-Sin " (a text inscribed

STARTLING DISCOVERIES AT SUSA 159

on a clay tablet from Ashur-bani-pal's library at Nineveh which associates the deeds of these two early rulers with certain augural phenomena) that Narâm-Sin had made an expedition to Sinai in the course of his reign and had conquered the king of the country. The new text gives contemporary confirmation of this assertion and furnishes us with additional information with regard to the name of the conquered ruler of Sinai and other details of the campaign.

That monuments of such great interest to the early history of Chaldæa should have been found at Susa in Persia was sufficiently startling, but an easy explanation was at first forthcoming from the fact that Narâm-Sin's stele of victory had been used by the later Elamite king, Shutruk-Nakhkhunte, for an inscription of his own; this he had engraved in seven long lines along the great cone in front of Narâm-Sin, which is probably intended to represent the peak of the mountain. From the fact that it had been used in this way by Shutruk-Nakhkhunte, it seemed permissible to infer that it had been captured in the course of a campaign and brought to Susa as a trophy of war. But we shall see later on that the existence of early Babylonian inscriptions and monuments in the mound of the acropolis at Susa is not to be explained in this way, but was due to the wide extension of both Sumerian and Semitic influence throughout Western Asia from the very earliest periods. This subject will be treated more fully in the chapter dealing with the early history of Elam.

The upper surface of the tell of the acropolis at

Susa for a depth of nearly two metres contains remains of the buildings and antiquities of the Achæmenian kings and others of both later and earlier dates. In these upper strata of the mound are found remains of the Arab, Sassanian, Parthian, Seleucian, and Persian periods, mixed indiscriminately with one another and with Elamite objects and materials of all ages, from

BABIL.

The most northern of the mounds which now mark the site of the ancient city of Babylon; used for centuries as a quarry for building materials.

that of the earliest patesis down to that of the Susian kings of the seventh century B. C. The reason of this mixture of the remains of many races and periods is that the later builders on the mound made use of the earlier building materials which they found preserved within it. Along the skirts of the mound may still be seen the foundations of the wall which formed the principal defence of the acropolis in the time of Xerxes, and in many places not only are the foundations pre-

THE FORTRESS OF SUSA

served but large pieces of the wall itself still rise above the surface of the soil. The plan of the wall is quite irregular, following the contours of the mound, and, though it is probable that the wall was strengthened and defended at intervals by towers, no trace of these now remains. The wall is very thick and built of un-

ROUGHLY HEWN SCULPTURE OF A LION STANDING OVER A FALLEN MAN, FOUND AT BABYLON.

The group probably represents Babylon or the Babylonian king triumphing over the country's enemies. The Arabs regard the figure as an evil spirit, and it is pitted with the marks of bullets shot at it. They also smear it with filth when they can do so unobserved; in the photograph some newly smeared filth may be seen adhering to the side of the lion.

burnt bricks, and the system of fortification seems to have been extremely simple at this period. The earlier citadel or fortress of the city of Susa was built at the top of the mound and must have been a more formidable stronghold than that of the Achæmenian kings, for, besides its walls, it had the additional protection of the steep slopes of the mound.

Below the depth of two metres from the surface of

the mound are found strata in which Elamite objects and materials are no longer mixed with the remains of later ages, but here the latest Elamite remains are found mingled with objects and materials dating from the earliest periods of Elam's history. The use of unburnt bricks as the principal material for buildings erected on the mound in all ages has been another cause of this mixture of materials, for it has little power of resistance to water, and a considerable rain-storm will wash away large portions of the surface and cause the remains of different strata to be mixed indiscriminately with one another. In proportion as the trenches were cut deeper into the mound the strata which were laid bare showed remains of earlier ages than those in the upper layers, though here also remains of different periods are considerably mixed. The only building that has hitherto been discovered at Susa by M. de Morgan, the ground plan of which was in a comparatively good state of preservation, was a small temple of the god Shushinak, and this owed its preservation to the fact that it was not built of unburnt brick, but was largely composed of burnt brick and plaques and tiles of enamelled terra-cotta.

But although the diggings of M. de Morgan at Susa have so far afforded little information on the subject of Elamite architecture, the separate objects found have enabled us to gain considerable knowledge of the artistic achievements of the race during the different periods of its existence. Moreover, the stelæ and stone records that have been recovered present a wealth of material for the study of the long history of Elam and of the kings who ruled in Babylonia during the earliest ages. The most famous of M. de Morgan's recent finds is the long code of laws drawn up by Hammurabi, the great-

GENERAL VIEW OF THE EXCAVATIONS ON THE KASR AT BABYLON.
Showing the depth in the mound to which the diggings are carried.

est king of the First Dynasty of Babylon.[1] This was engraved upon a huge block of black diorite, and was found in the tell of the acropolis in the winter of 1901-2. This document in itself has entirely revolutionized current theories as to the growth and origin

---

[1] It will be noted that the Babylonian dynasties are referred to throughout this volume as "First Dynasty," "Second Dynasty," "Third Dynasty," etc. They are thus distinguished from the Egyptian dynasties, the order of which is indicated by Roman numerals, e. g. "Ist Dynasty," "IId Dynasty," "IIId Dynasty."

of the principal ancient legal codes. It proves that Babylonia was the fountainhead from which many later races borrowed portions of their legislative systems. Moreover, the subjects dealt with in this code of laws embrace most of the different classes of the Babylonian people, and it regulates their duties and their relations to one another in their ordinary occupations and pursuits. It therefore throws much light upon early Babylonian life and customs, and we shall return to it in the chapter dealing with these subjects.

The American excavators at Nippur, under the direction of Mr. Haynes, have done much in the past to increase our knowledge of Sumerian and early Babylonian history, but the work has not been continued in recent years, and, unfortunately, little progress has been made in the publication of the material already accumulated. In fact, the leadership in American excavation has passed from the University of Pennsylvania to that of Chicago. This progressive university has sent out an expedition, under the general direction of Prof. R. F. Harper (with Dr. E. J. Banks as director of excavations), which is doing excellent work at Bismya, and, although it is too early yet to expect detailed accounts of their achievements, it is clear that they have already met with considerable success. One of their recent finds consists of a white marble statue of an early Sumerian king named Daudu, which was set up in the temple of E-shar in the city of Udnun, of which he was ruler. From its archaic style of workmanship it may be placed in the earliest period of

Sumerian history, and may be regarded as an earnest of what may be expected to follow from the future labours of Prof. Harper's expedition.

At Fâra and at Abû Hatab in Babylonia, the Deutsch-Orient Gesellschaft, under Dr. Koldewey's direction, has excavated Sumerian and Babylonian re-

WITHIN THE PALACE OF NEBUCHADNEZZAR II.

mains of the early period. At the former site they unearthed the remains of many private houses and found some Sumerian tablets of accounts and commercial documents, but little of historical interest; and an inscription, which seems to have come from Abû Hatab, probably proves that the Sumerian name of the city whose site it marks was Kishurra. But the main centre of German activity in Babylonia is the city of Babylon itself, where for the last seven years Dr. Koldewey has conducted excavations, unearthing the palaces of Nebuchadnezzar II on the mound termed the Kasr, identifying the temple of E-sagila under the mound called Tell Amran ibn-Ali, tracing the course

EXCAVATIONS IN THE TEMPLE OF NINIB AT BABYLON.
In the middle distance may be seen the metal trucks running on light rails which are employed on the work for the removal of the débris from the diggings.

of the sacred way between E-sagila and the palace-mound, and excavating temples dedicated to the goddess Ninmakh and the god Ninib. Dr. Andrae, Dr. Koldewey's assistant, has also completed the excavation of the temple dedicated to Nabû at Birs Nimrud. On the principal mound at this spot, which marks the site of the ancient city of Borsippa, traces of the ziggurat, or temple tower, may still be seen rising from the soil, the temple of Nabû lying at a lower level below the steep slope of the mound, which is mainly made up of débris from the ziggurat. Dr. Andrae has recently left Babylonia for Assyria, where his excavations at Sherghat, the site of the ancient Assyrian city of Ashur,

THE PRINCIPAL MOUND OF BIRS NIMRUD, WHICH MARKS THE SITE OF THE ANCIENT CITY OF BORSIPPA.

are confidently expected to throw considerable light on the early history of that country and the customs of the people, and already he has made numerous finds of considerable interest.

Since the early spring of 1903 excavations have been conducted at Kuyunjik, the site of the city of Nineveh, by Messrs. L. W. King and R. C. Thompson on behalf of the Trustees of the British Museum, and have resulted in the discovery of many early remains in the lower strata of the mound, in addition to the finding of new portions of the two palaces already known and partly excavated, the identification of a third palace, and the finding of an ancient temple dedicated to Nabû, whose existence had already been inferred from a study of the Assyrian inscriptions.[1] All these diggings at

THE PRINCIPAL MOUND AT SHERGHAT, WHICH MARKS THE SITE OF ASHUR, THE ANCIENT CAPITAL OF THE ASSYRIANS.

Babylon, at Ashur, and at Nineveh throw more light upon the history of the country during the Assyrian and Neo-Babylonian periods, and will be referred to later in the volume. Meanwhile, we will return to the

[1] It may be noted that excavations are also being actively carried on in Palestine at the present time. Mr. Macalister has for some years been working for the Palestine Exploration Fund at Gezer; Dr. Schumacher is digging at Megiddo for the German Palestine Society; and Prof. Sellin is at present excavating at Taanach (Ta'annak) and will shortly start work at Dothan. Good work on remains of later historical periods is also being carried on under the auspices of the Deutsch-Orient Gesellschaft at Ba'albek and in Galilee. It would be tempting to include here a summary of the very interesting results

RIVAL CITIES

diggings described at the beginning of this chapter, as affording new information concerning the earliest periods of Chaldæan history.

A most interesting inscription has recently been discovered by Capt. Cros at Telloh, which throws considerable light on the rivalry which existed between the cities of Shirpurla and Gishkhu, and at the same time furnishes valuable material for settling the chronology

THE MOUND OF KUYUNJIK, WHICH FORMED ONE OF THE PALACE MOUNDS OF THE ANCIENT ASSYRIAN CITY OF NINEVEH.

of the earliest rulers whose inscriptions have been found at Nippur and their relations to contemporary rulers in Shirpurla. The cities of Gishkhu and Shirpurla were

that have recently been achieved in this fruitful field of archæological research, for it is true that these excavations may strictly be said to bear on the history of a portion of Western Asia. But the problems which they raise would more naturally be discussed in a work dealing with recent excavation and research in relation to the Bible, and to have summarized them adequately would have increased the size of the present volume considerably beyond its natural limits. They have therefore not been included within the scope of the present probably situated not far from one another, and their rivalry is typical of the history of the early city-states of Babylonia. The site of the latter city, as has already been said, is marked by the mounds of Telloh on the east bank of the Shatt el-Hai, the natural stream joining the Tigris and Euphrates, which has been improved and canalized by the dwellers in Southern Babylonia from the earliest period. The site of Gishkhu may be

WINGED BULL IN THE PALACE OF SENNACHERIB ON KUYUNJIK, THE PRINCIPAL MOUND MARKING THE SITE OF NINEVEH.

set with considerable probability not far to the north of Telloh on the opposite bank of the Shatt el-Hai. These two cities, situated so close to one another, exercised considerable political influence, and though less is known of Gishkhu than of the more famous Babylonian cities such as Ur, Erech, and Larsam, her proximity to Shirpurla gave her an importance which she might not otherwise have possessed. The earliest knowledge we possess of the relations existing between

Gishkhu and Shirpurla refers to the reign of Mesilim, King of Kish, the period of whose rule may be provisionally set before that of Sargon of Agade, *i. e.* about 4000 B. C.

At this period there was rivalry between the two cities, in consequence of which Mesilim, King of Kish, was called in as arbitrator. A record of the treaty of delimitation that was drawn up on this occasion has been preserved upon the recently discovered cone of Entemena. This document tells us that at the command of the god Enlil, described as "the king of the countries," Ningirsu, the chief god of Shirpurla, and the god of Gishkhu decided to draw up a line of division between their respective territories, and that Mesilim, King of Kish, acting under the direction of his own god Kadi, marked out the frontier and set up a stele between the two territories to commemorate the fixing of the boundary.

This policy of fixing the boundary by arbitration seems to have been successful, and to have secured peace between Shirpurla and Gishkhu for some generations. But after a period which cannot be accurately determined a certain patesi of Gishkhu, named Ush, was filled with ambition to extend his territory at the expense of Shirpurla. He therefore removed the stele which Mesilim had set up, and, invading the plain of Shirpurla, succeeded in conquering and holding a district named Gu-edin. But Ush's successful raid was not of any permanent benefit to his city, for he was in his turn defeated by the forces of Shirpurla, and his successor upon the throne, a patesi named Enakalli, abandoned a policy of aggression, and concluded with Eannadu, patesi of Shirpurla, a solemn treaty concerning the boundary between their realms, the text of which has been preserved to us upon the famous Stele of Vultures in the Louvre.[1]

According to this treaty Gu-edin was restored to Shirpurla, and a deep ditch was dug between the two territories which should permanently indicate the line of demarcation. The stele of Mesilim was restored to its place, and a second stele was inscribed and set up as a memorial of the new treaty. Enakalli did not negotiate the treaty on equal terms with Eannadu, for he only secured its ratification by consenting to pay heavy tribute in grain for the supply of the great temples of Ningirsu and Ninâ in Shirpurla. It would appear that under Eannadu the power and influence of Shirpurla were extended over the whole of Southern Babylonia, and reached even to the borders of Elam. At any rate, it is clear that during his lifetime the city of Gishkhu was content to remain in a state of subjection to its more powerful neighbour. But it was always ready to seize any opportunity of asserting itself and of attempting to regain its independence. Accordingly, after Eannadu's death the men of Gishkhu again took the offensive. At this time Urlumma, the son and successor of Enakalli, was on the throne of Gishkhu, and he organized the forces of the city and led them out to

[1] A fragment of this stele is also preserved in the British Museum. It is published in *Cuneiform Texts in the British Museum*, Pt. vii.

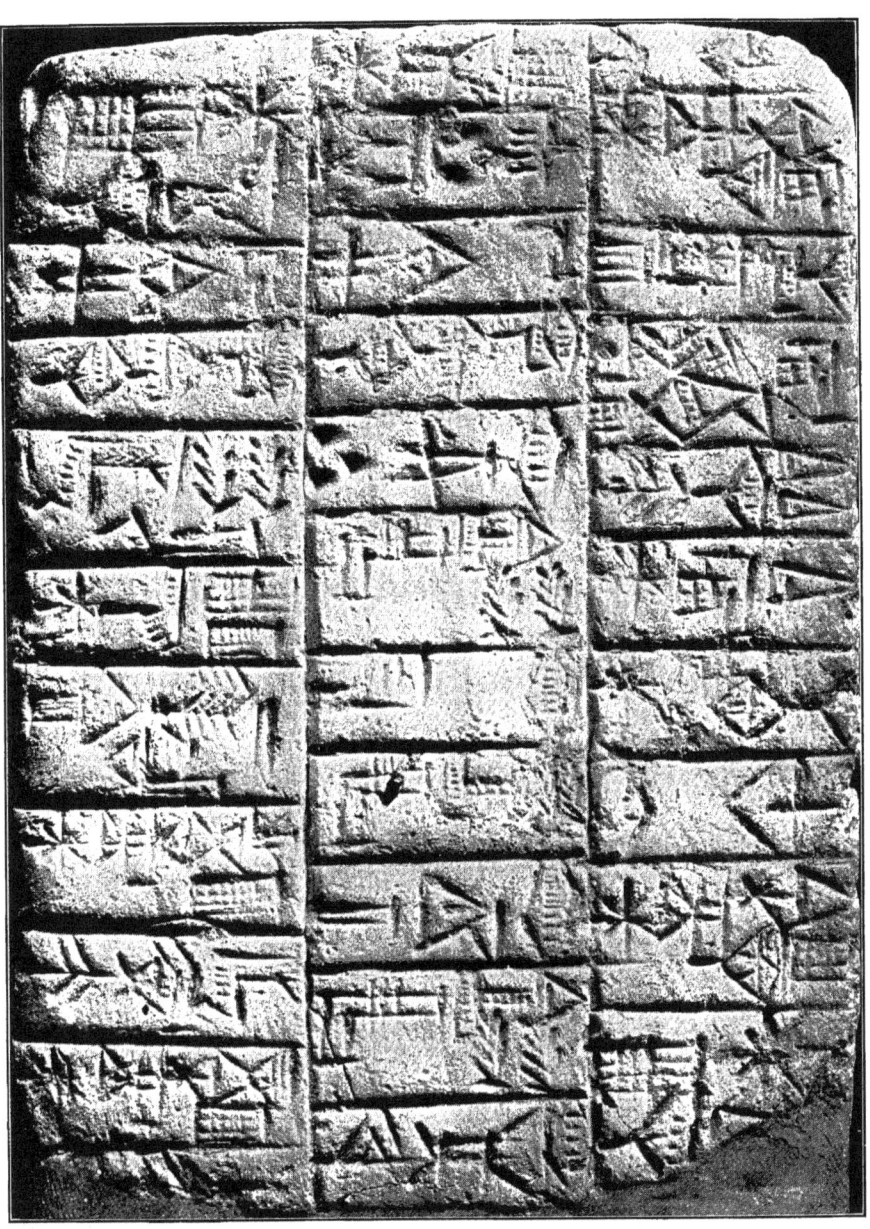

Clay Memorial-tablet of Eannadu.

One of the most powerful of the patesis or viceroys of Shirpurla. The characters of the inscription well illustrate the pictorial origin of the Sumerian system of writing. Photograph by Messrs. Mansell & Co.

battle. His first act was to destroy the frontier ditches named after Ningirsu and Ninâ, the principal god and goddess of Shirpurla, which Eannadu, the powerful foe of Gishkhu, had caused to be dug. He then tore down the stele on which the terms of Eannadu's treaty had been engraved and broke it into pieces by casting it into the fire, and the shrines which Eannadu had built near the frontier, and had consecrated to the gods of Shirpurla, he razed to the ground. But again Shirpurla in the end proved too strong for Gishkhu. The ruler in Shirpurla at this time was Enannadu, who had succeeded his brother Eannadu upon the throne. He marched out to meet the invading forces of the men of Gishkhu, and a battle was fought in the territory of Shirpurla. According to one account, the forces of Shirpurla were victorious, while on the cone of Entemena no mention is made of the issue of the combat. The result may not have been decisive, but Enannadu's action at least checked Urlumma's encroachments for the time.

It would appear that the death of the reigning patesi in Shirpurla was always the signal for an attack upon that city by the men of Gishkhu. They may have hoped that the new ruler would prove a less successful leader than the last, or that the accession of a new monarch might give rise to internal dissensions in the city which would weaken Shirpurla's power of resisting a sudden attack. As Eannadu's death had encouraged Urlumma to lead out the men of Gishkhu, so the death of Enannadu seemed to him a good opportunity to make another bid for victory. But this time the result of the battle was not indecisive. Entemena had succeeded his father Enannadu, and he led out to victory the forces of Shirpurla. The battle was fought near the canal Lummagirnun-ta, and when the men of Gishkhu were put to flight they left sixty of their fellows lying dead upon the banks of the canal. Entemena tells us that the bones of these warriors were left to bleach in the open plain, but he seems to have buried those of the men of Gishkhu who fell in the pursuit, for he records that in five separate places he piled up burial-mounds in which the bodies of the slain were interred. Entemena was not content with merely inflicting a defeat upon the army of Gishkhu and driving it back within its own borders, for he followed up his initial advantage and captured the capital itself. He deposed and imprisoned Urlumma, and chose one of his own adherents to rule as patesi of Gishkhu in his stead. The man he appointed for this high office was named Ili, and he had up to that time been priest in Ninab. Entemena summoned him to his presence, and, after marching in a triumphal procession from Girsu in the neighbourhood of Shirpurla to the conquered city, proceeded to invest him with the office of patesi of Gishkhu.

Entemena also repaired the frontier ditches named after Ningirsu and Ninâ, which had been employed for purposes of irrigation as well as for marking the frontier; and he gave instructions to Ili to employ the men dwelling in the district of Karkar on this work, as a punishment for the active part they had taken in the

ENTERPRISE OF ENTEMENA

recent raid into the territory of Shirpurla. Entemena also restored and extended the system of canals in the region between the Tigris and the Euphrates, lining one of the principal channels with stone. He thus added

MARBLE GATE-SOCKET BEARING AN INSCRIPTION OF ENTEMENA, A POWERFUL PATESI, OR VICEROY, OF SHIRPURLA.

In the photograph the gate-socket is resting on its side so as to show the inscription, but when in use it was set flat upon the ground and partly buried below the level of the pavement of the building in which it was used. It was fixed at the side of a gateway and the pivot of the heavy gate revolved in the shallow hole or depression in its centre. As stone is not found in the alluvial soil of Babylonia, the blocks for gate-sockets had to be brought from great distances and they were consequently highly prized. The kings and patesis who used them in their buildings generally had their names and titles engraved upon them, and they thus form a valuable class of inscriptions for the study of the early history. Photograph by Messrs. Mansell & Co.

greatly to the wealth of Shirpurla by increasing the area of territory under cultivation, and he continued to exercise authority in Gishkhu by means of officers appointed by himself. A record of his victory over Gishkhu was inscribed by Entemena upon a number of clay cones, that the fame of it might be preserved in future days to the honour of Ningirsu and the goddess Ninâ. He ends this record with a prayer for the preservation of the frontier. If ever in time to come the men of Gishkhu should break out across the frontier-ditch of Ningirsu, or the frontier-ditch of Ninä, in order to seize or lay waste the lands of Shirpurla, whether they be men of the city of Gishkhu itself or men of the mountains, he prays that Enlil may destroy them and that Ningirsu may lay his curse upon them; and if ever the warriors of his own city should be called upon to defend it, he prays that they may be full of courage and ardour for their task.

The greater part of this information with regard to the struggles between Gishkhu and Shirpurla, between the period of Mesilim, King of Kish, and that of Entemena, is supplied by the inscription of the latter ruler which has been found written around a small cone of clay. There is little doubt that the text was also engraved by the orders of Entemena upon a stone stele which was set up, like those of Mesilim and Eannadu, upon the frontier. Other copies of the inscription were probably engraved and erected in the cities of Gishkhu and Shirpurla, and to ensure the preservation of the record Entemena probably had numerous copies of it made upon small cones of clay which were preserved and possibly buried in the structure of the temples of

Shirpurla. Entemena's foresight in this matter has been justified by results, for, while his great memorials of stone have perished, the preservation of one of his small cones has sufficed to make known to later ages his own and his forefathers' prowess in their continual contests with their ancient rival Gishkhu.

After the reign of Entemena we have little information with regard to the relations between Gishkhu and Shirpurla, though it is probable that the effects of his decisive victory continued to exercise a moderating influence on Gishkhu's desire for expansion and secured a period of peaceful development for Shirpurla without the continual fear of encroachments on the part of her turbulent neighbour. We may assume that this period of tranquillity continued during the reigns of Enannadu II, Enlitarzi, and Lugal-anda, but, when in the reign of Urukagina the men of Gishkhu once more emerge from their temporary obscurity, they appear as the authors of deeds of rapine and bloodshed committed on a scale that was rare even in that primitive age.

In the earlier stages of their rivalry Gishkhu had always been defeated, or at any rate checked, in her actual conflicts with Shirpurla. When taking the aggressive the men of Gishkhu seem generally to have confined themselves to the seizure of territory, such as the district of Gu-edin, which was situated on the western bank of the Shatt el-Hai and divided from their own lands only by the frontier-ditch. If they ever actually crossed the Shatt el-Hai and raided the lands on its eastern bank, they never ventured to attack the city of Shirpurla itself. And, although their raids were attended with some success in their initial stages, the ruling patesis of Shirpurla were always strong enough to check them; and on most occasions they carried the war into the territory of Gishkhu, with the result that they readjusted the boundary on their own terms. But it would appear that all these primitive Chaldæan cities were subject to alternate periods of expansion and defeat, and Shirpurla was not an exception to the rule. It was probably not due so much to Urukagina's personal qualities or defects as a leader that Shirpurla suffered the greatest reverse in her history during his reign, but rather to Gishkhu's gradual increase in power at a time when Shirpurla herself remained inactive, possibly lulled into a false sense of security by the memory of her victories in the past. Whatever may have been the cause of Gishkhu's final triumph, it is certain that it took place in Urukagina's reign, and that for many years afterwards the hegemony of Southern Babylonia remained in her hands, while Shirpurla for a long period passed completely out of existence as an independent or semi-independent state.

The evidence of the catastrophe that befell Shirpurla at this period is furnished by a small clay tablet recently found at Telloh during Captain Cros's excavations on that site. The document on which the facts in question are recorded had no official character, and in all probability it had not been stored in any library or record chamber. The actual spot at Telloh where it was found was to the north of the mound in which the most ancient buildings have been recovered, and at the depth of two metres below the surface. No other tablets appear to have been found near it, but that fact in itself would not be sufficient evidence on which to base any theory as to its not having originally formed part of the archives of the city. Its unofficial character is attested by the form of the tablet and the manner in which the information upon it is arranged. In shape there is little to distinguish the document from the tablets of accounts inscribed in the reign of Urukagina, great numbers of which have been found recently at Telloh. Roughly square in shape, its edges are slightly convex, and the text is inscribed in a series of narrow columns upon both the obverse and the reverse. The text itself is not a carefully arranged composition, such as are the votive and historical inscriptions of early Sumerian rulers. It consists of a series of short sentences enumerating briefly and without detail the separate deeds of violence and sacrilege performed by the men of Gishkhu after their capture of the city. It is little more than a catalogue or list of the shrines and temples destroyed during the sack of the city, or defiled by the blood of the men of Shirpurla who were slain therein. No mention is made in the list of the palace of the Urukagina, or of any secular building, or of the dwellings of the citizens themselves. There is little doubt that these also were despoiled and destroyed by the victorious enemy, but the writer of the tablet is not concerned for the moment with the fate of his city or his fellow citizens. He appears to be overcome with the thought of the deeds of sacrilege committed against his gods; his mind is entirely taken up with the magnitude of the insult offered to the god Ningirsu, the city-god of Shirpurla. His bare enumeration of the deeds of sacrilege and violence loses little by its brevity, and, when he has ended the list of his accusations against the men of Gishkhu, he curses the goddess to whose influence he attributes their success.

No composition at all like this document has yet been recovered, and as it is not very long we may here give a translation of the text. It will be seen that the writer plunges at once into the subject of his charges against the men of Gishkhu. No historical *résumé* prefaces his accusations, and he gives no hint of the circumstances that have rendered their delivery possible. The temples of his city have been profaned and destroyed, and his indignation finds vent in a mere enumeration of their titles. To his mind the facts need no comment, for to him it is barely conceivable that such sacred places of ancient worship should have been defiled. He launches his indictment against Gishkhu in the following terms: " The men of Gishkhu have set fire to the temple of E-ki [. . .], they have set fire to Antashura, and they have carried away the silver and the precious stones therefrom! They have shed blood in the palace of Tirash, they have shed blood in Abzubanda, they have shed blood in the shrine of Enlil and in the shrine of the Sun-god, they have shed blood in Akhush, and they have carried away the silver and the precious stones therefrom! They have shed blood in the Gikana of the sacred grove of the goddess Ninmakh, and they have carried away the silver and the precious stones therefrom! They have shed blood in Baga, and they have carried away the silver and the precious stones therefrom! They have shed blood in Abzu-ega, they have set fire to the temple of Gatumdug, and they have carried away the silver and the precious stones therefrom, and have destroyed her statue! They have set fire to the . . . of the temple E-anna of the goddess Ninni, and they have carried away the silver and the precious stones therefrom, and have destroyed her statue! They have shed blood in Shapada, and they have carried away the silver and precious stones therefrom! They have . . . in Khenda, they have shed blood in the temple of Nindar in the town of Kiab, and they have carried away the silver and the precious stones therefrom! They have set fire to the temple of Dumuzi-abzu in the town of Kinunir, and they have carried away the silver and the precious stones therefrom! They have set fire to the temple of Lugaluru, and they have carried away the silver and the precious stones therefrom! They have shed blood in E-engura, the temple of the goddess Ninâ, and they have carried away the silver and the precious stones therefrom! They have shed blood in Sag . . . , the temple of Amageshtin, and the silver and the precious stones of Amageshtin have they carried away! They have removed the grain from Ginarbaniru, the field of the god Ningirsu, so much of it as was under cultivation! The men of Gishkhu, by the despoiling of

Shirpurla, have committed a transgression against the god Ningirsu! The power that is come unto them, from them shall be taken away! Of transgression on the part of Urukagina, King of Girsu, there is none. As for Lugalzaggisi, patesi of Gishkhu, may his goddess Nidaba bear on her head (the weight of) this transgression!"

Such is the account, which has come down to us from the rough tablet of some unknown scribe, of the greatest misfortune experienced by Shirpurla during the long course of her history. Many of the great temples mentioned in the text as among those which were burnt down and despoiled of their treasures are referred to more than once in the votive and historical inscriptions of earlier rulers of Shirpurla, who occupied the throne before the ill-fated Urukagina. The names of some of them, too, are to be found in the texts of the later patesis of that city, so that it may be concluded that in course of time they were rebuilt and restored to their former splendour. But there is no doubt that the despoiling and partial destruction of Shirpurla in the reign of Urukagina had a lasting effect upon the fortunes of that city, and effectively curtailed her influence among the greater cities of Southern Babylonia.

We may now turn our attention to the leader of the men of Gishkhu, under whose direction they achieved their final triumph over their ancient, and for long years more powerful, rival Shirpurla. The writer of our tablet mentions his name in the closing words of his text when he curses him and his goddess for the destruction and sacrilege that they have wrought. "As for Lugalzaggisi," he says, "patesi of Gishkhu, may his goddess Nidaba bear on her head (the weight of) this transgression!" Now the name of Lugalzaggisi has been found upon a number of fragments of vases made of white calcite stalagmite which were discovered by Mr. Haynes during his excavations at Nippur. All the vases were engraved with the same inscription, so that it was possible by piecing the fragments of text together to obtain a more or less complete copy of the records which were originally engraved upon each of them. From these records we learned for the first time, not only the name of Lugalzaggisi, but the fact that he founded a powerful coalition of cities in Babylonia at what was obviously a very early period in the history of the country. In the text he describes himself as "King of Erech, king of the world, the priest of Ana, the hero of Nidaba, the son of Ukush, patesi of Gishkhu, the hero of Nidaba, the man who was favourably regarded by the sure eye of the King of the Lands (*i. e.* the god Enlil), the great patesi of Enlil, unto whom understanding was granted by Enki, the chosen of the Sun-god, the exalted minister of Enzu, endowed with strength by the Sun-god, the worshipper of Ninni, the son who was conceived by Nidaba, who was nourished by Ninkharsag with the milk of life, the attendant of Umu, priestess of Erech, the servant who was trained by Ninagidkhadu, the mistress of Erech, the great minister of the gods." Lugalzaggisi then goes on to describe the extent of his dominion, and he says: "When the god Enlil, the lord of the countries, bestowed upon Lugalzaggisi the kingdom of the world, and granted unto him success in the sight of the world, when he filled the lands with his power, and conquered them from the rising of the sun unto the setting of the same, at that time he made straight his path from the Lower Sea of the Tigris and Euphrates unto the Upper Sea, and he granted him dominion over all from the rising of the sun unto the setting of the same, so that he caused the lands to dwell in peace."

Now when first the text of this inscription was published there existed only vague indications of the date to be assigned to Lugalzaggisi and the kingdom that he founded. It was clear from the titles which he bore, that, though Gishkhu was his native place, he had extended his authority far beyond that city and had chosen Erech as his capital. Moreover, he claimed an empire extending from " the Lower Sea of the Tigris and Euphrates unto the Upper Sea." There is no doubt that the Lower Sea here mentioned is the Persian Gulf, and it has been suggested that the Upper Sea may be taken to be the Mediterranean, though it may possibly have been Lake Van or Lake Urmi. But whichever of these views might be adopted, it was clear that Lugalzaggisi was a great conqueror, and had achieved the right to assume the high-sounding title of *lugal kalama*, " king of the world." In these circumstances it was of the first importance for the study of primitive Chaldæan history and chronology to ascertain approximately the period at which Lugalzaggisi reigned.

The evidence on which such a question could be provisionally settled was of the vaguest and most uncertain character, but such as it was it had to suffice, in the absence of more reliable data. In settling all problems connected with early Chaldæan chronology, the starting-point was, and in fact still is, the period of Sargon I, King of Agade, inasmuch as the date of his reign is settled, according to the reckoning of the scribes of Nabonidus, as about 3800 B. C.' It is true that this date has been called in question, and ingenious suggestions for amending it have been made by some writers, while others have rejected it altogether, holding that it merely represented a guess on the part of the late Babylonians and could be safely ignored in the chronological schemes which they brought forward. But nearly every fresh discovery made in the last few years has tended to confirm some point in the traditions current among the later Babylonians with regard to the earlier history of their country. Consequently, reliance may be placed with increased confidence on the truth of such traditions as a whole, and we may continue to accept those statements which yet await confirmation from documents more nearly contemporary with the early period to which they refer. It is true that such a date as that assigned by Nabonidus to Sargon is not to be regarded as absolutely fixed, for Nabonidus is obviously speaking in round numbers, and we may allow for some minor inaccuracies in the calculations of his scribes. But it is certain that the later Babylonian priests and scribes had a wealth of historical material at their disposal which has not come down to us. We may therefore accept the date given by Nabonidus for Sargon of Agade and his son Narâm-Sin as approximately accurate, and this is also the opinion of the majority of writers on early Babylonian history.

The diggings at Nippur furnished indications that certain inscriptions found on that site and written in a very archaic form of script were to be assigned to a period earlier than that of Sargon. One class of evidence was obtained from a careful study of the different levels at which the inscriptions and the remains of buildings were found. At a comparatively deep level in the mound inscriptions of Sargon himself were recovered, along with bricks stamped with the name of Narâm-Sin, his son. It was, therefore, a reasonable conclusion roughly to date the particular stratum in which these objects were found to the period of the empire established by Sargon, with its centre at Agade. Later on excavations were carried to a lower level, and remains of buildings were discovered which appeared to belong to a still earlier period of civilization. An altar was found standing in a small enclosure surrounded by a kind of curb. Near by were two immense clay vases which appeared to have been placed on a ramp or inclined plane leading up to the altar, and remains were also found of a massive brick building in which was an arch of brick. No inscriptions were actually found at this level, but in the upper level assigned to Sargon were a number of texts which might very probably be assigned to the pre-Sargonic period. None of these were complete, and they had the appearance of having been intentionally broken into small fragments. There was therefore something to be said for the theory that they might have been inscribed by the builders of the construction in the lowest levels of the mound, and that they were destroyed and scattered by some conqueror who had laid their city in ruins.

But all such evidence derived from noting the levels at which inscriptions are found is in its nature extremely uncertain and liable to many different interpretations, especially if the strata show signs of having been disturbed. Where a pavement or building is still intact, with the inscribed bricks of the builder remaining in their original positions, conclusions may be confidently drawn with regard to the age of the building and its relative antiquity to the strata above and below it. But the strata in the lowest levels at Nippur, as we have seen, were not in this condition, and such evidence as they furnished could only be accepted if confirmed by independent data. Such confirmation was to be found by examination of the early inscriptions themselves.

It has been remarked that most of them were broken into small pieces, as though by some invader of the country; but this was not the case with certain gate-sockets and great blocks of diorite which were too hard and big to be easily broken. Moreover, any conqueror of a city would be unlikely to spend time and labour in destroying materials which might be usefully employed in the construction of other buildings which he himself might erect. Stone could not be obtained in the alluvial plains of Babylonia and had to be quarried in the mountains and brought great distances. From any building of his predecessors which he razed to the ground, an invader would therefore remove the gate-sockets and blocks of stone for his own use, supposing

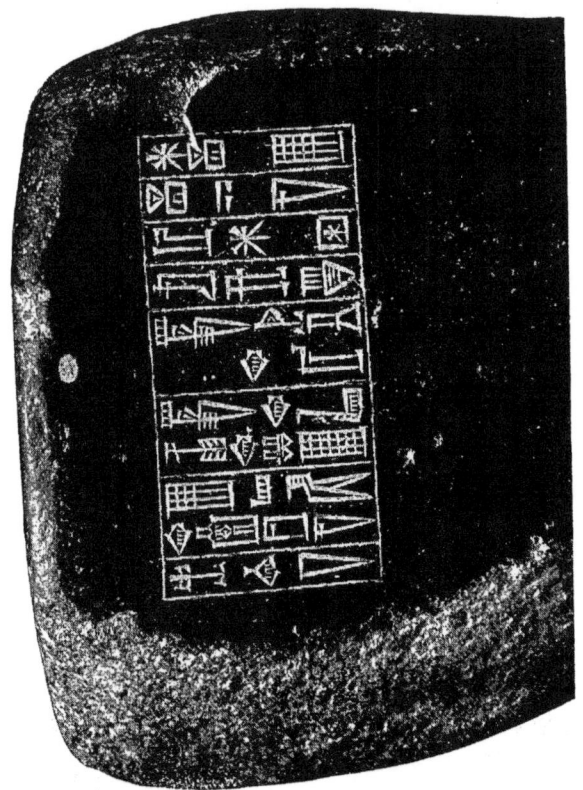

STONE GATE-SOCKET BEARING AN INSCRIPTION OF UR-ENGUR, AN EARLY KING OF THE CITY OF UR.
Photograph by Messrs. Mansell & Co.

he contemplated building on the site. If he left the city in ruins and returned to his own country, some subsequent king, when clearing the ruined site for building operations, might come across the stones, and he would not leave them buried, but would use them for his own construction. And this is what actually did happen in the case of some of the building materials of one of these early kings, from the lower strata of Nippur. Certain of the blocks which bore the name of Lugalkigubnidudu had been used again by Sargon, King of Agade, who engraved his own name upon them without obliterating the name of the former king.

It followed that Lugalkigubnidudu belonged to the pre-Sargonic period, and, although the same conclusive evidence was not forthcoming in the case of Lugalzaggisi, he also without much hesitation was set in this early period, mainly on the strength of the archaic forms of the characters employed in his inscriptions. In fact, they were held to be so archaic that, not only was he said to have reigned before Sargon of Agade, but he was set in the very earliest period of Chaldæan history, and his empire was supposed to have been contemporaneous with the very earliest rulers of Shirpurla. The new inscription found by Captain Cros will cause this opinion to be considerably modified. While it corroborates the view that Lugalzaggisi is to be set in the pre-Sargonic period, it proves that he lived and reigned very shortly before him. As we have already seen, he was the contemporary of Urukagina, who belongs to the middle period of the history of Shirpurla. Lugalzaggisi's capture and sack of the city of Shirpurla was only one of a number of conquests which he achieved. His father Ukush had been merely patesi of the city of Gishkhu, but he himself was not content with the restricted sphere of authority which such a position implied, and he eventually succeeded in enforcing his authority over the greater part of Babylonia. From the fact that he styles himself King of Erech, we may conclude that he removed his capital from Ukush to that city, after having probably secured its submission by force of arms. In fact, his title of "king of the world" can only have been won as the result of many victories, and Captain Cros's tablet gives us a glimpse of the methods by which he managed to secure himself against the competition of any rival. The capture of Shirpurla must have been one of his earliest achievements, for its proximity to Gishkhu rendered its reduction a necessary prelude to any more extensive plan of conquest. But the kingdom which Lugalzaggisi founded cannot have endured long.

Under Sargon of Agade, the Semites gained the upper hand in Babylonia, and Erech, Gishkhu, and Shirpurla, as well as the other ancient cities in the land, fell in turn under his domination and formed part of the extensive empire which he ruled.

Concerning the later rulers of city-states of Babylonia which succeeded the disruption of the empire founded by Sargon of Agade and consolidated by Narâm-Sin, his son, the excavations have little to tell us which has not already been made use of by Prof. Maspero in his history of this period.[1] Ur, Isin, and

[1] The tablets found at Telloh by the late M. de Sarzec, and published during his lifetime, fall into two main classes, which date from different periods in early Chaldæan history. The great majority belong to the period when the city of Ur held pre-eminence among the cities of Southern Babylonia, and they are

Larsam succeeded one another in the position of leading city in Babylonia, holding Nippur, Eridu, Erech, Shirpurla, and the other chief cities in a condition of semi-dependence upon themselves. We may note that the true reading of the name of the founder of the dynasty of Ur has now been ascertained from a syllabary to be Ur-Engur; and an unpublished chronicle in the British Museum relates that his son Dungi cared greatly for the city of Eridu, but sacked Babylon and carried off its spoil, together with the treasures from E-sagila, the great temple of Marduk. Such episodes must have been common at this period when each city was striving for hegemony. Meanwhile, Shirpurla remained the centre of Sumerian influence in Babylonia, and her patesis were content to owe allegiance to so powerful a ruler as Dungi, King of Ur, while at all times exercising complete authority within their own jurisdiction.

During the most recent diggings that have been carried out at Telloh a find of considerable value to the history of Sumerian art has been made. The find is also of great general interest, since it enables us to identify a portrait of Gudea, the most famous of the later Sume-

dated in the reigns of Dungi, Bur-Sin, Gamil-Sin, and Ine-Sin. The other and smaller collection belongs to the earlier period of Sargon and Narâm-Sin; while many of the tablets found in M. de Sarzec's last diggings, which were published after his death, are to be set in the great gap between these two periods. Some of those recently discovered, which belong to the period of Dungi, contain memoranda concerning the supply of food for the maintenance of officials stopping at Shirpurla in the course of journeys in Babylonia and Elam, and they throw an interesting light on the close and constant communication which took place at this time between the great cities of Mesopotamia and the neighbouring countries.

rian patesis. In the course of excavating the Tell of Tablets Captain Cros found a little seated statue made of diorite. It was not found in place, but upside down, and appeared to have been thrown with other débris scattered in that portion of the mound. On lifting it

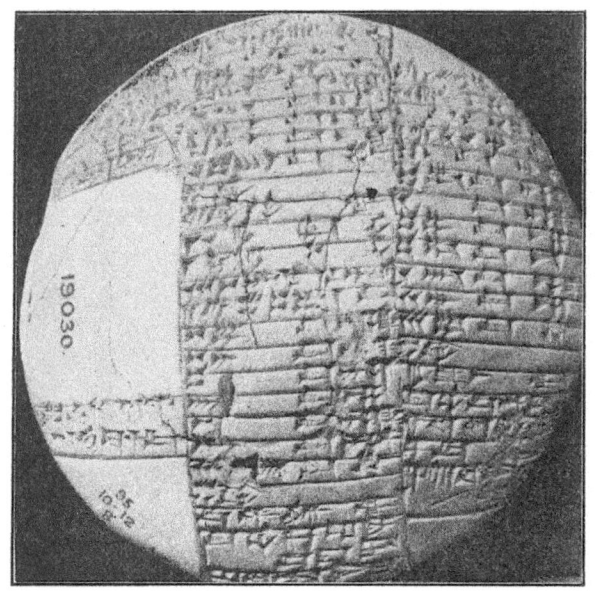

TABLET INSCRIBED IN SUMERIAN WITH DETAILS OF A SURVEY OF CERTAIN PROPERTY.

Probably situated in the neighbourhood of Telloh. The circular shape is very unusual, and appears to have been used only for survey-tablets. Photograph by Messrs. Mansell & Co.

from the trench it was seen that the head of the statue was broken off, as is the case with all the other statues of Gudea found at Telloh. The statue bore an inscription of Gudea, carefully executed and well preserved, but it was smaller than other statues of the same ruler that had been already recovered, and the absence of the head thus robbed it of any extraordinary interest. On its arrival at the Louvre, M. Léon Heuzey was struck by its general resemblance to a Sumerian head of diorite formerly discovered by M. de Sarzec at Telloh, which has been preserved in the Louvre for many years. On applying the head to the newly found statue, it was found to fit it exactly, and to complete the monument, and we are thus enabled to identify the features of Gudea. From a photographic reproduction of this statue, it is seen that the head is larger than it should be, in proportion to the body, a characteristic which is also apparent in a small Sumerian statue preserved in the British Museum.

Gudea caused many statues of himself to be made out of the hard diorite which he brought for that purpose from the Sinaitic peninsula, and from the inscriptions preserved upon them it is possible to ascertain the buildings in which they were originally placed. Thus one of the statues previously found was set up in the temple of Ninkharsag, two others in E-ninnû, the temple of the god Ningirsu, three more in the temple of the goddess Bau, one in E-anna, the temple of the goddess Ninni, and another in the temple of Gatumdug. The newly found statue of the king was made to be set up in the temple erected by Gudea at Girsu in honour of the god Ningishzida, as is recorded in the inscription engraved on the front of the king's robe, which reads as follows:

"In the day when the god Ningirsu, the strong warrior of Enlil, granted unto the god Ningishzida, the son of Ninazu, the beloved of the gods, (the guardianship of) the foundation of the city and of the hills and valleys, on that day Gudea, patesi of Shirpurla, the just man who loveth his god, who for his master Ningirsu hath constructed his temple E-ninnû, called the shining Imgig, and his temple E-pa, the temple of the seven zones of heaven, and for the goddess Ninâ, the queen, his lady, hath constructed the temple Sirara-shum, which riseth higher than (all) the temples in the world, and hath constructed their temples for the great gods of Lagash, built for his god Ningishzida his temple in Girsu. Whosoever shall proclaim the god Ningirsu as his god, even as I proclaim him, may he do no harm unto the temple of my god! May he proclaim the name of this temple! May that man be my friend, and may he proclaim my name! Gudea hath made the statue, and ' Unto - Gudea - the - builder - of - the - temple - hath life-been-given ' hath he called its name, and he hath brought it into the temple."

The long name which Gudea gave to the statue, " Unto - Gudea - the - builder - of - the - temple - hath - life-been-given," is characteristic of the practice of the Sumerian patesis, who always gave long and symbolical names to statues, stelæ, and sacred objects dedicated and set up in their temples. The occasion on which the temple was built, and this statue erected within it, seems to have been the investiture of the god Ningishzida with special and peculiar powers, and it possibly inaugurated his introduction into the pantheon of Shirpurla. Ningishzida is called in the inscription the son of Ninazu, who was the husband of the Queen of the Underworld.

In one of his aspects he was therefore probably a god of the underworld himself, and it is in this character that he was appointed by Ningirsu as guardian of the city's foundations. But "the hills and valleys" (*i.e.* the open country) were also put under his jurisdiction, so that in another aspect he was a god of vegetation. It is therefore not improbable that, like the god Dumuzi, or Tammuz, he was supposed to descend into the underworld in winter, ascending to the surface of the earth with the earliest green shoots of vegetation in the spring.[1]

A most valuable contribution has recently been made to our knowledge of Sumerian religion and of the light in which these early rulers regarded the cult and worship of their gods, by the complete interpretation of the long texts inscribed upon the famous cylinders of Gudea, the patesi of Shirpurla, which have been preserved for many years in the Louvre. These two great cylinders of baked clay were discovered by the late M. de Sarzec so long ago as the year 1877, during the first period of his diggings at Telloh, and, although the general nature of their contents has long been recognized, no complete translation of the texts inscribed upon them had been published until a few months ago. M. Thureau-Dangin, who has made the early Sumerian texts his special study, has devoted himself to their interpretation for some years past, and he has just issued the first part of his monograph upon them. In view of the importance of the texts and of the light they

[1] *Cf.* Thureau-Dangin, *Rev. d'Assyr.*, vol. vi. (1904), p. 24.

throw upon the religious beliefs and practices of the early Sumerians, a somewhat detailed account of their contents may here be given.

The occasion on which the cylinders were made was the rebuilding by Gudea of E-ninnû, the great temple of the god Ningirsu, in the city of Shirpurla. The two cylinders supplement one another, one of them having been inscribed while the work of construction was still in progress, the other after the completion of the temple, when the god Ningirsu had been installed within his shrine with due pomp and ceremony. It would appear that Southern Babylonia had been suffering from a prolonged drought, and that the water in the rivers and canals had fallen, so that the crops had suffered and the country was threatened with famine. Gudea was at a loss to know by what means he might restore prosperity to his country, when one night he had a dream, and it was in consequence of this dream that he eventually erected one of the most sumptuously appointed of Sumerian temples. By this means he secured the return of Ningirsu's favour and that of the other gods, and his country once more enjoyed the blessings of peace and prosperity.

In the opening words of the first of his cylinders Gudea describes how the great gods themselves took counsel and decreed that he should build the temple of E-ninnû and thereby restore to his city the supply of water it had formerly enjoyed. He records that on the day on which the destinies were fixed in heaven and upon earth, Enlil, the chief of the gods, and Ningirsu, the city-god of Shirpurla, held converse. And Enlil, turning to Ningirsu, said: "In my city that which is fitting is not done. The stream doth not rise. The stream of Enlil doth not rise. The high waters shine not, neither do they show their splendour. The stream of Enlil bringeth not good water like the Tigris. Let the King (*i. e.* Ningirsu) therefore proclaim the temple. Let the decrees of the temple E-ninnû be made illustrious in heaven and upon earth!" The great gods did not communicate their orders directly to Gudea, but conveyed their wishes to him by means of a dream. And while the patesi slept a vision of the night came to him, and he beheld a man whose stature was so great that it equalled the heavens and the earth. And by the crown he wore upon his head Gudea knew that the figure must be a god. And by his side was the divine eagle, the emblem of Shirpurla, and his feet rested upon the whirlwind, and a lion was crouching upon his right hand and upon his left. And the figure spoke to the patesi, but he did not understand the meaning of the words. Then it seemed to Gudea that the sun rose from the earth and he beheld a woman holding in her hand a pure reed, and she carried also a tablet on which was a star of the heavens, and she seemed to take counsel with herself. And while Gudea was gazing he seemed to see a second man who was like a warrior; and he carried a slab of lapis lazuli and on it he drew out the plan of a temple. And before the patesi himself it seemed that a fair cushion was placed, and upon the cushion was set a mould, and within the mould was a brick, the brick of destiny. And on the right hand the patesi beheld an ass which lay upon the ground.

Such was the dream which Gudea beheld in a vision of the night, and he was troubled because he could not interpret it. So he decided to go to the goddess Ninâ, who could divine all mysteries of the gods, and beseech her to tell him the meaning of the vision. But before applying to the goddess for her help, he thought it best to secure the mediation of the god Ningirsu and the goddess Gatumdug, in order that they should use their influence with Ninâ to induce her to reveal the interpretation of the dream. So the patesi set out to the temple of Ningirsu, and, having offered a sacrifice and poured out fresh water, he prayed to the god that his sister, Ninâ, the child of Eridu, might be prevailed upon to give him help. And the god hearkened to his prayer. Then Gudea made offerings, and before the sleeping-chamber of the goddess Gatumdug he offered a sacrifice and poured out fresh water. And he prayed to the goddess, calling her his queen and the child of the pure heaven, who gave life to the countries and befriended and preserved the people or the man on whom she looked with favour.

"I have no mother," cried Gudea, "but thou art my mother! I have no father, but thou art a father to me!" And the goddess Gatumdug gave ear to the patesi's prayer. Thus encouraged by her favour and that of Ningirsu, Gudea set out for the temple of the goddess Ninâ.

On his arrival at the temple, the patesi offered a

sacrifice and poured out fresh water, as he had already done when approaching the presence of Ningirsu and Gatumdug. And he prayed to Ninâ, as the goddess who divines the secrets of the gods, beseeching her to interpret the vision that had been sent to him; and he then recounted to her the details of his dream. When the patesi had finished his story, the goddess addressed him and told him that she would explain the meaning of his dream to him. And this was the interpretation of the dream. The man whose stature was so great that it equalled the heavens and the earth, whose head was that of a god, at whose side was the divine eagle, whose feet rested on the whirlwind, while a lion couched on his right hand and on his left, was her brother, the god Ningirsu. And the words which he uttered were an order to the patesi that he should build the temple E-ninnû. And the sun which rose from the earth before the patesi was the god Ningishzida, for like the sun he goes forth from the earth. And the maiden who held a pure reed in her hand, and carried the tablet with the star, was her sister, the goddess Nidaba: the star was the pure star of the temple's construction, which she proclaimed. And the second man, who was like a warrior and carried the slab of lapis lazuli, was the god Nindub, and the plan of the temple which he drew was the plan of E-ninnû. And the brick which rested in its mould upon the cushion was the sacred brick of E-ninnû. And as for the ass which lay upon the ground, that, the goddess said, was the patesi himself.

Having interpreted the meaning of the dream, the

goddess Ninâ proceeded to give Gudea instruction as to how he should go to work to build the temple. She told him first of all to go to his treasure-house and bring forth his treasures from their sealed cases, and out of these to make certain offerings which he was to place near the god Ningirsu, in the temple in which he was dwelling at that time. The offerings were to consist of a chariot, adorned with pure metal and precious stones; bright arrows in a quiver; the weapon of the god, his sacred emblem, on which Gudea was to inscribe his own name; and finally a lyre, the music of which was wont to soothe the god when he took counsel with himself. Ninâ added that if the patesi carried out her instructions and made the offerings she had specified, Ningirsu would reveal to him the plan on which the temple was to be built, and would also bless him. Gudea bowed himself down in token of his submission to the commands of the goddess, and proceeded to execute them forthwith. He brought out his treasures, and from the precious woods and metals which he possessed his craftsmen fashioned the objects he was to present, and he set them in Ningirsu's temple near to the god. He worked day and night, and, having prepared a suitable spot in the precincts of the temple at the place of judgment, he spread out upon it as offerings a fat sheep and a kid and the skin of a young female kid. Then he built a fire of cypress and cedar and other aromatic woods, to make a sweet savour, and, entering the inner chamber of the temple, he offered a prayer to Ningirsu. He said that he wished to build the temple, but he had received no sign that this was the will of the god, and he prayed for a sign.

While he prayed the patesi was stretched out upon the ground, and the god, standing near his head, then answered him. He said that he who should build his temple was none other than Gudea, and that he would give him the sign for which he asked. But first he described the plan on which the temple was to be built, naming its various shrines and chambers and describing the manner in which they were to be fashioned and adorned. And the god promised that when Gudea should build the temple, the land would once more enjoy abundance, for Ningirsu would send a wind which should proclaim to the heavens the return of the waters. And on that day the waters would fall from the heavens, the water in the ditches and canals would rise, and water would gush out from the dry clefts in the ground. And the great fields would once more produce their crops, and oil would be poured out plenteously in Sumer, and wool would again be weighed in great abundance. In that day the god would go to the mountain where dwelt the whirlwind, and he would himself direct the wind which should give the land the breath of life. Gudea must therefore work day and night at the task of building the temple. One company of men was to relieve another at its toil, and during the night the men were to kindle lights so that the plain should be as bright as day. Thus the builders would build continuously. Men were also to be sent to the mountains to cut down cedars and pines and other trees and bring their trunks to the city, while masons were to go to the mountains and were to cut and transport huge blocks of stone to be used in the construction of the temple. Finally the god gave Gudea the sign for which he asked. The sign was that he should feel his side touched as by a flame, and thereby he should know that he was the man chosen by Ningirsu to carry out his commands.

Gudea bowed his head in submission, and his first act was to consult the omens, and the omens were favourable. He then proceeded to purify the city by special rites, so that the mother when angered did not chide her son, and the master did not strike his servant's head, and the mistress, though provoked by her handmaid, did not smite her face. And Gudea drove all the evil wizards and sorcerers from the city, and he purified and sanctified the city completely. Then he kindled a great fire of cedar and other aromatic woods, to make a sweet savour for the gods, and prayers were offered day and night; and the patesi addressed a prayer to the Anunnaki, or Spirits of the Earth, who dwelt in Shirpurla, and assigned a place to them in the temple. Then, having completed his purification of the city itself, he consecrated its immediate surroundings. Thus he consecrated the district of Gu-edin, whence the revenues of Ningirsu were derived, and the lands of the goddess Ninâ with their populous villages. And he consecrated the wild and savage bulls which no man could turn aside, and the cedars which were sacred to Ningirsu, and the cattle of the plains. And he consecrated the armed men, and the famous warriors, and the warriors of the Sun-god. And the emblems of the god Ningirsu, and of the two great goddesses, Ninâ and Ninni, he installed before them in their shrines.

Then Gudea sent far and wide to fetch materials for the construction of the temple. And the Elamite came from Elam, and men of Susa came from Susa, and men brought wood from the mountains of Sinai and Melukhkha. And into the mountain of cedars, where no man before had penetrated, the patesi cut a road, and he brought cedars and beams of other precious woods in great quantities to the city. And he also made a road into the mountain where stone was quarried, into places where no man before had penetrated. And he carried great blocks of stone down from the mountain and loaded them into barges and brought them to the city. And the barges brought bitumen and plaster, and they were loaded as though they were carrying grain, and all manner of great things were brought to the city. Copper ore was brought from the mountain of copper in the land of Kimash, and gold was brought in powder from the mountains, and silver was brought from the mountains and porphyry from the land of Melukhkha, and marble from the mountain of marble. And the patesi installed goldsmiths and silversmiths, who wrought in these precious metals, for the adornment of the temple; and he brought smiths who worked in copper and lead, who were priests of Nin-tu-kalama. In his search for fitting materials for the building of the temple, Gudea journeyed from the lower country to the upper country, and from the upper country to the lower country he returned.

The only other materials now wanting for the construction of the temple were the sun-dried bricks of clay, of which the temple platform and the structure of the temple itself were in the main composed. Their manufacture was now inaugurated by a symbolical ceremony carried out by the patesi in person. At dawn he performed an ablution with the fitting rites that accompanied it, and when the day was more advanced he slew a bull and a kid as sacrifices, and he then entered the temple of Ningirsu, where he prostrated himself. And he took the sacred mould and the fair cushion on which it rested in the temple, and he poured a libation into the mould. Afterwards, having made offerings of honey and butter, and having burnt incense, he placed the cushion and the mould upon his head and carried it to the appointed place. There he placed clay in the mould, shaping it into a brick, and he left the brick in its mould within the temple. And last of all he sprinkled oil of cedar-wood around.

The next day at dawn Gudea broke the mould and set the brick in the sun. And the Sun-god was rejoiced at the brick that he had fashioned. And Gudea took the brick and raised it on high towards the heavens, and he carried the brick to his people. In this way the patesi inaugurated the manufacture of the sun-dried bricks for the temple, the sacred brick which he had made being the symbol and pattern of the innumerable bricks to be used in its construction. He then marked out the plan of the temple, and the text states that he devoted himself to the building of the temple like a young man who has begun building a house and allows no pleasure to interfere with his task. And he chose out skilled workmen and employed them on the building, and he was filled with joy. The gods, too, are stated to have helped with the building, for Enki fixed the temennu of the temple, and the goddess Ninâ looked after its oracles, and Gatumdug, the mother of Shirpurla, fashioned bricks for it morning and evening, while the goddess Bau sprinkled aromatic oil of cedarwood. Gudea himself laid its foundations, and as he did so he blessed the temple seven times, comparing it to the sacred brick, to the holy libation-vase, to the divine eagle of Shirpurla, to a terrible couching panther, to the beautiful heavens, to the day of offerings, and to the morning light which brightens the land. He caused the temple to rise towards heaven like a mountain, or like a cedar growing in the desert. He built it of bricks of Sumer, and the timbers which he set in place were as strong as the dragon of the deep.

While he was engaged on the building Gudea took counsel of the god Enki, and he built a fountain for the gods, where they might drink. With the great stones which he had brought and fashioned he built a reservoir and a basin for the temple. And seven of the great stones he set up as stelæ, and he gave them favourable names. The text then recounts the various parts and shrines of the temple, and it describes their splendours in similes drawn from the heavens and the earth and the abyss, or deep, beneath the earth. The temple itself is described as being like the crescent of the new moon, or like the sun in the midst of the stars, or like a mountain of lapis lazuli, or like a mountain of shining marble. Parts of it are said to have been terrible and strong as a savage bull, or a lion, or the antelope of the abyss, or the monster Lakhamu who dwells in the abyss, or the sacred leopard that inspires terror. One of the doors of the temple was guarded by a figure of the hero who slew the monster with six heads, and at another door was a good dragon, and at another a lion; opposite the city were set figures of the seven heroes, and facing the rising sun was fixed the emblem of the Sun-god. Figures of other heroes and favourable monsters were set up as guardians of other portions of the temple. The fastenings of the main entrance were decorated with dragons shooting out their tongues, and the bolt of the great door was fashioned like a raging hound.

After this description of the construction and adornment of the temple the text goes on to narrate how Gudea arranged for its material endowment. He stalled oxen and sheep, for sacrifice and feasting, in the outhouses and pens within the temple precincts, and he heaped up grain in its granaries. Its storehouses he filled with spices so that they were like the Tigris when its waters are in flood, and in its treasure-chambers he piled up precious stones, and silver, and lead in abundance. Within the temple precincts he planted a sacred garden which was like a mountain covered with vines; and on the terrace he built a great reservoir, or tank, lined with lead, in addition to the great stone reservoir within the temple itself. He constructed a special dwelling-place for the sacred doves, and among the flowers of the temple garden and under the shade of the great trees the birds of heaven flew about unmolested.

The first of the two great cylinders of Gudea ends at this point in the description of the temple, and it is evident that its text was composed while the work of building was still in progress. Moreover, the writing of the cylinder was finished before the actual work of building the temple was completed, for the last column of the text concludes with a prayer to Ningirsu to make it glorious during the progress of the work, the prayer ending with the words, " O Ningirsu, glorify it! Glorify the temple of Ningirsu during its construction! " The text of the second of the two great cylinders is shorter than that of the first, consisting of twenty-four instead of thirty columns of writing, and it was composed and written after the temple was completed. Like the first of the cylinders, it concludes with a prayer to Ningirsu on behalf of the temple, ending with the similar refrain, " O Ningirsu, glorify it! Glorify the temple of Ningirsu after its construction! " The first cylinder, as we have seen, records how it came about that Gudea decided to rebuild the temple E-ninnû in honour of Ningirsu. It describes how, when the land was suffering from drought and famine, Gudea had a dream, how Ninâ interpreted the dream to mean that he must rebuild the temple, and how Ningirsu himself promised that this act of piety would restore abundance and prosperity to the land. Its text ends with the long description of the sumptuous manner in which the patesi carried out the work, the most striking points of which we have just summarized. The narrative of the second cylinder begins at the moment when the building of the temple was finished, and when all was ready for the great god Ningirsu to be installed therein, and its text is taken up with a description of the ceremonies and rites with which this solemn function was carried out. It presents us with a picture, drawn from life, of the worship and cult of the ancient Sumerians in actual operation. In view of its importance from the point of view of the study and comparison of the Sumerian and Babylonian religious systems, its contents also may be summarized. We will afterwards discuss briefly the information furnished by both the cylinders on the Sumerian origin of many of the religious beliefs and practices which were current among the later Semitic inhabitants of Babylonia and Assyria.

When Gudea had finished building the new temple of E-ninnû, and had completed the decoration and adornment of its shrines, and had planted its gardens and stocked its treasure-chambers and storehouses, he applied himself to the preliminary ceremonies and religious preparations which necessarily preceded the actual function of transferring the statue of the god Ningirsu from his old temple to his new one. Gudea's first act was to install the Anunnaki, or Spirits of the Earth, in the new temple, and when he had done this, and had supplied additional sheep for their sacrifices and food in abundance for their offerings, he prayed to them to give him their assistance and to pronounce a prayer at his side when he should lead Ningirsu into his new dwelling-place. The text then describes how Gudea went to the old temple of Ningirsu, accompanied by his protecting spirits who walked before him and behind him. Into the old temple he carried sumptuous offerings, and when he had set them before the god, he addressed him in prayer and said: "O my King, Ningirsu! O Lord, who curbest the raging waters! O Lord, whose word surpasseth all others! O Son of Enlil, O warrior, what commands shall I faithfully carry out? O Ningirsu, I have built thy temple, and with joy would I lead thee therein, and my goddess Bau would I install at thy side." We are told that the god accepted Gudea's prayer, and thereby he gave his consent to be removed from the old temple of E-ninnû to his new one which bore the same name.

But the ceremony of the god's removal was not carried out at once, for the due time had not arrived. The year ended, and the new year came, and then "the month of the temple" began. The third day of the month was that appointed for the installation of Ningirsu. Gudea meanwhile had sprinkled the ground with oil, and set out offerings of honey and butter and wine, and grain mixed with milk, and dates, and food untouched by fire, to serve as food for the gods; and the gods themselves had assisted in the preparations for the reception of Ningirsu. The god Asaru made ready the temple itself, and Ninmada performed the ceremony of purification. The god Enki issued oracles, and the god Nindub, the supreme priest of Eridu, brought incense. Ninâ performed chants within the temple, and brought black sheep and holy cows to its folds and stalls. This record of the help given by the other gods we may interpret as meaning that the priests attached to the other great Sumerian temples took part in the preparation of the new temple, and added their offerings to the temple stores. To many of the gods, also, special shrines within the temple were assigned.

When the purification of E-ninnû was completed and the way between the old temple and the new made ready, all the inhabitants of the city prostrated themselves on the ground. "The city," says Gudea, "was like the mother of a sick man who prepareth a potion for him, or like the cattle of the plain which lie down together, or like the fierce lion, the master of the plain, when he coucheth." During the day and the night before the ceremony of removal, prayers and supplications were uttered, and at the first light of dawn on the appointed day the god Ningirsu went into his new temple "like a whirlwind," the goddess Bau entering at his side "like the sun rising over Shirpurla." She entered beside his couch, like a faithful wife, whose cares are for her own household, and she dwelt beside his ear and bestowed abundance upon Shirpurla.

As the day began to brighten and the sun rose, Gudea set out as offerings in the temple a fat ox and a fat sheep, and he brought a vase of lead and filled it with wine, which he poured out as a libation, and he performed incantations. Then, having duly established Ningirsu and Bau in the chief shrine, he turned his attention to the lesser gods and installed them in their appointed places in the temple, where they would be always ready to assist Ningirsu in the temple ceremonies and in the issue of his decrees for the welfare of the city and its inhabitants. Thus he established the god Galalim, the son of Ningirsu, in a chosen spot in the great court in front of the temple, where, under the orders of his father, he should direct the just and curb the evil-doer; he would also by his presence strengthen and preserve the temple, while his special duty was to guard the throne of destiny and, on behalf of Ningirsu, to place the sceptre in the hands of the reigning patesi. Near to Ningirsu and under his orders Gudea also established the god Dunshaga, whose function it was to sanctify the temple and to look after its libations and offerings, and to see to the due performance of the ceremonies of ablution. This god would offer water to Ningirsu with a pure hand, he would pour out libations of wine and strong drink, and would tend the oxen, sheep, kids, and other offerings which were brought to the temple night and day. To the god Lugalkurdub, who was also installed in the temple, was assigned the privilege of holding in his hand the mace with the seven heads, and it was his duty to open the door of the Gate of Combat. He guarded the sacred weapons of Ningirsu and destroyed the countries of his enemies. He was Ningirsu's chief leader in battle, and another god with lesser powers was associated with him as his second leader.

Ningirsu's counsellor was the god Lugalsisa, and he also had his appointed place in E-ninnû. It was his duty to receive the prayers of Shirpurla and render them propitious; he superintended and blessed Ningirsu's journey when he visited Eridu or returned from that city, and he made special intercessions for the life of Gudea. The minister of Ningirsu's harim was the god Shakanshabar, and he was installed near to Ningirsu that he might issue his commands, both great and small. The keeper of the harim was the god Urizu, and it was his duty to purify the water and sanctify the grain, and he tended Ningirsu's sleeping-chamber and saw that all was arranged therein as was fitting. The driver of Ningirsu's chariot was the god Ensignun; it was his duty to keep the sacred chariot as bright as the stars of heaven, and morning and evening to tend and feed Ningirsu's sacred ass, called Ug-kash, and the ass of Eridu. The shepherd of Ningirsu's kids was the god Enlulim, and he tended the sacred she-goat who suckled the kids, and he guarded her so that the serpent should not steal her milk. This god also looked after the oil and the strong drink of E-ninnû, and saw that its store increased.

Ningirsu's beloved musician was the god Ushumgabkalama, and he was installed in E-ninnû that he might take his flute and fill the temple court with joy. It was his privilege to play to Ningirsu as he listened in his harim, and to render the life of the god pleasant in E-ninnû. Ningirsu's singer was the god Lugaligikhusham, and he had his appointed place in E-ninnû, for he could appease the heart and soften anger; he could stop the tears which flowed from weeping eyes, and could lessen sorrow in the sighing heart. Gudea also installed in E-ninnû the seven twin-daughters of the goddess Bau, all virgins, whom Ningirsu had begotten. Their names were Zarzaru, Impaë, Urenuntaëa, Khegirnuna, Kheshaga, Gurmu, and Zarmu. Gudea installed them near their father that they might offer favourable prayers.

The cultivator of the district of Gu-edin was the god Gishbare, and he was installed in the temple that he might cause the great fields to be fertile, and might make the wheat glisten in Gu-edin, the plain assigned to Ningirsu for his revenues. It was this god's duty also to tend the machines for irrigation, and to raise the water into the canals and ditches of Shirpurla, and thus to keep the city's granaries well filled. The god Kal was the guardian of the fishing in Gu-edin, and his chief duty was to place fish in the sacred pools. The steward of Gu-edin was the god Dimgalabzu, whose duty it was to keep the plain in good order, so that the birds might abound there and the beasts might raise their young in peace; he also guarded the special privilege, which the plain enjoyed, of freedom from any tax levied upon the increase of the cattle pastured there. Last of all Gudea installed in E-ninnû the god Lugalenuruazagakam, who looked after the construction of houses in the city and the building of fortresses upon the city wall; in the temple it was his privilege to raise on high a battle-axe made of cedar.

All these lesser deities, having close relations to the god Ningirsu, were installed by Gudea in his temple in close proximity to him, that they might be always ready to perform their special functions. But the greater deities also had their share in the inauguration of the temple, and of these Gudea specially mentions Ana, Enlil, Ninkharsag, Enki, and Enzu, who all assisted in rendering the temple's lot propitious. For at least three of the greater gods (Ana, Enlil, and the goddess Ninmakh) Gudea erected shrines near one another and probably within the temple's precincts, and, as the passage which records this fact is broken, it is possible that the missing portion of the text recorded the building of shrines to other deities. In any case, it is clear that the composer of the text represents all the great gods as beholding the erection and inauguration of Ningirsu's new temple with favour.

After the account of the installation of Ningirsu, and his spouse Bau, and his attendant deities, the text records the sumptuous offerings which Gudea placed within Ningirsu's shrine. These included another chariot drawn by an ass, a seven-headed battle-axe, a sword with nine emblems, a bow with terrible arrows and a quiver decorated with wild beasts and dragons shooting out their tongues, and a bed which was set within the god's sleeping-chamber. On the couch in the shrine the goddess Bau reclined beside her lord Ningirsu, and ate of the great victims which were sacrificed in their honour.

When the ceremony of installation had been successfully performed, Gudea rested, and for seven days he feasted with his people. During this time the maid was the equal of her mistress, and master and servant consorted together as friends. The powerful and the humble man lay down side by side, and in place of evil speech only propitious words were heard. The rich man did not wrong the orphan and the strong man did not oppress the widow. The laws of Ninâ and Ningirsu were observed, justice was bright in the sunlight, and the Sun-god trampled iniquity under foot. The building of the temple also restored material prosperity to the land, for the canals became full of water and fish swarmed in the pools, the granaries were filled with grain and the flocks and herds brought forth their increase. The city of Shirpurla was satiated with abundance.

Such is a summary of the account which Gudea has left us of his rebuilding of the temple E-ninnû, of the reasons which led him to undertake the work, and of the results which followed its completion. It has often been said that the inscriptions of the ancient Sumerians are without much intrinsic value, that they mainly consist of dull votive formulæ, and that for general interest the best of them cannot be compared with the later inscriptions of the Semitic inhabitants of Mesopotamia. This reproach, for which until recently there was considerable justification, has been finally removed by the working out of the texts upon Gudea's cylinders. For picturesque narrative, for wealth of detail, and for striking similes, it would be hard to find their superior in

Babylonian and Assyrian literature. They are, in fact, very remarkable compositions, and in themselves justify the claim that the Sumerians were possessed of a literature in the proper sense of the term.

But that is not their only value, for they give a vivid picture of ancient Sumerian life and of the ideals and aims which actuated the people and their rulers. The Sumerians were essentially an unmilitary race. That they could maintain a stubborn fight for their territory is proved by the prolonged struggle maintained by Shirpurla against her rival Gishkhu, but neither ruler nor people was inflamed by love of conquest for its own sake. They were settled in a rich and fertile country, which supplied their own wants in abundance, and they were content to lead a peaceful life therein, engaged in agricultural and industrial pursuits, and devoted wholly to the worship of their gods. Gudea's inscriptions enable us to realize with what fervour they carried out the rebuilding of a temple, and how the whole resources of the nation were devoted to the successful completion of the work. It is true that the rebuilding of E-ninnû was undertaken in a critical period when the land was threatened with famine, and the peculiar magnificence with which the work was carried out may be partly explained as due to the belief that such devotion would ensure a return of material prosperity. But the existence of such a belief is in itself an index to the people's character, and we may take it that the record faithfully represents the relations of the Sumerians to their gods, and the important place which worship and ritual occupied in the national life.

Moreover, the inscriptions of Gudea furnish much valuable information with regard to the details of Sumerian worship and the elaborate organization of the temples. From them we can reconstruct a picture of one of these immense buildings, with its numerous shrines and courts, surrounded by sacred gardens and raising its ziggurat, or temple tower, high above the surrounding city. Within its dark chambers were the mysterious figures of the gods, and what little light could enter would have been reflected in the tanks of sacred water sunk to the level of the pavement. The air within the shrines must have been heavy with the smell of incense and of aromatic woods, while the deep silence would have been broken only by the chanting of the priests and the feet of those that bore offerings. Outside in the sunlight cedars and other rare trees cast a pleasant shade, and birds flew about among the flowers and bushes in the outer courts and on the garden terraces. The area covered by the temple buildings must have been enormous, for they included the dwellings of the priests, stables and pens for the cattle, sheep, and kids employed for sacrifice, and treasure-chambers and storehouses and granaries for the produce from the temple lands.

We also get much information with regard to the nature of the offerings and the character of the ceremonies which were performed. We may mention as of peculiar interest Gudea's symbolical rite which preceded the making of the sun-dried bricks, and the ceremony of the installation of Ningirsu in the presence of the prostrate city. The texts also throw an interesting light on the truly Oriental manner in which, when approaching one deity for help, the coöperation and assistance of other deities were first secured. Thus Gudea solicited the intercession of Ningirsu and Gatumdug before applying to the goddess Ninâ to interpret his dream. The extremely human character of the gods themselves is also well illustrated. Thus we gather from the texts that Ningirsu's temple was arranged like the palace of a Sumerian ruler and that he was surrounded by gods who took the place of the attendants and ministers of his human counterpart. His son was installed in a place of honour and shared with him the responsibility of government. Another god was his personal attendant and cupbearer, who offered him fair water and looked after the ablutions. Two more were his generals, who secured his country against the attacks of foes. Another was his counsellor, who received and presented petitions from his subjects and superintended his journeys. Another was the head of his harim, a position of great trust and responsibility, while a keeper of the harim looked after the practical details. Another god was the driver of his chariot, and it is interesting to note that the chariot was drawn by an ass, for horses were not introduced into Western Asia until a much later period. Other gods performed the functions of head shepherd, chief musician, chief singer, head cultivator and inspector of irrigation, inspector of the fishing, land steward, and architect. His household also included his wife and his seven virgin daughters. In addition to the account of the various functions performed by these lesser deities, the texts also furnish valuable facts with regard to the characters and attributes of the greater gods and goddesses, such as the attributes of Ningirsu himself, and the character of Ninâ as the goddess who divined and interpreted the secrets of the gods.

But perhaps the most interesting conclusions to be drawn from the texts relate to the influence exerted by the ancient Sumerians upon Semitic beliefs and practices. It has, of course, long been recognized that the later Semitic inhabitants of Babylonia and Assyria drew most of their culture from the Sumerians, whom they displaced and absorbed. Their system of writing, the general structure of their temples, the ritual of their worship, the majority of their religious compositions, and many of their gods themselves are to be traced to a Sumerian origin, and much of the information obtained from the cylinders of Gudea merely confirms or illustrates the conclusions already deduced from other sources. As instances we may mention the belief in spirits, which is illustrated by the importance attached to the placating of the Anunnaki, or Spirits of the Earth, to whom a special place and special offerings were assigned in E-ninnû. The Sumerian origin of ceremonies of purification is confirmed by Gudea's purification of the city before beginning the building of the temple, and again before the transference of the god from his old temple to the new one. The consultation of omens, which was so marked a feature of Babylonian and Assyrian life, is seen in actual operation under the Sumerians; for, even after Gudea had received direct instructions from Ningirsu to begin building his temple, he did not proceed to carry them out until he had consulted the omens and found that they were favourable. Moreover, the references to mythological beings, such as the seven heroes, the dragon of the deep, and the god who slew the dragon, confirm the opinion that the creation legends and other mythological compositions of the Babylonians were derived by them from Sumerian sources. But there are two incidents in the narrative which are on a rather different plane and are more startling in their novelty. One is the story of Gudea's dream, and the other the sign which he sought from his god. The former is distinctly apocalyptic in character, and both may be paralleled in what is regarded as purely Semitic literature. That such conceptions existed among the Sumerians is a most interesting fact, and although the theory of independent origin is possible, their existence may well have influenced later Semitic beliefs.

CHAPTER V

ELAM AND BABYLON, THE COUNTRY OF THE SEA AND THE KASSITES

UP to five years ago our knowledge of Elam and of the part she played in the ancient world was derived, in the main, from a few allusions to the country to be found in the records of Babylonian and Assyrian kings. It is true that a few inscriptions of the native rulers had been found in Persia, but they belonged to the late periods of her history, and the majority consisted of short dedicatory formulæ and did not supply us with much historical information. But the excavations carried on since then by M. de Morgan at Susa have revealed an entirely new chapter of ancient Oriental history, and have thrown a flood of light upon the position occupied by Elam among the early races of the East.

Lying to the north of the Persian Gulf and to the east of the Tigris, and rising from the broad plains nearer the coast to the mountainous districts within its borders on the east and north, Elam was one of the nearest neighbours of Chaldæa. A few facts concerning her relations with Babylonia during certain periods of her history have long been known, and her struggles with the later kings of Assyria are known in some detail; but for her history during the earliest periods we have had to trust mainly to conjecture. That in the earlier as in the later periods she should have been in constant antagonism with Babylonia might legitimately be suspected, and it is not surprising that we should find an echo of her early struggles with Chaldæa in the legends which were current in the later periods of Babylonian history. In the fourth and fifth tablets, or sections, of the great Babylonian epic which describes the exploits of the Babylonian hero Gilgamesh, a story is told of an expedition undertaken by Gilgamesh and his friend Ea-bani against an Elamite despot named Khumbaba. It is related in the poem that Khumbaba was feared by all who dwelt near him, for his roaring was like the storm, and any man perished who was rash enough to enter the cedar-wood in which he dwelt. But Gilgamesh, encouraged by a dream sent him by Shamash, the Sun-god, pressed on with his friend, and, having entered the wood, succeeded in slaying Khumbaba and in cutting off his head. This legend is doubtless based on episodes in early Babylonian and Elamite history. Khumbaba may not have been an actual historical ruler, but at least he represents or personifies the power of Elam, and the success of Gilgamesh no doubt reflects the aspirations with which many a Babylonian expedition set out for the Elamite frontier.

Incidentally it may be noted that the legend possibly had a still closer historical parallel, for the name of

Khumbaba occurs as a component in a proper name upon one of the Elamite contracts found recently by M. de Morgan at Mal-Amir. The name in question is written *Khumbaba-arad-ili*, " Khumbaba, the servant of God," and it proves that at the date at which the contract was written (about 1300 - 1000 B. C.) the name of Khumbaba was still held in remembrance, possibly as that of an early historical ruler of the country.

In her struggles with Chaldæa, Elam was not successful during the earliest historical period of which we have obtained information; and, so far as we can tell at present, her princes long continued to own allegiance to the Semitic rulers whose influence was predominant from time to time in the plains of Lower Mesopotamia. Tradition relates that two of the earliest Semitic rulers whose names are known to us, Sargon and Narâm-Sin, kings of Agade, held sway in Elam, for in the "Omens" which were current in a later period concerning them, the former is credited with the conquest of the whole country, while of the latter it is related that he conquered Apirak, an Elamite district, and captured its king. Some doubts were formerly cast upon these traditions inasmuch as they were found in a text containing omens or forecasts, but these doubts were removed by the discovery of contemporary documents by which the later traditions were confirmed. Sargon's conquest of Elam, for instance, was proved to be historical by a reference to the event in a date-formula upon tablets belonging to his reign. Moreover, the event has received further confirmation from an unpublished tablet in the British Museum, containing a copy of the original chronicle from which the historical extracts in the "Omens" were derived. The portion of the composition inscribed upon this tablet does not contain the lines referring to Sargon's conquest of Elam, for these occurred in an earlier section of the composition; but the recovery of the tablet puts beyond a doubt the historical character of the traditions preserved upon the omen-tablet as a whole, and the conquest of Elam is thus confirmed by inference. The new text does recount the expedition undertaken by Narâm-Sin, the son of Sargon, against Apirak, and so furnishes a direct confirmation of this event.

Another early conqueror of Elam, who was probably of Semitic origin, was Alu-usharshid, king of the city of Kish, for, from a number of his inscriptions found near those of Sargon at Nippur in Babylonia, we learn that he subdued Elam and Para'se, the district in which the city of Susa was probably situated. From a small mace-head preserved in the British Museum we know of another conquest of Elam by a Semitic ruler of this early period. The mace-head was made and engraved by the orders of Mutabil, an early governor of the city of Dûr-ilu, to commemorate his own valour as the man "who smote the head of the hosts" of Elam. Mutabil was not himself an independent ruler, and his conquest of Elam must have been undertaken on behalf of the suzerain to whom he owed allegiance, and thus his victory cannot be classed in the same category as those of his predecessors. A similar remark applies to the success against the city of Anshan in Elam, achieved by Gudea, the Sumerian ruler of Shirpurla, inasmuch as he was a patesi, or viceroy, and not an independent king. Of greater duration was the influence exercised over Elam by the kings of Ur, for bricks and contract-tablets have been found at Susa proving that Dungi, one of the most powerful kings of Ur, and Bur-Sin, Ine-Sin, and Gamil-Sin, kings of the second dynasty in that city, all in turn included Elam within the limits of their empire.

Such are the main facts which until recently had been ascertained with regard to the influence of early Babylonian rulers in Elam. The information is obtained mainly from Babylonian sources, and until recently we have been unable to fill in any details of the picture from the Elamite side. But this inability has now been removed by M. de Morgan's discoveries. From the inscribed bricks, cones, stelæ, and statues that have been brought to light in the course of his excavations at Susa, we have recovered the name of a succession of native Elamite rulers. All those who are to be assigned to this early period, during which Elam owed allegiance to the kings of Babylonia, ascribe to themselves the title of *patesi*, or viceroy, of Susa, in acknowledgment of their dependence. Their records consist principally of building inscriptions and foundation memorials, and they commemorate the construction or repair of temples, the cutting of canals, and the like. They do not, therefore, throw much light upon the problems connected with the external history of Elam during this early period, but we obtain from them a glimpse of the internal administration of the country. We see a nation without ambition to extend its boundaries, and content, at any rate for the time, to owe allegiance to foreign rulers, while the energies of its native princes are devoted exclusively to the cultivation of the worship of the gods and to the amelioration of the conditions of the life of the people in their charge.

A difficult but interesting problem presents itself for solution at the outset of our inquiry into the history of this people as revealed by their lately recovered inscriptions,—the problem of their race and origin. Found at Susa in Elam, and inscribed by princes bearing purely Elamite names, we should expect these votive and memorial texts to be written entirely in the Elamite language. But such is not the case, for many of them are written in good Semitic Babylonian. While some are entirely composed in the tongue which we term Elamite or Anzanite, others, so far as their language and style is concerned, might have been written by any early Semitic king ruling in Babylonia. Why did early princes of Susa make this use of the Babylonian tongue?

At first sight it might seem possible to trace a parallel in the use of the Babylonian language by kings and officials in Egypt and Syria during the fifteenth century B. C., as revealed in the letters from Tell el-Amarna. But a moment's thought will show that the cases are not similar. The Egyptian or Syrian scribe employed Babylonian as a medium for his official foreign correspondence because Babylonian at that period was the *lingua franca* of the East. But the object of the early Elamite rulers was totally different. Their inscribed bricks and memorial stelæ were not intended for the eyes of foreigners, but for those of their own descendants. Built into the structure of a temple, or buried beneath the edifice, one of their principal objects was to preserve the name and deeds of the writer from oblivion. Like similar documents found on the sites of Assyrian and Babylonian cities, they sometimes include curses upon any impious man, who, on finding the inscription after the temple shall have fallen into ruins, should in any way injure the inscription or deface the writer's name. It will be obvious that the writers of these inscriptions intended that they should be intelligible to those who might come across them in the future. If, therefore, they employed the Babylonian as well as the Elamite language, it is clear that they expected that their future readers might be either Babylonian or Elamite; and this belief can only be explained on the supposition that their own subjects were of mixed race.

It is therefore certain that at this early period of Elamite history Semitic Babylonians and Elamites dwelt side by side in Susa and retained their separate languages. The problem therefore resolves itself into the inquiry: which of these two peoples occupied the country first? Were the Semites at first in sole possession, which was afterwards disputed by the incursion of Elamite tribes from the north and east? Or were the Elamites the original inhabitants of the land, into which the Semites subsequently pressed from Babylonia?

A similar mixture of races is met with in Babylonia itself in the early period of the history of that country. There the early Sumerian inhabitants were gradually dispossessed by the invading Semite, who adopted the civilization of the conquered race, and took over the system of cuneiform writing, which he modified to suit his own language. In Babylonia the Semites eventually predominated and the Sumerians as a race disappeared, but during the process of absorption the two languages were employed indiscriminately. The kings of the First Babylonian Dynasty wrote their votive inscriptions sometimes in Sumerian, sometimes in Semitic Babylonian; at other times they employed both languages for the same text, writing the record first in Sumerian and afterwards appending a Semitic translation by the side; and in the legal and commercial documents of the period the old Sumerian legal forms and phrases were retained intact. In Elam we may suppose that the use of the Sumerian and Semitic languages was the same.

It may be surmised, however, that the first Semitic incursions into Elam took place at a much later period than those into Babylonia, and under very different conditions. When overrunning the plains and cities of the Sumerians, the Semites were comparatively uncivilized, and, so far as we know, without a system of writing of their own. The incursions into Elam must have taken place under the great Semitic conquerors, such as Sargon and Narâm-Sin and Alu-usharshid. At this period they had fully adopted and modified the Sumerian characters to express their own Semitic tongue, and on their invasion of Elam they brought their system of writing with them. The native princes of Elam, whom they conquered, adopted it in turn for many of their votive texts and inscribed monuments when they wished to write them in the Babylonian language.

Such is the most probable explanation of the occurrence in Elam of inscriptions in the Old Babylonian language, written by native princes concerning purely domestic matters. But a further question now suggests itself. Assuming that this was the order in which events took place, are we to suppose that the first Semitic invaders of Elam found there a native population in a totally undeveloped stage of civilization? Or did they find a population enjoying a comparatively high state of culture, different from their own, which they proceeded to modify and transform? Luckily, we have not to fall back on conjecture for an answer to these questions, for a recent discovery at Susa has furnished material from which it is possible to reconstruct in outline the state of culture of these early Elamites.

This interesting discovery consists of a number of clay tablets inscribed in the proto-Elamite system of writing, a system which was probably the only one in use in the country during the period before the Semitic invasion. The documents in question are small, roughly formed tablets of clay very similar to those employed in the early periods of Babylonian history, but the signs and characters impressed upon them offer the greatest contrast to the Sumerian and early Babylonian characters with which we are familiar. Although they cannot be fully deciphered at present, it is probable that they are tablets of accounts, the signs upon them consisting of lists of figures and what are probably ideographs for things. Some of the ideographs, such as that

CLAY TABLET, FOUND AT SUSA, BEARING AN INSCRIPTION
IN THE EARLY PROTO-ELAMITE CHARACTER.
The photograph is taken from M de Morgan's *Délégation en Perse, Mém.*, t. VI, pl. 23.

for " tablet," with which many of the texts begin, are very similar to the Sumerian or Babylonian signs for the same objects; but the majority are entirely different and have been formed and developed upon a system of their own. On these tablets, in fact, we have a new class of cuneiform writing in an early stage of its development, when the hieroglyphic or pictorial character of the ideographs was still prominent. Although the meaning of the majority of these ideographs has not yet been identified, Père Scheil, who has edited the texts, has

CLAY TABLET, RECENTLY FOUND AT SUSA, BEARING AN INSCRIPTION IN THE EARLY PROTO-ELAMITE CHARACTER.
The photograph is reproduced from M. de Morgan's *Délégation en Perse, Mém.*, t. vi, pl. 22.

succeeded in making out the system of numeration. He has identified the signs for unity, 10, 100, and 1,000, and for certain fractions,[1] and the signs for these figures are quite different from those employed by the Sumerians.

[1] *E. g.* $\frac{1}{2}$, $\frac{1}{3}$, $\frac{2}{3}$, $\frac{1}{4}$, $\frac{3}{4}$, $\frac{1}{5}$, $\frac{2}{5}$, $\frac{1}{6}$, $\frac{5}{6}$, $\frac{5}{12}$, $\frac{7}{12}$, $1\frac{1}{2}$, etc. See *Délégation en Perse, Mémoires*, tome vi (1905), pp. 115 *ff*.

The system, too, is different, for it is a decimal, and not a sexagesimal, system of numeration.

That in its origin this form of writing had some connection with that employed and, so far as we know, invented by the ancient Sumerians is possible.[1] But it shows small trace of Sumerian influence, and the disparity in the two systems of numeration is a clear indication that, at any rate, it broke off and was isolated from the latter at a very early period. Having once been adopted by the early Elamites, it continued to be used by them for long periods with but small change or modification. Employed far from the centre of Sumerian civilization, its development was slow, and it seems to have remained in its ideographic state, while the system employed by the Sumerians, and adopted by the Semitic Babylonians, was developed along syllabic lines.

It was without doubt this proto-Elamite system of writing which the Semites from Babylonia found employed in Elam on their first incursions into that country. They brought with them their own more convenient form of writing, and, when the country had once been finally subdued, the subject Elamite princes adopted the foreign system of writing and language from their conquerors for memorial and monumental inscriptions. But the ancient native writing was not

[1] It is, of course, also possible that the system of writing had no connection in its origin with that of the Sumerians, and was invented independently of the system employed in Babylonia. In that case, the signs which resemble certain of the Sumerian characters must have been adopted in a later stage of its development. Though it would be rash to dogmatize on the subject, the view that connects its origin with the Sumerians appears on the whole to fit in best with the evidence at present available.

MODIFIED BABYLONIAN WRITING

entirely ousted, and continued to be employed by the common people of Elam for the ordinary purposes of daily life. That this was the case at least until the reign of Karibu-sha-Shushinak, one of the early subject native rulers, is clear from one of his inscriptions engraved upon a block of limestone to commemorate the dedication of what were probably some temple furnishings in honour of the god Shushinak. The main part of the inscription is written in Semitic Babylonian, and below there is an addition to the text written in proto-Elamite. characters, probably enumerating the offerings which the Karibu - sha - Shushinak decreed should be made for the future in honour of the god.[1] In course of time this proto-Elamite system of writing by means of ideographs seems to have died out, and a modified form of the Babylonian system was adopted by the Elamites for writing their own language phonetically. It is in this phonetic char-

BLOCK OF LIMESTONE, FOUND AT SUSA, BEARING INSCRIPTIONS OF KARIBU - SHA - SHUSHINAK.

The photograph is taken from M. de Morgan's *Délégation en Perse, Mém.*, t. vi, pl. 2.

---

[1] We have assumed that both inscriptions were the work of Karibu-sha-Shushinak. But it is also possible that the second one in proto-Elamite charac-

acter that the so-called "Anzanite" texts of the later Elamite princes were composed.

Karibu-sha-Shushinak, whose recently discovered bilingual inscription has been referred to above, was one of the earlier of the subject princes of Elam, and he probably reigned at Susa not later than B. C. 3000. He styles himself "patesi of Susa, governor of the land of Elam," but we do not know at present to what contemporary king in Babylonia he owed allegiance. The longest of his inscriptions that have been recovered is engraved upon a stele of limestone and records the building of the Gate of Shushinak at Susa and the cutting of a canal; it also recounts the offerings which Karibu-sha-Shushinak dedicated on the completion of the work. It may here be quoted as an example of the class of votive inscriptions from which the names of these early Elamite rulers have been recovered. The inscription runs as follows: "For the god Shushinak, his lord, Karibu-sha-Shushinak, the son of Shimbi-ishkhuk, patesi of Susa, governor of the land of Elam,— when he set the (door) of his Gate in place, . . . in the Gate of the god Shushinak, his lord, and when he had opened the canal of Sidur, he set up in face thereof his canopy, and he set planks of cedar-wood for its gate. A sheep in the interior thereof, and sheep without, he appointed (for sacrifice) to him each day. On days of festival he caused the people to sing songs in the Gate

---

ters was added at a later period. From its position on the stone it is clear that it was written after and not before Karibu-sha-Shushinak's inscription in Semitic Babylonian. See the photographic reproduction.

of the god Shushinak. And twenty measures of fine oil he dedicated to make his gate beautiful. Four *magi* of silver he dedicated; a censer of silver and gold he dedicated for a sweet odour; a sword he dedicated; an axe with four blades he dedicated, and he dedicated silver in addition for the mounting thereof. . . . A righteous judgment he judged in the city! As for the man who shall transgress his judgment or shall remove his gift, may the gods Shushinak and Shamash, Bêl and Ea, Ninni and Sin, Ninkharsag and Nati — may all the gods uproot his foundation, and his seed may they destroy!"

It will be seen that Karibu-sha-Shushinak takes a delight in enumerating the details of the offerings he has ordained in honour of his city-god Shushinak, and this religious temper is peculiarly characteristic of the princes of Elam throughout the whole course of their history. Another interesting point to notice in the inscription is that, although the writer invokes Shushinak, his own god, and puts his name at the head of the list of deities whose vengeance he implores upon the impious, he also calls upon the gods of the Babylonians. As he wrote the inscription itself in Babylonian, in the belief that it might be recovered by some future Semitic inhabitant of his country, so he included in his imprecations those deities whose names he conceived would be most reverenced by such a reader. In addition to Karibu-sha-Shushinak the names of a number of other patesis, or viceroys, have recently been recovered, such as Khutran-tepti, and Idadu I and his son Kal-Rukhuratir, and his grandson Idadu II. All these probably ruled after Karibu-sha-Shushinak, and may be set in the early period of Babylonian supremacy in Elam.

It has been stated above that the allegiance which these early Elamite princes owed to their overlords in Babylonia was probably reflected in the titles which they bear upon their inscriptions recently found at Susa. These titles are " *patesi* of Susa, *shakkannak* of Elam," which may be rendered as " viceroy of Susa, governor of Elam." But inscriptions have been found on the same site belonging to another series of rulers, to whom a different title is applied. Instead of referring to themselves as viceroys of Susa and governors of Elam, they bear the title of *sukkal* of Elam, of Siparki, and of Susa. Siparki, or Sipar, was probably the name of an important section of Elamite territory, and the title *sukkalu*, " ruler," probably carries with it an idea of independence of foreign control which is absent from the title of *patesi*. It is therefore legitimate to trace this change of title to a corresponding change in the political condition of Elam; and there is much to be said for the view that the rulers of Elam who bore the title of *sukkalu* reigned at a period when Elam herself was independent, and may possibly have exercised a suzerainty over the neighbouring districts of Babylonia.

The worker of this change in the political condition of Elam and the author of her independence was a king named Kutir-Nakhkhunte or Kutir-Na'khunde, whose name and deeds have been preserved in later Assyrian records, where he is termed Kudur-Nankhundi and

Kudur-Nakhundu.[1] This ruler, according to the Assyrian king Ashur-bani-pal, was not content with throwing off the yoke under which his land had laboured for so long, but carried war into the country of his suzerain and marched through Babylonia devastating and despoiling the principal cities. This successful Elamite campaign took place, according to the computation of the later Assyrian scribes, about the year 2280 B.C., and it is probable that for many years afterwards the authority of the King of Elam extended over the plains of Babylonia. It has been suggested that Kutir-Nakhkhunte, after including Babylonia within his empire, did not remain permanently in Elam, but may have resided for a part of each year, at least, in Lower Mesopotamia. His object, no doubt, would have been to superintend in person the administration of his empire and to check any growing spirit of independence among his local governors. He may thus have appointed in Susa itself a local governor who would carry on the business of the country during his absence, and, under the king himself, would wield supreme authority. Such governors may have been the sukkali, who, unlike the patesi, were independent of foreign control, but yet did not enjoy the full title of "king."

It is possible that the sukkalu who ruled in Elam during the reign of Kutir-Nakhkhunte was named Temti-agun, for a short inscription of this ruler has been recovered, in which he records that he built and

[1] For references to the passages where the name occurs, see King, *Letters of Hammurabi*, vol. i, p. lv *f.*

dedicated a certain temple with the object of ensuring the preservation of the life of Kutir-Na'khundi. If we may identify the Kutir-Na'khundi of this text with the great Elamite conqueror, Kutir-Nakhkhunte, it follows that Temti-agun, the sukkal of Susa, was his subordinate. The inscription mentions other names which are possibly those of rulers of this period, and reads as follows: " Temti-agun, sukkal of Susa, the son of the sister of Sirukdu', hath built a temple of bricks at Ishme-karab for the preservation of the life of Kutir-Na'khundi, and for the preservation of the life of Lila-irtash, and for the preservation of his own life, and for the preservation of the life of Temti-khisha-khanesh and of Pil-kishamma-khashduk." As Lila-irtash is mentioned immediately after Kutir-Na'khundi, he was possibly his son, and he may have succeeded him as ruler of the empire of Elam and Babylonia, though no confirmation of this view has yet been discovered. Temti-khisha-khanesh is mentioned immediately after the reference to the preservation of the life of Temti-agun himself, and it may be conjectured that the name was that of Temti-agun's son, or possibly that of his wife, in which event the last two personages mentioned in the text may have been the sons of Temti-agun.

This short text affords a good example of one class of votive inscriptions from which it is possible to recover the names of Elamite rulers of this period, and it illustrates the uncertainty which at present attaches to the identification of the names themselves and the order in which they are to be arranged. Such uncertainty necessarily exists when only a few texts have been recovered, and it will disappear with the discovery of additional monuments by which the results already arrived at may be checked. We need not here enumerate all the names of the later Elamite rulers which have been found in the numerous votive inscriptions recovered during the recent excavations at Susa. The order in which they should be arranged is still a matter of considerable uncertainty, and the facts recorded by them in such inscriptions as we possess mainly concern the building and restoration of Elamite temples and the decoration of shrines, and they are thus of no great historical interest. These votive texts are well illustrated by a remarkable find of foundation deposits made last year by M. de Morgan in the temple of Shushinak at Susa, consisting of figures and jewelry of gold and silver, and objects of lead, bronze, iron, stone, and ivory, cylinder-seals, mace-heads, vases, etc. This is the richest foundation deposit that has been recovered on any ancient site, and its archæological interest in connection with the development of Elamite art is great. But in no other way does the find affect our conception of the history of the country, and we may therefore pass on to a consideration of such recent discoveries as throw new light upon the course of history in Western Asia.

With the advent of the First Dynasty in Babylon Elam found herself face to face with a power prepared to dispute her claims to exercise a suzerainty over the plains of Mesopotamia. It is held by many writers that the First Dynasty of Babylon was of Arab origin, and there is much to be said for this view. M. Pognon was the first to start the theory that its kings were not purely Babylonian, but were of either Arab or Aramæan extraction, and he based his theory on a study of the forms of the names which some of them bore. The name of Samsu-iluna, for instance, means "the sun is our god," but the form of the words of which the name is composed betray foreign influence. Thus in Babylonian the name for "sun" or the Sun-god would be *Shamash* or *Shamshu*, not *Samsu;* in the second half of the name, while *ilu* ("god") is good Babylonian, the ending *na*, which is the pronominal suffix of the first person plural, is not Babylonian, but Arabic. We need not here enter into a long philological discussion, and the instance already cited may suffice to show in what way many of the names met in the Babylonian inscriptions of this period betray a foreign, and possibly an Arabic, origin. But whether we assign the forms of these names to Arabic influence or not, it may be regarded as certain that the First Dynasty of Babylon had its origin in the incursion into Babylonia of a new wave of Semitic immigration. The invading Semites brought with them fresh blood and unexhausted energy, and, finding many of their own race in scattered cities and settlements throughout the country, they succeeded in establishing a purely Semitic dynasty, with its capital at Babylon, and set about the task of freeing the country from any vestiges of foreign control. Many centuries earlier Semitic kings had ruled in Babylonian cities, and Semitic empires had been formed there. Sar-

Brick Stamped with an Inscription of Kudur-mabug.
Photograph by Messrs. Mansell & Co.

importance for one city, while it might never have been heard of in another district; thus it sometimes happened that the same event was not adopted throughout the whole country for designating a particular year, and the result was that different systems of dating were employed in different parts of Babylonia. Moreover, when a particular system had been in use for a considerable time, it required a very good memory to retain the order and period of the various events referred to in the date-formulæ, so as to fix in a moment the date of a document by its mention of one of them. In order to assist themselves in their task of fixing dates in this manner, the scribes of the First Dynasty of Babylon drew up lists of the titles of the years, arranged in chronological order under the reigns of the kings to which they referred. Some of these lists have been recovered, and they are of the greatest assistance in fixing the chronology, while at the same time they furnish us with considerable information concerning the history of the period of which we should otherwise have been in ignorance.

From these lists of date-formulæ, and from the dates themselves which are found upon the legal and commercial tablets of the period, we learn that Kish, Kasallu, and Isin all gave trouble to the earlier kings of the First Dynasty, and had in turn to be subdued. Elam did not watch the diminution of her influence in Babylonia without a struggle to retain it. Under Kudurmabug, who was prince or governor of the districts lying along the frontier of Elam, the Elamites struggled hard to maintain their position in Babylonia, making the city of Ur the centre from which they sought to check the growing power of Babylon. From bricks that have been recovered from Mukayyer, the site of the city of Ur, we learn that Kudur-mabug rebuilt the temple in that city dedicated to the Moon-god, which is an indication of the firm hold he had obtained upon the city. It was obvious to the new Semitic dynasty in Babylon that, until Ur and the neighbouring city of Larsam had been captured, they could entertain no hope of removing the Elamite yoke from Southern Babylonia. It is probable that the earlier kings of the dynasty made many attempts to capture them, with varying success. An echo of one of their struggles in which they claimed the victory may be seen in the date-formula for the fourteenth year of the reign of Sin-muballit, Hammurabi's father and predecessor on the throne of Babylon. This year was referred to in the documents of the period as "the year in which the people of Ur were slain with the sword." It will be noted that the capture of the city is not commemorated, so that we may infer that the slaughter of the Elamites which is recorded did not materially reduce their influence, as they were left in possession of their principal stronghold. In fact, Elam was not signally defeated in the reign of Kudur-mabug, but in that of his son Rim-Sin. From the date-formulæ of Hammurabi's reign we learn that the struggle between Elam and Babylon was brought to a climax in the thirtieth year of his reign, when it is recorded in the formulæ that he defeated the Elamite army and overthrew Rîm-Sin, while in the following year we gather that he added the land of Emutbal, that is, the western district of Elam, to his dominions.

An unpublished chronicle in the British Museum gives us further details of Hammurabi's victory over the Elamites, and at the same time makes it clear that the defeat and overthrow of Rim-Sin was not so crushing as has hitherto been supposed. This chronicle relates that Hammurabi attacked Rîm-Sin, and, after capturing the cities of Ur and Larsam, carried their spoil to Babylon. Up to the present it has been supposed that Hammurabi's victory marked the end of Elamite influence in Babylonia, and that thenceforward the supremacy of Babylon was established throughout the whole of the country. But from the new chronicle we gather that Hammurabi did not succeed in finally suppressing the attempts of Elam to regain her former position. It is true that the cities of Ur and Larsam were finally incorporated in the Babylonian empire, and the letters of Hammurabi to Sin-idinnam, the governor whom he placed in authority over Larsam, afford abundant evidence of the stringency of the administrative control which he established over Southern Babylonia. But Rim-Sin was only crippled for the time, and, on being driven from Ur and Larsam, he retired beyond the Elamite frontier and devoted his energies to the recuperation of his forces against the time when he should feel himself strong enough again to make a bid for victory in his struggle against the growing power of Babylon. It is probable that he made no further attempt to renew the contest during the life of Hammurabi, but after Samsu-iluna, the son of Hammurabi, had succeeded to the Babylonian throne, he appeared in

SEMITIC BABYLONIAN CONTRACT-TABLET, INSCRIBED IN THE REIGN OF HAMMURABI WITH A DEED RECORDING THE DIVISION OF PROPERTY.

The actual tablet is on the right; that which appears to be another and larger tablet on the left is the hollow clay case in which the tablet on the right was originally enclosed. Photograph by Messrs. Mansell & Co.

Babylonia at the head of the forces he had collected, and attempted to regain the cities and territory he had lost. The portion of the text of the chronicle relating to the war between Rim-Sin and Samsu-iluna is broken so that it is not possible to follow the campaign in detail, but it appears that Samsu-iluna defeated Rim-Sin, and possibly captured him or burnt him alive in a palace in which he had taken refuge.

With the final defeat of Rim-Sin by Samsu-iluna it is probable that Elam ceased to be a thorn in the side of the kings of Babylon and that she made no further attempts to extend her authority beyond her own frontiers. But no sooner had Samsu-iluna freed his country from all danger from this quarter than he found himself faced by a new foe, before whom the dynasty eventually succumbed. This fact we learn from the unpublished chronicle to which reference has already been made, and the name of this new foe, as supplied by the chronicle, will render it necessary to revise all current schemes of Babylonian chronology. Samsu-iluna's new foe was no other than Iluma-ilu, the first king of the Second Dynasty, and, so far from having been regarded as Samsu-iluna's contemporary, hitherto it has been imagined that he ascended the throne of Babylon one hundred and eighteen years after Samsu-iluna's death. The new information supplied by the chronicle thus proves two important facts: first, that the Second Dynasty, instead of immediately succeeding the First Dynasty, was partly contemporary with it; second, that during the period in which the two dynasties were contemporary they were at war with one another, the Second Dynasty gradually encroaching on the territory of the First Dynasty, until it eventually succeeded in capturing Babylon and in getting the whole of the country under its control. We also learn from the new chronicle that this Second Dynasty at first established itself in "the Country of the Sea," that is to say, the districts in the extreme south of Babylonia bordering on the Persian Gulf, and afterwards extended its borders northward until it gradually absorbed the whole of Babylonia. Before discussing the other facts supplied by the new chronicle, with regard to the rise and growth of the Country of the Sea, whose kings formed the so-called "Second Dynasty," it will be well to refer briefly to the sources from which the information on the period to be found in the current histories is derived.

All the schemes of Babylonian chronology that have been suggested during the last twenty years have been based mainly on the great list of kings which is preserved in the British Museum. This document was drawn up in the Neo-Babylonian or Persian period, and when complete it gave a list of the names of all the Babylonian kings from the First Dynasty of Babylon down to the time in which it was written. The names of the kings are arranged in dynasties, and details are given as to the length of their reigns and the total number of years each dynasty lasted. The beginning of the list which gave the names of the First Dynasty is wanting, but the missing portion has been restored from a smaller document which gives a list of the kings of the First and Second Dynasties only. In the great list of kings the dynasties are arranged one after the other, and it was obvious that its compiler imagined that they succeeded one another in the order in which he arranged them. But when the total number of years the dynasties lasted is learned, we obtain dates for the first dynasties in the list which are too early to agree with other chronological information supplied by the historical inscriptions. The majority of writers have accepted the figures of the list of kings and have been content to ignore the discrepancies; others have sought to reconcile the available data by ingenious emendations of the figures given by the list and the historical inscriptions, or have omitted the Second Dynasty entirely from their calculations. The new chronicle, by showing that the First and Second Dynasties were partly contemporaneous, explains the discrepancies that have hitherto proved so puzzling.

It would be out of place here to enter into a detailed discussion of Babylonian chronology, and therefore we will confine ourselves to a brief description of the sequence of events as revealed by the new chronicle. According to the list of kings, Iluma-ilu's reign was a long one, lasting for sixty years, and the new chronicle gives no indication as to the period of his reign at which active hostilities with Babylon broke out. If the war occurred in the latter portion of his reign, it would follow that he had been for many years organizing the forces of the new state he had founded in the south of Babylonia before making serious encroachments in the north; and in that case the incessant campaigns carried on by Babylon against Elam in the reigns of Hammurabi and Samsu-iluna would have afforded him the opportunity of establishing a firm foothold in the Country of the Sea without the risk of Babylonian interference. If, on the other hand, it was in the earlier part of his reign that hostilities with Babylon broke out, we may suppose that, while Samsu-iluna was devoting all his energies to crush Rim-Sin, the Country of the Sea declared her independence of Babylonian control. In this case we may imagine Samsu-iluna hurrying south, on the conclusion of his Elamite campaign, to crush the newly formed state before it had had time to organize its forces for prolonged resistance.

Whichever of these alternatives eventually may prove to be correct, it is certain that Samsu-iluna took the initiative in Babylon's struggle with the Country of the Sea, and that his action was due either to her declaration of independence or to some daring act of aggression on the part of this small state which had hitherto appeared too insignificant to cause Babylon any serious trouble. The new chronicle tells us that Samsu-iluna undertook two expeditions against the Country of the Sea, both of which proved unsuccessful. In the first of these he penetrated to the very shores of the Persian Gulf, where a battle took place in which Samsu-iluna was defeated, and the bodies of many of the Babylonian soldiers were washed away by the sea. In the second campaign Iluma-ilu did not await Samsu-iluna's attack, but advanced to meet him, and again defeated the Babylonian army. In the reign of Abêshu', Samsu-iluna's son and successor, Iluma-ilu appears to have undertaken fresh acts of aggression against

Babylon; and it was probably during one of his raids in Babylonian territory that Abêshu' attempted to crush the growing power of the Country of the Sea by the capture of its daring leader, Iluma-ilu himself. The new chronicle informs us that, with this object in view, Abêshu' dammed the river Tigris, hoping by this means to cut off Iluma-ilu and his army, but his stratagem did not succeed, and Iluma-ilu got back to his own territory in safety.

The new chronicle does not supply us with further details of the struggle between Babylon and the Country of the Sea, but we may conclude that all similar attempts on the part of the later kings of the First Dynasty to crush or restrain the power of the new state were useless. It is probable that from this time forward the kings of the First Dynasty accepted the independence of the Country of the Sea upon their southern border as an evil which they were powerless to prevent. They must have looked back with regret to the good times the country had enjoyed under the powerful sway of Hammurabi, whose victorious arms even their ancient foes, the Elamites, had been unable to withstand. But, although the chronicle does not recount the further successes achieved by the Country of the Sea, it records a fact which undoubtedly contributed to hasten the fall of Babylon and bring the First Dynasty to an end. It tells us that in the reign of Samsu-ditana, the last king of the First Dynasty, the men of the land of Khattu (the Hittites from Northern Syria) marched against him in order to conquer the land of Akkad; in other words, they marched down the Euphrates and invaded Northern Babylonia. The chronicle does not state how far the invasion was successful, but the appearance of a new enemy from the northwest must have divided the Babylonian forces and thus have reduced their power of resisting pressure from the Country of the Sea. Samsu-ditana may have succeeded in defeating the Hittites and in driving them from his country; but the fact that he was the last king of the First Dynasty proves that in his reign Babylon itself fell into the hands of the king of the Country of the Sea.

The question now arises, To what race did the people of the Country of the Sea belong? Did they represent an advance-guard of the Kassite tribes, who eventually succeeded in establishing themselves as the Third Dynasty in Babylon? Or were they the Elamites who, when driven from Ur and Larsam, retreated southwards and maintained their independence on the shores of the Persian Gulf? Or did they represent some fresh wave of Semitic immigration? That they were not Kassites is proved by the new chronicle which relates how the Country of the Sea was conquered by the Kassites, and how the dynasty founded by Iluma-ilu thus came to an end. There is nothing to show that they were Elamites, and if the Country of the Sea had been colonized by fresh Semitic tribes, so far from opposing their kindred in Babylon, most probably they would have proved to them a source of additional strength and support. In fact, there are indications that the people of the Country of the Sea are to be referred to an older stock than the Elamites, the Semites, or the Kassites. In the dynasty of the Country of the Sea there is no doubt that we may trace the last successful struggle of the ancient Sumerians to retain possession of the land which they had held for so many centuries before the invading Semites had disputed its possession with them.

Evidence of the Sumerian origin of the kings of the Country of the Sea may be traced in the names which several of them bear. Ishkibal, Gulkishar, Peshgaldaramash, A-dara-kalama, Akur-ul-ana, and Melam-kurkura, the names of some of them, are all good Sumerian names, and Shushshi, the brother of Ishkibal, may also be taken as a Sumerian name. It is true that the first three kings of the dynasty, Iluma-ilu, Itti-ili-nibi, and Damki-ilishu, and the last king of the dynasty, Eagamil, bear Semitic Babylonian names, but there is evidence that at least one of these is merely a Semitic rendering of a Sumerian equivalent. Iluma-ilu, the founder of the dynasty, has left inscriptions in which his name is written in its correct Sumerian form as Dingir-a-an, and the fact that he and some of his successors either bore Semitic names or appear in the late list of kings with their Sumerian names translated into Babylonian form may be easily explained by supposing that the population of the Country of the Sea was mixed and that the Sumerian and Semitic tongues were to a great extent employed indiscriminately. This supposition is not inconsistent with the suggestion that the dynasty of the Country of the Sea was Sumerian, and that under it the Sumerians once more became the predominant race in Babylonia.

The new chronicle also relates how the dynasty of the Country of the Sea succumbed in its turn before the incursions of the Kassites. We know that already under the First Dynasty the Kassite tribes had begun to make incursions into Babylonia, for the ninth year of Samsu-iluna was named in the date-formulæ after a Kassite invasion, which, as it was commemorated in this manner by the Babylonians, was probably successfully repulsed. Such invasions must have taken place from time to time during the period of supremacy attained by the Country of the Sea, and it was undoubtedly with a view to stopping such incursions for the future that Ea-gamil, the last king of the Second Dynasty, decided to invade Elam and conquer the mountainous districts in which the Kassite tribes had built their strongholds. This Elamite campaign of Ea-gamil is recorded by the new chronicle, which relates how he was defeated and driven from the country by Ulam-Buriash, the brother of Bitiliash the Kassite. Ulam-Buriash did not rest content with repelling Ea-gamil's invasion of his land, but pursued him across the border and succeeded in conquering the Country of the Sea and in establishing there his own administration. The gradual conquest of the whole of Babylonia by the Kassites no doubt followed the conquest of the Country of the Sea, for the chronicle relates how the process of subjugation, begun by Ulam-Buriash, was continued by his nephew Agum, and we know from the lists of kings that

Ea-gamil was the last king of the dynasty founded by Iluma-ilu. In this fashion the Second Dynasty was brought to an end, and the Sumerian element in the mixed population of Babylonia did not again succeed in gaining control of the government of the country.

It will be noticed that the account of the earliest Kassite rulers of Babylonia which is given by the new chronicle does not exactly tally with the names of the kings of the Third Dynasty as found upon the list of kings. On this document the first king of the dynasty is named Gandash, with whom we may probably identify Ulam-Buriash, the Kassite conqueror of the Country of the Sea; the second king is Agum, and the third is Bitiliashi. According to the new chronicle Agum was the son of Bitiliashi, and it would be improbable that he should have ruled in Babylonia before his father. But this difficulty is removed by supposing that the two names were transposed by some copyist. The different names assigned to the founder of the Kassite dynasty may be due to the existence of variant traditions, or Ulam-Buriash may have assumed another name on his conquest of Babylonia, a practice which was usual with the later kings of Assyria when they occupied the Babylonian throne.

The information supplied by the new chronicle with regard to the relations of the first three dynasties to one another is of the greatest possible interest to the student of early Babylonian history. We see that the Semitic empire founded at Babylon by Sumu-abu, and consolidated by Hammurabi, was not established on so firm a basis as has hitherto been believed. The later kings of the dynasty, after Elam had been conquered, had to defend their empire from encroachments on the south, and they eventually succumbed before the onslaught of the Sumerian element, which still remained in the population of Babylonia and had rallied in the Country of the Sea. This dynasty in its turn succumbed before the invasion of the Kassites from the mountains in the western districts of Elam, and, although the city of Babylon retained her position as the capital of the country throughout these changes of government, she was the capital of rulers of different races, who successively fought for and obtained the control of the fertile plains of Mesopotamia.

It is probable that the Kassite kings of the Third Dynasty exercised authority not only over Babylonia but also over the greater part of Elam, for a number of inscriptions of Kassite kings of Babylonia have been found by M. de Morgan at Susa. These inscriptions consist of grants of land written on roughly shaped stone stelæ, a class which the Babylonians themselves called *kudurru*, while they have been frequently referred to by modern writers as "boundary-stones." This latter term is not very happily chosen, for it suggests that the actual monuments themselves were set up on the limits of a field or estate to mark its boundary. It is true that the inscription on a kudurru enumerates the exact position and size of the estate with which it is concerned, but the kudurru was never actually used to mark the boundary. It was preserved as a title-deed, in the house of the owner of the estate or possibly in the temple of his god, and formed his charter or title-deed to which he could appeal in case of any dispute arising as to his right of ownership. One of the kudurrus found by M. de Morgan records the grant of a number of estates near Babylon by Nazimaruttash, a king of the Third or Kassite Dynasty, to the god Marduk, that is to say they were assigned by the king to the service of E-sagila, the great temple of Marduk at Babylon. All the crops and produce from the land were granted for the supply of the temple, which was to enjoy the property without the payment of any tax or tribute. The text also records the gift of considerable tracts of land in the same district to a private individual named Kashakti-Shugab, who was to enjoy a similar freedom from taxation so far as the lands bestowed upon him were concerned.

A KUDURRU OR "BOUNDARY-STONE."

Inscribed with a text of Nazimaruttash, a king of the Third or Kassite Dynasty, conferring certain estates near Babylon on the temple of Marduk and on a certain man named Kashakti-Shugab. The photograph is reproduced from M. de Morgan's *Délégation en Perse, Mém.*, t. ii, pl. 18.

This freedom from taxation is specially enacted by the document in the words: "Whensoever in the days that are to come the ruler of the country, or one of the governors, or directors, or wardens of these districts, shall make any claim with regard to these estates, or shall attempt to impose the payment of a tithe or tax upon them, may all the great gods whose names are commemorated, or whose arms are portrayed, or whose dwelling-places are represented, on this stone, curse him with an evil curse and blot out his name!"

Incidentally, this curse illustrates one of the most striking characteristics of the kudurrus, or "boundary-stones," viz. the carved figures of gods and representations of their emblems, which all of them bare in addition to the texts inscribed upon them. At one time it was thought that these symbols were to be connected with the signs of the zodiac and various constellations and stars, and it was suggested that they might have been intended to represent the relative positions of the heavenly bodies at the time the document was drawn up. But this text of Nazimaruttash and other similar documents that have recently been discovered prove that the presence of the figures and emblems of the gods upon the stones is to be explained on another and far more simple theory. They were placed there as guardians of the property to which the kudurru referred, and it was believed that the carving of their figures or emblems upon the stone would ensure their intervention in case of any attempted infringement of the rights and privileges which it was the object of the document to commemorate and preserve. A photographic reproduction of one side of the kudurru of Nazi-maruttash is shown in the accompanying illustration. There will be seen a representation of Gula or Bau, the mother of the gods, who is portrayed as seated on her throne and wearing the four-horned head-dress and a long robe that reaches to her feet. In the field are emblems of the Sun-god, the Moon-god, Ishtar, and other deities, and the representation of divine emblems and dwelling-places is continued on another face of the stone round the corner towards which Gula is looking. The other two faces of the document are taken up with the inscription.

An interesting note is appended to the text inscribed upon the stone, beginning under the throne and feet of Marduk and continuing under the emblems of the gods upon the other side. This note relates the history of the document in the following words: " In those days Kashakti-Shugab, the son of Nusku-na'id, inscribed (this document) upon a memorial of clay, and he set it before his god. But in the reign of Marduk-aplu-iddina, king of hosts, the son of Melishikhu, King of Babylon, the wall fell upon this memorial and crushed it. Shukhuli-Shugab, the son of Nibishiku, wrote a copy of the ancient text upon a new stone stele, and he set it (before the god)." It will be seen, therefore, that this actual stone that has been recovered was not the document drawn up in the reign of Nazimaruttash, but a copy made under Marduk-aplu-iddina, a later king of the Third Dynasty. The original deed was drawn up to preserve the rights of Kashakti-Shugab, who shared the grant of land with the temple of Marduk. His share was less than half that of the temple, but, as both were situated in the same district, he was careful to enumerate and describe the temple's share, to prevent any encroachment on his rights by the Babylonian priests.

It is probable that such grants of land were made to private individuals in return for special services which they had rendered to the king. Thus a broken kudurru among M. de Morgan's finds records the confirmation of a man's claims to certain property by Bitiliash II, the claims being based on a grant made to the man's ancestor by Kurigalzu for services rendered to the king during his war with Assyria. One of the finest specimens of this class of charters or title-deeds has been found at Susa, dating from the reign of Melishikhu, a king of the Third Dynasty. The document in question records a grant of certain property in the district of Bit-Pir-Shadû-rabû, near the cities Agade and Dûr-Kurigalzu, made by Melishikhu to Marduk-aplu-iddina, his son, who succeeded him upon the throne of Babylon. The text first gives details with regard to the size and situation of the estates included in the grant of land, and it states the names of the high officials who were entrusted with the duty of measuring them. The remainder of the text defines and secures the privileges granted to Marduk-aplu-iddina together with the land, and, as it throws considerable light upon the system of land tenure at the period, an extract from it may here be translated.

KUDURRU, OR "BOUNDARY-STONE."

Inscribed with a text of Melishikhu, one of the kings of the Third or Kassite Dynasty of Babylon, recording a grant of certain property to Marduk-aplu-iddina, his son. The photograph is reproduced from M. de Morgan's *Délégation en Perse, Mém.*, t. ii, pl. 24.

"To prevent the encroachment on his land," the inscription runs, "thus hath he (*i. e.* the king) established his (Marduk-aplu-iddina's) charter. On his land taxes and tithes shall they not impose; ditches, limits, and boundaries shall they not displace; there shall be no plots, stratagems, or claims (with regard to his possession); for forced labour or public work for the prevention of floods, for the maintenance and repair of the royal canal under the protection of the towns of Bit-Sikkamidu and Damik-Adad, among the gangs levied in the towns of the district of Ninâ-Agade, they shall not call out the people of his estate; they are not liable to forced labour on the sluices of the royal canal, nor are they liable for building dams, nor for closing the canal, nor for digging out the bed thereof. A cultivator of his lands, whether hired or belonging to the estate, and the men who receive his instructions (*i. e.* his overseers) shall no governor of Bit-Pir-Shadû-rabû cause to leave his lands, whether by the order of the king, or by the order of the governor, or by the order of whosoever may be at Bit-Pir-Shadû-rabû. On wood, grass, straw, corn, and every other sort of crop, on his carts and yoke, on his ass and man-servant, shall they make no levy. During the scarcity of water in the canal running between the Rati-Anzanim canal and the canal of the royal district, on the waters of his ditch for irrigation shall they make no levy; from the ditch of his reservoir shall they not draw water, neither shall they divert (his water for) irrigation, and other land shall they not irrigate nor water therewith. The grass of his lands shall they not mow; the beasts belonging to the king or to a governor, which may be assigned to the district of Bit-Pir-

Shadû-rabû, shall they not drive within his boundary, nor shall they pasture them on his grass. He shall not be forced to build a road or a bridge, whether for the king, or for the governor who may be appointed in the district of Bit-Pir-Shadû-rabû, neither shall he be liable for any new form of forced labour, which in the days that are to come a king, or a governor appointed in the district of Bit-Pir-Shadû-rabû, shall institute and exact, nor for forced labour long fallen into disuse which may be revived anew. To prevent encroachment on his land the king hath fixed the privileges of his domain, and that which appertaineth unto it, and all that he hath granted unto him; and in the presence of Shamash, and Marduk, and Anunitu, and the great gods of heaven and earth, he hath inscribed them upon a stone, and he hath left it as an everlasting memorial with regard to his estate."

The whole of the text is too long to quote, and it will suffice to note here that Melishikhu proceeds to appeal to future kings to respect the land and privileges which he has granted to his son, Marduk-aplu-iddina, even as he himself has respected similar grants made by his predecessors on the throne; and the text ends with some very vivid curses against any one, whatever his station, who should make any encroachments on the privileges granted to Marduk-aplu-iddina, or should alter or do any harm to the memorial-stone itself. The emblems of the gods whom Melishikhu invokes to avenge any infringement of his grant are sculptured upon one side of the stone, for, as has already been remarked, it was believed that by carving them upon the memorial-stone their help in guarding the stone itself and its enactments was assured.

From the portion of the text inscribed upon the stone which has just been translated it is seen that the owner of land in Babylonia in the period of the Kassite kings, unless he was granted special exemption, was liable to furnish forced labour for public works to the state or to his district, to furnish grazing and pasture for the flocks and herds of the king or governor, and to pay various taxes and tithes on his land, his water for irrigation, and his crops. From the numerous documents of the First Dynasty of Babylon that have been recovered and published within the last few years we know that similar customs were prevalent at that period, so that it is clear that the successive conquests to which the country was subjected, and the establishment of different dynasties of foreign kings at Babylon, did not to any appreciable extent affect the life and customs of the inhabitants of the country or even the general character of its government and administration. Some documents of a commercial and legal nature, inscribed upon clay tablets during the reigns of the Kassite kings of Babylon, have been found at Nippur, but they have not yet been published, and the information we possess concerning the life of the people in this period is obtained indirectly from kudurrus or boundary-stones, such as those of Nazimaruttash and Melishikhu which have been already described. Of documents relating to the life of the people under the rule of the kings of the

Country of the Sea we have none, and, with the exception of the unpublished chronicle which has been described earlier in this chapter, our information for this period is confined to one or two short votive inscriptions. But the case is very different with regard to the reigns of the Semitic kings of the First Dynasty of Babylon. Thousands of tablets relating to legal and commercial transactions during this period have been recovered, and more recently a most valuable series of royal letters, written by Hammurabi and other kings of his dynasty, has been brought to light. Moreover, the recently discovered code of laws drawn up by Hammurabi contains information of the greatest interest with regard to the conditions of life that were prevalent in Babylonia at that period. From these three sources it is possible to draw up a comparatively full account of early Babylonian life and customs.

Upper Part of the Stele of Hammurabi, King of Babylon.

The stele is inscribed with his great code of laws. The Sun-god is represented as seated on a throne in the form of a temple façade, and his feet are resting upon the mountains. Photograph by Messrs. Mansell & Co.

CHAPTER VI

EARLY BABYLONIAN LIFE AND CUSTOMS

IN tracing the ancient history of Mesopotamia and the surrounding countries it is possible to construct a narrative which has the appearance of being comparatively full and complete. With regard to Babylonia it may be shown how dynasty succeeded dynasty, and for long periods together the names of the kings have been recovered and the order of their succession fixed with certainty. But the number and importance of the original documents on which this connected narration is based vary enormously for different periods. Gaps occur in our knowledge of the sequence of events, which with some ingenuity may be bridged over by means of the native lists of kings and the genealogies furnished by the historical inscriptions. On the other hand, as if to make up for such parsimony, the excavations have yielded a wealth of material for illustrating the conditions of early Babylonian life which prevailed in such periods. The most fortunate of these periods, so far as the recovery of its records is concerned, is undoubtedly the period of the Semitic kings of the First Dynasty of Babylon, and in particular the reign of its greatest ruler, Hammurabi. When M. Maspero wrote his history, thousands of clay tablets, inscribed with legal and commercial documents and dated in the reigns of these early kings, had already been recovered, and the information they furnished was duly summarized by him.[1] But since that time two other sources of information have been made available which have largely increased our knowledge of the constitution of the early Babylonian state, its system of administration, and the conditions of life of the various classes of the population.

One of these new sources of information consists of a remarkable series of royal letters, written by kings of the First Dynasty, which has been recovered and is now preserved in the British Museum. The letters were addressed to the governors and high officials of various great cities in Babylonia, and they contain the king's orders with regard to details of the administration of the country which had been brought to his notice. The range of subjects with which they deal is enormous, and there is scarcely one of them which does not add to our knowledge of the period.[2] The other new source of information is the great code of laws, drawn up by Ham-

---

[1] Most of these tablets are preserved in the British Museum. The principal works in which they have been published are *Cuneiform Texts in the British Museum* (1896; etc.), Strassmaier's *Altbabylonischen Verträge aus Warka*, and Meissner's *Beiträge zum altbabylonischen Privatrecht*. A number of similar tablets of this period, preserved in the Pennsylvania Museum, will shortly be published by Dr. Ranke.

[2] See King, *Letters and Inscriptions of Hammurabi*, 3 vols. (1898–1900).

murabi for the guidance of his people and defining the
duties and privileges of all classes of his subjects, the
discovery of which at Susa has been described in a previous chapter. The laws are engraved on a great stele
of diorite in no less than forty-nine columns of writing,
of which forty-four are preserved,[1] and at the head of
the stele is sculptured a representation of the king receiving them from Shamash, the Sun-god.[2]

This code shows to what an extent the administration of law and justice had been developed in Babylonia
in the time of the First Dynasty. From the contracts
and letters of the period we already knew that regular
judges and duly appointed courts of law were in existence, and the code itself was evidently intended by the
king to give the royal sanction to a great body of legal
decisions and enactments which already possessed the
authority conferred by custom and tradition. The
means by which such a code could have come into existence are illustrated by the system of procedure adopted
in the courts at this period. After a case had been heard
and judgment had been given, a summary of the case
and of the evidence, together with the judgment, was
drawn up and written out on tablets in due legal form
and phraseology. A list of the witnesses was appended,
and, after the tablet had been dated and sealed, it was
stored away among the legal archives of the court,
where it was ready for production in the event of any
future appeal or case in which the recorded decision

---

[1] See Scheil, *Délégation en Perse, Mémoires*, tome iv (1902).
[2] See illustration.

was involved. This procedure represents an advanced stage in the system of judicial administration, but the care which was taken for the preservation of the judgments given was evidently traditional, and would naturally give rise in course of time to the existence of a recognized code of laws.

Moreover, when once a judgment had been given and had been duly recorded it was irrevocable, and if any judge attempted to alter such a decision he was severely punished. For not only was he expelled from his judgment-seat, and debarred from exercising judicial functions in the future, but, if his judgment had involved the infliction of a penalty, he was obliged to pay twelve times the amount to the man he had condemned. Such an enactment must have occasionally given rise to hardship or injustice, but at least it must have had the effect of imbuing the judges with a sense of their responsibility and of instilling a respect for their decisions in the minds of the people. A further check upon injustice was provided by the custom of the elders of the city, who sat with the judge and assisted him in the carrying out of his duties; and it was always open to a man, if he believed that he could not get justice enforced, to make an appeal to the king. It is not our present purpose to give a technical discussion of the legal contents of the code, but rather to examine it with the object of ascertaining what light it throws upon ancient Babylonian life and customs, and the conditions under which the people lived.

The code gives a good deal of information with regard to the family life of the Babylonians, and, above all, proves the sanctity with which the marriage-tie was invested. The claims that were involved by marriage were not lightly undertaken. Any marriage, to be legally binding, had to be accompanied by a duly executed and attested marriage-contract. If a man had taken a woman to wife without having carried out this necessary preliminary, the woman was not regarded as his wife in the legal sense. On the other hand, when once such a marriage-contract had been drawn up, its inviolability was stringently secured. A case of proved adultery on the part of a man's wife was punished by the drowning of the guilty parties, though the husband of the woman, if he wished to save his wife, could do so by an appeal to the king. Similarly, death was the penalty for a man who ravished another man's betrothed wife while she was still living in her father's house, but in this case the girl's innocence and inexperience were taken into account, and no penalty was enforced against her and she was allowed to go free. Where the adultery of a wife was not proved, and only depended on the accusation of the husband, the woman could clear herself by swearing her own innocence; if, however, the accusation was not brought by the husband himself, but by others, the woman could clear herself by submitting to the ordeal by water; that is to say, she would plunge into the Euphrates; if the river carried her away and she were drowned, it was regarded as proof that the accusation was well founded; if, on the contrary, she survived and got safely to the bank, she was considered innocent and was forthwith allowed to return to her household completely vindicated.

It will have been seen that the duty of chastity on the part of a married woman was strictly enforced, but the husband's responsibility to properly maintain his wife was also recognized, and in the event of his desertion she could under certain circumstances become the wife of another man. Thus, if he left his city and fled from it of his own free will and deserted his wife, he could not reclaim her on his return, since he had not been forced to leave the city, but had done so because he hated it. This rule did not apply to the case of a man who was taken captive in battle. In such circumstances the wife's action was to be guided by the condition of her husband's affairs. If the captive husband possessed sufficient property on which his wife could be maintained during his captivity in a strange land, she had no reason nor excuse for seeking another marriage. If under these circumstances she became another man's wife, she was to be prosecuted at law, and, her action being the equivalent of adultery, she was to be drowned. But the case was regarded as altered if the captive husband had not sufficient means for the maintenance of his wife during his absence. The woman would then be thrown on her own resources, and if she became the wife of another man she incurred no blame. On the return of the captive he could reclaim his wife, but the children of the second marriage would remain with their own father. These regulations for the conduct of a woman, whose husband was captured in battle, give an intimate picture of the manner in which the constant wars of this early period affected the lives of those who took part in them.

Under the Babylonians at the period of the First Dynasty divorce was strictly regulated, though it was far easier for the man to obtain one than for the woman. If we may regard the copies of Sumerian laws, which have come down to us from the late Assyrian period, as parts of the code in use under the early Sumerians, we must conclude that at this earlier period the law was still more in favour of the husband, who could divorce his wife whenever he so desired, merely paying her half a mana as compensation. Under the Sumerians the wife could not obtain a divorce at all, and the penalty for denying her husband was death. These regulations were modified in favour of the woman in Hammurabi's code; for under its provisions, if a man divorced his wife or his concubine, he was obliged to make proper provision for her maintenance. Whether she were barren or had borne him children, he was obliged to return her marriage portion; and in the latter case she had the custody of the children, for whose maintenance and education he was obliged to furnish the necessary supplies. Moreover, at the man's death she and her children would inherit a share of his property. When there had been no marriage portion, a sum was fixed which the husband was obliged to pay to his divorced wife, according to his status. In cases where the wife was proved to have wasted her household and to have entirely failed in her duty, her husband could divorce her without paying any compensation, or could make her a slave in his house, and the extreme penalty for this offence was death. On the other hand, a woman could not be divorced because she had contracted a permanent disease; and, if she desired to divorce her husband and could prove that her past life had been seemly, she could do so, returning to her father's house and taking her marriage portion with her.

It is not necessary here to go very minutely into the regulations given by the code with regard to marriage portions, the rights of widows, the laws of inheritance, and the laws regulating the adoption and maintenance of children. The customs that already have been described with regard to marriage and divorce may serve to indicate the spirit in which the code is drawn up and the recognized status occupied by the wife in the Babylonian household. The extremely independent position enjoyed by women in the early Babylonian days is illustrated by the existence of a special class of women, to which constant reference is made in the contracts and letters of the period. When the existence of this class of women was first recognized from the references to them in the contract-tablets inscribed at the time of the First Dynasty, they were regarded as priestesses, but the regulations concerning them which occur in the code of Hammurabi prove that their duties were not strictly sacerdotal, but that they occupied the position of votaries. The majority of those referred to in the inscriptions of this period were vowed to the service of E-babbara, the temple of the Sun-god at Sippara, and of

E-sagila, the great temple of Marduk at Babylon, but it is probable that all the great temples in the country had classes of female votaries attached to them. From the evidence at present available it may be concluded that the functions of these women bore no resemblance to that of the sacred prostitutes devoted to the service of the goddess Ishtar in the city of Erech. They seem to have occupied a position of great influence and independence in the community, and their duties and privileges were defined and safeguarded by special legislation.

Generally they lived together in a special building, or convent, attached to the temple, but they had considerable freedom and could leave the convent and also contract marriage. Their vows, however, while securing them special privileges, entailed corresponding responsibilities. Even when married a votary was still obliged to remain a virgin, and, should her husband desire to have children, she could not bear them herself, but must provide him with a maid or concubine. Also she had to maintain a high standard of moral conduct, for any breach of which severe penalties were enforced. Thus, if a votary who was not living in the convent opened a beer-shop, or should enter one for drink, she ran the risk of being put to death. But the privileges she enjoyed were also considerable, for even when unmarried she enjoyed the status of a married woman, and if any man slandered her he incurred the penalty of branding on the forehead. Moreover, a married votary, though she could not bear her husband children, was secured in her position as the permanent head of his household. The concubine she might give to her husband was always the wife's inferior, even after bearing him children, and should the former attempt to put herself on a level of equality with the votary, the latter might brand her as a slave and put her with the female slaves. If the concubine proved barren she could be sold. The votary could also possess property, and on taking her vows was provided with a portion by her father exactly as though she were being given in marriage. Her portion was vested in herself and did not become the property of the order of votaries, nor of the temple to which she was attached. The proceeds of her property were devoted to her own maintenance, and on her father's death her brothers looked after her interests, or she might farm the property out. Under certain circumstances she could inherit property and was not obliged to pay taxes on it, and such property she could bequeath at her own death; but upon her death her portion returned to her own family unless her father had assigned her the privilege of bequeathing it. That the social position enjoyed by a votary was considerable is proved by the fact that many women of good family, and even members of the royal house, took vows. The existence of the order and its high repute indicate a very advanced conception of the position of women among the early Babylonians.

From the code of Hammurabi we also gather considerable information with regard to the various classes of which the community was composed and to their relative social positions. For the purposes of legislation the community was divided into three main classes or sections, which corresponded to well-defined strata in the social system. The lowest of these classes consisted of the slaves, who must have formed a considerable portion of the population. The class next above them comprised the large body of free men, who were possessed of a certain amount of property but were poor and humble, as their name, *mushkênu*, implied. These we may refer to as the middle class. The highest, or upper class, in the Babylonian community embraced all the officers and ministers attached to the court, the higher officials and servants of the state, and the owners of considerable lands and estates. The differences which divided and marked off from one another the two great classes of free men in the population of Babylonia is well illustrated by the scale of payments as compensation for injury which they were obliged to make or were entitled to receive. Thus, if a member of the upper class were guilty of stealing an ox, or a sheep, or an ass, or a pig, or a boat, from a temple or a private house, he had to pay the owner thirty times its value as compensation, whereas if the thief were a member of the middle class he only had to pay ten times its price, but if he had no property and so could not pay compensation he was put to death. The penalty for manslaughter was less if the assailant was a man of the middle class, and such a man could also divorce his wife more cheaply, and was privileged to pay his doctor or surgeon a smaller fee for a successful operation.

But the privileges enjoyed by a man of the middle class were counterbalanced by a corresponding diminution of the value at which his life and limbs were assessed. Thus, if a doctor by carrying out an operation unskilfully caused the death of a member of the upper class, or inflicted a serious injury upon him, such as the loss of an eye, the punishment was the amputation of both hands, but no such penalty seems to have been exacted if the patient were a member of the middle class. If, however, the patient were a slave of a member of the middle class, in the event of death under the operation, the doctor had to give the owner another slave, and in the event of the slave losing his eye, he had to pay the owner half the slave's value. Penalties for assault were also regulated in accordance with the social position and standing of the parties to the quarrel. Thus, if one member of the upper class knocked out the eye or the tooth of one of his equals, his own eye or his own tooth was knocked out as a punishment, and if he broke the limb of one of the members of his own class, he had his corresponding limb broken; but if he knocked out the eye of a member of the middle class, or broke his limb, he suffered no punishment in his own person, but was fined one mana of silver, and for knocking out the tooth of such a man he was fined one-third of a mana. If two members of the same class were engaged in a quarrel, and one of them made a peculiarly improper assault upon the other, the assailant was only fined, the fine being larger if the quarrel was between members of the upper class. But if such an assault was made by one man upon another who was of higher rank than himself, the assailant was punished by being publicly beaten in the presence of the assembly, when he received sixty stripes from a scourge of ox-hide. These regulations show the privileges and responsibilities which pertained to the two classes of free men in the Babylonian community, and they indicate the relative social positions which they enjoyed.

Both classes of free men could own slaves, though it is obvious that they were more numerous in the households and on the estates of members of the upper class. The slave was the absolute property of his master and could be bought and sold and employed as a deposit for a debt, but, though slaves as a class had few rights of their own, in certain circumstances they could acquire them. Thus, if the owner of a female slave had begotten children by her he could not use her as the payment for a debt, and in the event of his having done so he was obliged to ransom her by paying the original amount of the debt in money. It was also possible for a male slave, whether owned by a member of the upper or of the middle class, to marry a free woman, and if he did so, his children were free and did not become the property of his master. Also, if the free woman whom the slave married brought with her a marriage portion from her father's house, this remained her own property on the slave's death, and supposing the couple had acquired other property during the time they lived together as man and wife, the owner of the slave could only claim half of such property, the other half being retained by the free woman for her own use and for that of her children.

Generally speaking, the lot of the slave was not a particularly hard one, for he was a recognized member of his owner's household, and, as a valuable piece of property, it was obviously to his owner's interest to keep him healthy and in good condition. In fact, the value of the slave is attested by the severity of the penalty imposed for abducting a male or female slave from the owner's house and removing him or her from the city; for a man guilty of this offence was put to death. The same penalty was imposed for harbouring and taking possession of a runaway slave, whereas a fixed reward was paid by the owner to any one by whom a runaway slave was captured and brought back. Special legislation was also devised with the object of rendering the theft of slaves difficult and their detection easy. Thus, if a brander put a mark upon a slave without the owner's consent, he was liable to have his hands cut off, and if he could prove that he did so through being deceived by another man, that man was put to death. For bad offences slaves were liable to severe punishments, such as cutting off the ear, which was the penalty for denying his master, and also for making an aggravated assault on a member of the upper class of free men. But it is clear that on the whole the slave was well looked after. He was also not condemned to remain perpetually a slave, for while still in his master's service it was possible for him, under certain conditions, to acquire property of his own, and if he did so he was able with his master's consent to purchase his freedom. If a slave were captured by the enemy and taken to a foreign land and sold, and were then brought back by his new owner to his own country, he could claim his liberty without having to pay any purchase-money to either of his masters.

The code of Hammurabi also contains detailed regulations concerning the duties of debtors and creditors, and it throws an interesting light on the commercial life of the Babylonians at this early period. For instance, it reveals the method by which a wealthy man, or a merchant, extended his business and obtained large profits by trading with other towns. This he did by employing agents who were under certain fixed obligations to him, but acted independently so far as their trading was concerned. From the merchant these agents would receive money or grain or wool or oil or any sort of goods wherewith to trade, and in return they paid a fixed share of their profits, retaining the remainder as the recompense for their own services. They were thus the earliest of commercial travellers. In order to prevent fraud between the merchant and the agent special regulations were framed for the dealings they had with one another. Thus, when the agent received from the merchant the money or goods to trade with, it was enacted that he should at the time of the transaction give a properly executed receipt for the amount he had received. Similarly, if the agent gave the merchant money in return for the goods he had received and in token of his good faith, the merchant had to give a receipt to the agent, and in reckoning their accounts after the agent's return from his journey, only such amounts as were specified in the receipts were

CLAY CONTRACT TABLET AND ITS OUTER CASE.
Dating from the period of the First Dynasty of Babylon.

to be regarded as legal obligations. If the agent forgot to obtain his proper receipt he did so at his own risk.

Travelling at this period was attended with some risk, as it is in the East at the present day, and the caravan with which an agent travelled was liable to attack from brigands, or it might be captured by enemies of the country from which it set out. It was right that loss from this cause should not be borne by the agent, who by trading with the goods was risking his own life, but should fall upon the merchant who had merely advanced the goods and was safe in his own city. It is plain, however, that disputes frequently arose in consequence of the loss of goods through a caravan being attacked and robbed, for the code states clearly the responsibility of the merchant in the matter. If in the course of his journey an enemy had forced the agent to give up some of the goods he was carrying, on his return the agent had to specify the amount on oath, and he was then acquitted of all responsibility in the matter. If he attempted to cheat his employer by misappropriating the money or goods advanced to him, on being convicted of the offence before the elders of the city, he was obliged to repay the merchant three times the amount he had taken. On the other hand, if the merchant attempted to defraud his agent by denying that the due amount had been returned to him, he was obliged on conviction to pay the agent six times the amount as compensation. It will thus be seen that the law sought to protect the agent from the risk of being robbed by his more powerful employer.

The merchant sometimes furnished the agent with goods which he was to dispose of in the best markets he could find in the cities and towns along his route, and sometimes he would give the agent money with which to purchase goods in foreign cities for sale on his return. If the venture proved successful the merchant and his agent shared the profits between them, but if the agent made bad bargains he had to refund to the merchant the value of the goods he had received; if the merchant had not agreed to risk losing any profit, the amount to be refunded to him was fixed at double the value of the goods advanced. This last enactment gives an indication of the immense profits which were obtained by both the merchant and the agent from this system of foreign

A TRACK IN THE DESERT.

trade, for it is clear that what was regarded as a fair profit for the merchant was double the value of the goods disposed of. The profits of a successful journey would also include a fair return to the agent for the trouble and time involved in his undertaking. Many of the contract tablets of this early period relate to such commercial journeys, which show that various bargains were made between the different parties interested, and sometimes such contracts, or partnerships, were entered into, not for a single journey only, but for long periods.

We may therefore conclude that at the time of the First Dynasty of Babylon, and probably for long centuries before that period, the great trade-routes of the East were crowded with traffic. With the exception that donkeys and asses were employed for beasts of burden and were not supplemented by horses and camels until a much later period, a camping-ground in the desert on one of the great trade-routes must have pre-

A CAMPING-GROUND IN THE DESERT, BETWEEN BIREJIK AND URFA.

sented a scene similar to that of a caravan camping in the desert at the present day. The rough tracks beaten by the feet of men and beasts are the same to-day as they were in that remote period. We can imagine a body of these early travellers approaching a walled city at dusk and hastening their pace to get there before the gates were shut. Such a picture as that of the approach to the city of Samarra, with its mediæval walls, may be taken as having had its counterpart in many a city of the early Babylonians. The caravan route leads through the desert to the city gate, and if we substitute two massive temple towers for the domes of the mosques that rise above the wall, little else in the picture need be changed.

The houses, too, at this period must have resembled the structures of unburnt brick of the present day, with their flat mud tops, on which the inmates sleep at night during the hot season, supported on poles and brush-

APPROACH TO THE CITY OF SAMARRA, SITUATED ON THE LEFT BANK OF THE TIGRIS.

A small caravan is here seen approaching the city at sunset before the gates are shut. Samarra was only founded in A.D. 834, by the Khalif el-Motasim, the son of Harûn er-Rashîd, but customs in the East do not change, and the photograph may be used to illustrate the approach of an early Babylonian caravan to a walled city of the period.

wood. The code furnishes evidence that at that time, also, the houses were not particularly well built and were liable to fall, and, in the event of their doing so, it very justly fixes the responsibility upon the builder. It is clear from the penalties for bad workmanship enforced upon the builder that considerable abuses had existed in the trade before the time of Hammurabi, and it is not improbable that the enforcement of the penalties succeeded in stamping them out. Thus, if a builder built a house for a man, and his work was not sound and the house fell and crushed the owner so that he died, it was enacted that the builder himself should be put to death. If the fall of the house killed the

A SMALL CARAVAN IN THE MOUNTAINS OF KURDISTAN.

owner's son, the builder's own son was to be put to death. If one or more of the owner's slaves were killed, the builder had to restore him slave for slave. Any damage which the owner's goods might have suffered from the fall of the house was to be made good by the builder. In addition to these penalties the builder was obliged to rebuild the house, or any portion of it that had fallen through not being properly secured, at his own cost. On the other hand, due provisions were made for the payment of the builder for sound work; and as the houses of the period rarely, if ever, consisted

THE CITY OF MOSUL.

Situated on the right bank of the Tigris opposite the mounds which mark the site of the ancient city of Nineveh. The flat-roofed houses which may be distinguished in the photograph a e very similar in form and construction to those employed by the ancient Assyrians and Babylonians.

of more than one story, the scale of payment was fixed by the area of ground covered by the building.

From the code of Hammurabi we also gain considerable information with regard to agricultural pursuits in ancient Babylonia, for elaborate regulations are given concerning the landowner's duties and responsibilities, and his relations to his tenants. The usual practice in hiring land for cultivation was for the tenant to pay his rent in kind, by assigning a certain proportion of the crop, generally a third or a half, to the owner. If a tenant hired certain land for cultivation he was bound to till it and raise a crop, and should he neglect to do so he had to pay the owner what was reckoned as the average rent of the land, and he had also to break up the land and plough it before handing it back. As the rent of a field was usually reckoned at harvest, and its amount depended on the size of the crop, it was only

THE VILLAGE OF NEBI YUNUS.

Built on one of the mounds marking the site of the Assyrian city of Nineveh. The mosque in the photograph is built over the traditional site of the prophet Jonah's tomb. The flat-roofed houses of the modern dwellers on the mound can be well seen in the picture.

fair that damage to the crop from flood or storm should not be made up by the tenant; thus it was enacted by the code that any loss from such a cause should be shared equally by the owner of the field and the farmer, though if the latter had already paid his rent at the time the damage occurred he could not make a claim for repayment. It is clear from the enactments of the code that disputes were frequent, not only between farmers and landowners, but also between farmers and shepherds. It is certain that the latter, in the attempt to find pasture for the flocks, often allowed their sheep to feed off the farmers' fields in the spring. This practice the code set itself to prevent by fixing a scale of compensation to be paid by any shepherd who caused his sheep to graze on cultivated land without the owner's consent. If the offence was committed in the early spring, when the crop was still small, the farmer was to harvest the crop and receive a considerable price in kind as compensation for the shepherd. But if it occurred later on in the spring, when the sheep had been brought in from the meadows and turned into the great common field at the city gate, the offence would less probably be due to accident and the damage to the crop would be greater. In these circumstances the shepherd had to take over the crop and pay the farmer very heavily for his loss.

The planting of gardens and orchards was encouraged, and a man was allowed to use a field for this purpose without paying a yearly rent. He might plant it and tend it for four years, and in the fifth year of his tenancy the original owner of the field took half of the garden in payment, while the other half the planter of the garden kept for himself. If a bare patch had been left in the garden it was to be reckoned in the planter's half. Regulations were framed to ensure the proper carrying out of the planting, for if the tenant neglected to do this during the first four years, he was still liable to plant the plot he had taken without receiving his half, and he had to pay the owner compensation

Portrait-sculpture of Hammurabi, King of Babylon.
From a stone slab in the British Museum.

in addition, which varied in amount according to the original condition of the land. If a man hired a garden, the rent he paid to the owner was fixed at two-thirds of its produce. Detailed regulations are also given in the code concerning the hire of cattle and asses, and the compensation to be paid to the owner for the loss or ill-treatment of his beasts. These are framed on the just principle that the hirer was responsible only for damage or loss which he could have reasonably prevented. Thus, if a lion killed a hired ox or ass in the open country, or if an ox was killed by lightning, the loss fell upon the owner and not on the man who hired the beast. But if the hirer killed the ox through carelessness or by beating it unmercifully, or if the beast broke its leg while in his charge, he had to restore another ox to the owner in place of the one he had hired. For lesser damages to the beast the hirer had to pay compensation on a fixed scale. Thus, if the ox had its eye knocked out during the period of its hire, the man who hired it had to pay to the owner half its value; while for a broken horn, the loss of the tail, or a torn muzzle, he paid a quarter of the value of the beast.

Fines were also levied for carelessness in looking after cattle, though in cases of damage or injury, where carelessness could not be proved, the owner of a beast was not held responsible. A bull might go wild at any time and gore a man, however careful and conscientious the owner might be, and in these circumstances the injured man could not bring an action against the owner. But if a bull had already gored a man, and, although it was known to be vicious, the owner had not blunted its horns or shut it up, in the event of its goring and killing a free man, he had to pay half a mana of silver. One-third of a mana was the price paid for a slave who was killed. A landed proprietor who might hire farmers to cultivate his fields inflicted severe fines for acts of dishonesty with regard to the cattle, provender, or seed-corn committed to their charge. If a man stole the provender for the cattle he had to make it good, and he was also liable to the punishment of having his hands cut off. In the event of his being convicted of letting out the oxen for hire, or stealing the seed-corn so that he did not produce a crop, he had to pay very heavy compensation, and, if he could not pay, he was liable to be torn to pieces by the oxen in the field he should have cultivated.

In a dry land like Babylonia, where little rain falls and that in only one season of the year, the irrigation of his fields forms one of the most important duties of the agriculturist. The farmer leads the water to his fields along small irrigation-canals or channels above the level of the soil, their sides being formed of banks of earth. It is clear that similar methods were employed by the early Babylonians. One such channel might supply the fields of several farmers, and it was the duty of each man through whose land the channel flowed to keep its banks on his land in repair. If he omitted to strengthen his bank or dyke, and the water forced a breach and flooded his neighbour's field, he had to pay compensation in kind for any crop that was ruined;

while if he could not pay, he and his goods were sold, and his neighbours, whose fields had been damaged through his carelessness, shared the money.

The land of Babylonian farmers was prepared for irrigation before it was sown by being divided into a number of small square or oblong tracts, each separated from the others by a low bank of earth, the seed being afterwards sown within the small squares or patches. Some of the banks running lengthwise through the field were made into small channels, the ends of which were carried up to the bank of the nearest main irrigation canal. No system of gates or sluices was employed, and when the farmer wished to water one of his fields he simply broke away the bank opposite one of his small channels and let the water flow into it. He would let the water run along this small channel until it reached the part of his land he wished to water. He then blocked the channel with a little earth, at the same time breaking down its bank so that the water flowed over one of the small squares and thoroughly soaked it. When this square was finished he filled up the bank and repeated the process for the next square, and so on until he had watered the necessary portion of the field. When this was finished he returned to the main channel and stopped the flow of the water by blocking up the hole he had made in the dyke. The whole process was, and to-day still is, extremely simple, but it needs care and vigilance, especially in the case of extensive irrigation when water is being carried into several parts of an estate at once. It will be obvious that any carelessness on the part of the irrigator in not shutting off the water in time may lead to extensive damage, not only to his own fields, but to those of his neighbours. In the early Babylonian period, if a farmer left the water running in his channel, and it flooded his neighbour's field and hurt his crop, he had to pay compensation according to the amount of damage done.

It was stated above that the irrigation-canals and little channels were made above the level of the soil so that the water could at any point be tapped and allowed to flow over the surrounding land; and in a flat country like Babylonia it will be obvious that some means had to be employed for raising the water from its natural level to the higher level of the land. As we should expect, reference is made in the Babylonian inscriptions to irrigation-machines, and, although their exact form and construction are not described, they must have been very similar to those employed at the present day. The modern inhabitants of Mesopotamia employ four sorts of contrivances for raising the water into their irrigation-channels; three of these are quite primitive, and are those most commonly employed. The method which gives the least trouble and which is used wherever the conditions allow is a primitive form of water-wheel. This can be used only in a river with a good current. The wheel is formed of rough boughs and branches nailed together, with spokes joining the outer rims to a roughly hewn axle. A row of rough earthenware cups or bottles are tied round the outer rim for picking up the water, and a few rough paddles are fixed so that they stick out beyond the rim. The wheel is then fixed in place near the bank of the river, its axle resting in pillars of rough masonry. As the current turns the wheel, the bottles on the rim dip below the surface and are raised up full. At the top of the wheel is fixed a trough made by hollowing half the trunk of a date-palm, and into this the bottles pour their water,

A MODERN MACHINE FOR IRRIGATION ON THE EUPHRATES.

which is conducted from the trough by means of a small aqueduct into the irrigation-channel on the bank.

The convenience of the water-wheel will be obvious, for the water is raised without the labour of man or beast, and a constant supply is secured day and night so long as the current is strong enough to turn the wheel. The water can be cut off by blocking the wheel or tying it up. These wheels are most common on the Euphrates, and are usually set up where there is a slight drop in the river bed and the water runs swiftly over shallows. As the banks are very high, the wheels are necessarily huge contrivances in order to reach the level of the fields, and their very rough construction causes them to creak and groan as they turn with the current. In a convenient place in the river several of these are sometimes set up side by side, and the noise of their combined creakings can be heard from a great distance. Some idea of what one of these machines looks like can be obtained from the illustration. At Hit on the Euphrates a line of gigantic water-wheels is built across the river, and the noise they make is extraordinary.

Where there is no current to turn one of these wheels, or where the bank is too high, the water must be raised by the labour of man or beast. The commonest method, which is the one employed generally on the Tigris, is to raise it in skins, which are drawn up by horses, donkeys, or cattle. A recess with perpendicular sides is cut into the bank, and a wooden spindle on wooden struts is supported horizontally over the recess. A rope running over the spindle is fastened to the skin, while the funnel end of the skin is held up by a second rope, running over a lower spindle, until its mouth is opposite the trough into which the water is to be poured. The beasts which are employed for raising the skin are fastened to the ends of the ropes, and they get a good purchase for their pull by being driven down a short cutting or inclined plane in the bank. To get a constant flow of water, two skins are usually employed, and as one is drawn up full the other is let down empty.

The third primitive method of raising water, which is commoner in Egypt than in Mesopotamia at the present day, is the *shadduf*, and is worked by hand. It consists of a beam supported in the centre, at one end of which is tied a rope with a bucket or vessel for raising the water, and at the other end is fixed a counterweight.[1] On an Assyrian bas-relief found at Kuyunjik are representations of the shadduf in operation, two of them being used, the one above the other, to raise the water to successive levels. These were probably the contrivances usually employed by the early Babylonians for raising the water to the level of their fields, and the fact that they were light and easily removed must have made them tempting objects to the dishonest farmer. Hammurabi therefore fixed a scale of compensation to be paid to the owner by a detected thief, which varied according to the class and value of the machine he stole.

The rivers and larger canals of Babylonia were used by the ancient inhabitants not only for the irrigation of their fields, but also as waterways for the transport of heavy materials. The recently published letters of Hammurabi and Abêshu' contain directions for the transportation of corn, dates, sesame seed, and wood, which were ordered to be brought in ships to Babylon, and the code of Hammurabi refers to the transportation by water of wool and oil. It is therefore clear that at

---

[1] The fourth class of machine for raising water employed in Mesopotamia at the present day consists of an endless chain of iron buckets running over a wheel. This is geared by means of rough wooden cogs to a horizontal wheel, the spindle of which has long poles fixed to it, to which horses or cattle are harnessed. The beasts go round in a circle and so turn the machine. The contrivance is not so primitive as the three described above, and the iron buckets are of European importation.

this period considerable use was made of vessels of different size for conveying supplies in bulk by water. The method by which the size of such ships and barges was reckoned was based on the amount of grain they were capable of carrying, and this was measured by the *gur*, the largest measure of capacity. Thus mention is made in the inscriptions of vessels of five, ten, fifteen, twenty, thirty, forty, fifty, sixty, and seventy-five gur capacity. A boat-builder's fee for building a vessel of sixty gur was fixed at two shekels of silver, and it was proportionately less for boats of smaller capacity. To ensure that the boat-builder should not scamp his work, regulations were drawn up to fix on him the responsibility for unsound work. Thus if a boat-builder were employed to build a vessel, and he put faulty work into its construction so that it developed defects within a year of its being launched, he was obliged to strengthen and rebuild it at his own expense.

The hire of a boatman was fixed at six gur of corn to be paid him yearly, but it is clear that some of the larger vessels carried crews commanded by a chief boatman, or captain, whose pay was probably on a larger scale. If a man let his boat to a boatman, the latter was responsible for losing or sinking it, and he had to replace it. A boatman was also responsible for the safety of his vessel and of any goods, such as corn, wool, oil, or dates, which he had been hired to transport, and if they were sunk through his carelessness he had to make good the loss. If he succeeded in refloating the boat after it had been sunk, he was only under obligation to pay the owner half its value in compensation for the damage it had sustained. In the case of a collision between two vessels, if one was at anchor at the time, the owner of the other vessel had to pay compensation for the boat that was sunk and its cargo, the owner of the latter estimating on oath the value of what had been sunk. Boats were also employed as ferries, and they must have resembled the primitive form of ferry-boat

KAIKS, OR NATIVE BOATS ON THE EUPHRATES AT BIREJIK.
Employed for ferrying caravans across the river.

in use at the present day, which is heavily built of huge timbers, and employed for transporting beasts as well as men across a river.

There is evidence that under the Assyrians rafts floated on inflated skins were employed for the transport of heavy goods, and these have survived in the keleks of the present day. They are specially adapted for the transportation of heavy materials, for they are carried down by the current, and are kept in the course by means of huge sweeps or oars. Being formed only of logs of wood and skins, they are not costly, for wood is plentiful in the upper reaches of the rivers. At the end of their journey, after the goods are landed, they are broken up. The wood is sold at a profit, and the skins, after being deflated, are packed on to donkeys to return by caravan. It is not improbable that such rafts were employed on the Tigris and the Euphrates from the earliest periods of Chaldæan history, though

THE MODERN BRIDGE OF BOATS ACROSS THE TIGRIS OPPOSITE MOSUL.

boats would have been used on the canals and more sluggish waterways.

In the preceding pages we have given a sketch of the more striking aspects of early Babylonian life, on which light has been thrown by recently discovered documents belonging to the period of the First Dynasty of Babylon. We have seen that, in the code of laws drawn up by Hammurabi, regulations were framed for settling disputes and fixing responsibilities under almost every condition and circumstance which might arise among the inhabitants of the country at that time; and the question naturally arises as to how far the code of laws was in actual operation. It is conceivable that the king may have held admirable convictions, but have been possessed of little power to carry them out and to see that his regulations were enforced. Luckily, we have not to depend on conjecture for settling the ques-

A SMALL KELEK, OR RAFT, UPON THE TIGRIS AT BAGHDAD.

tion, for Hammurabi's own letters which are now preserved in the British Museum afford abundant evidence of the active control which the king exercised over every department of his administration and in every province of his empire. In the earlier periods of history, when each city lived independently of its neighbours and had its own system of government, the need for close and frequent communication between them was not pressing, but this became apparent as soon as they were welded together and formed parts of an extended empire. Thus in the time of Sargon of Agade, about 3800 B. C., an extensive system of royal convoys was established between the principal cities. At Telloh the late M. de Sarzec came across numbers of lumps of clay bearing the seal impressions of Sargon and of his son Narâm-Sin, which had been used as seals and labels upon packages sent from Agade to Shirpurla. In the time of Dungi, King of Ur, there was a constant interchange of officials between the various cities of Babylonia and Elam, and during the more recent diggings at Telloh there have been found vouchers for the supply of food for their sustenance when stopping at Shirpurla in the course of their journeys. In the case of Hammurabi we have recovered some of the actual letters sent by the king himself to Sin-idinnam, his local governor in the city of Larsam, and from them we gain considerable insight into the principles which guided him in the administration of his empire.

The letters themselves, in their general characteristics, resembled the contract tablets of the period which have been already described. They were written on small clay tablets oblong in shape, and as they were only three or four inches long they could easily be carried about the person of the messenger into whose charge they were delivered. After the tablet was written it was enclosed in a thin envelope of clay, having been first powdered with dry clay to prevent its sticking to the envelope. The name of the person for whom the letter was intended was written on the outside of the envelope, and both it and the tablet were baked hard to ensure that they should not be broken on their travels. The recipient of the letter, on its being delivered to him, broke the outer envelope by tapping it sharply, and it then fell away in pieces, leaving the letter and its message exposed. The envelopes were very similar to those in which the contract tablets of the period were enclosed, of which illustrations have already been given, their only difference being that the text of the tablet was not repeated on the envelope, as was the case with the former class of documents.

The royal letters that have been recovered throw little light on military affairs and the prosecution of campaigns, for, being addressed to governors of cities and civil officials, most of them deal with matters affecting the internal administration of the empire. One letter indeed contains directions concerning the movements of two hundred and forty soldiers of "the King's Company" who had been stationed in Assyria, and another letter mentions certain troops who were quartered in the city of Ur. A third deals with the supply of clothing and oil for a section of the Babylonian army, and troops are also mentioned as having formed the escort for certain goddesses captured from the Elamites; while directions are sent to others engaged in a campaign upon the Elamite frontier. The letter which contains directions for the safe escort of the captured Elamite goddesses, and the one ordering the return of these same goddesses to their own shrines, show that foreign deities, even when captured from an enemy, were treated by the Babylonians with the same respect and reverence that was shown by them to their own gods and goddesses. Hammurabi gave directions in the first letter for the conveyance of the goddesses to Babylon with all due pomp and ceremony, sheep being supplied for sacrifice upon the journey, and their usual rites being performed by their own temple-women and priestesses. The king's voluntary restoration of the goddesses to their own country may have been due to the fact that, after their transference to Babylon, the army of the Babylonians suffered defeat in Elam. This misfortune would naturally have been ascribed by the king and the priests to the anger of the Elamite goddesses at being detained in a foreign land, and Hammurabi probably arrived at his decision that they should be escorted back in the hope of once more securing victory for the Babylonian arms.

The care which the king exercised for the due worship of his own gods and the proper supply of their temples is well illustrated from the letters that hâve been recovered, for he superintended the collection of the temple revenues, and the herdsmen and shepherds attached to the service of the gods sent their reports directly to him. He also took care that the observances of religious rites and ceremonies were duly carried out, and on one occasion he postponed the hearing of a lawsuit concerning the title to certain property which was in dispute, as it would have interfered with the proper observance of a festival in the city of Ur. The plaintiff in the suit was the chief of the temple bakers, and it was his duty to superintend the preparation of certain offerings for the occasion. In order that he should not have to leave his duties, the king put off the hearing of the case until after the festival had been duly celebrated. The king also exercised a strict control over the priests themselves, and received reports from the chief priests concerning their own subordinates, and it is probable that the royal sanction was obtained for all the principal appointments. The guild of soothsayers was an important religious class at this time, and they also were under the king's direct control. A letter written by Ammiditana, one of the later kings of the First Dynasty, to three high officials of the city of Sippar, contains directions with regard to certain duties to be carried out by the soothsayers attached to the service of the city, and indicates the nature of their functions. Ammiditana wrote to the officials in question, stating that there was a scarcity of corn in the city of Shagga, and he therefore ordered them to send a supply thither. But before the corn was brought into the city they were told to consult the soothsayers, who were to divine the future and ascertain whether the omens were favourable. If they proved to be so, the corn was to be brought in. We may conjecture that the king took this precaution, as he feared the scarcity of corn in Shagga was due to the anger of some local deity or spirit, and that, if this were the case, the bringing in of the corn would only lead to fresh troubles. This danger it was the duty of the soothsayers to prevent.

Another class of the priesthood, which we may infer was under the king's direct control, was the astrologers, whose duty it probably was to make reports to the king of the conjunctions of the heavenly bodies, with a view to ascertaining whether they portended good or evil to the state. No astrological reports written in this early period have been recovered, but at a later period under the Assyrian empire the astrologers reported regularly to the king on such matters, and it is probable that the practice was one long established. One of Hammurabi's letters proves that the king regulated the calendar, and it is legitimate to suppose that he sought the advice of his astrologers as to the times when intercalary months were to be inserted. The letter dealing with the calendar was written to inform Sin-idinnam, the governor of Larsam, that an intercalary month was to be inserted. " Since the year (*i. e.* the calendar) hath a deficiency," he writes, " let the month which is now beginning be registered as a second Elul," and the king adds that this insertion of an extra month will not justify any postponement in the payment of the regular tribute due from the city of Larsam, which had to be paid a month earlier than usual to make up for the month that was inserted. The intercalation of additional months was due to the fact that the Babylonian months were lunar, so that the calendar had to be corrected at intervals to make it correspond to the solar year.

From the description already given of the code of laws drawn up by Hammurabi it will have been seen that the king attempted to incorporate and arrange a set of regulations which should settle any dispute likely to arise with regard to the duties and privileges of all classes of his subjects. That this code was not a dead letter, but was actively administered, is abundantly proved by many of the letters of Hammurabi which have been recovered. From these we learn that the king took a very active part in the administration of justice in the country, and that he exercised a strict supervision, not only over the cases decided in the capital, but also over those which were tried in the other great cities and towns of Babylonia. Any private citizen was entitled to make a direct appeal to the king for justice, if he thought he could not obtain it in his local court, and it is clear from Hammurabi's letters that he always listened to such an appeal and gave it adequate consideration. The king was anxious to stamp out all corruption on the part of those who were invested with authority, and he had no mercy on any of his officers who were convicted of taking bribes. On one occasion when he had been informed of a case of bribery in the city of Dûr-gurgurri, he at once ordered the governor of the district in which Dûr-gurgurri lay to investigate the charge and send to Babylon those who were proved to be guilty, that they might be punished. He also ordered that the bribe should be confiscated and despatched to Babylon under seal, a wise provision which must have tended to discourage those who were inclined to tamper with the course of justice, while at the same time it enriched the state. It is probable that the king tried all cases of appeal in person when it was possible to do so. But if the litigants lived at a considerable distance from Babylon, he gave directions to his local officials on the spot to try the case. When he was convinced of the justice of any claim, he would decide the case himself and send instructions to the local authorities to see that his decision was duly carried out. It is certain that many disputes arose at this period in consequence of the extortions of money-lenders. These men frequently laid claim in a fraudulent manner to fields and estates which they had received in pledge as security for seed-corn advanced by them. In cases where fraud was proved Hammurabi had no mercy, and summoned the money-lender to Babylon to receive punishment, however wealthy and powerful he might be.

A subject frequently referred to in Hammurabi's letters is the collection of revenues, and it is clear that an elaborate system was in force throughout the country for the levying and payment of tribute to the state by the principal cities of Babylonia, as well as for the collection of rent and revenue from the royal estates and from the lands which were set apart for the supply of the great temples. Collectors of both secular and religious tribute sent reports directly to the king, and if there was any deficit in the supply which was expected from a collector he had to make it up himself; but the king was always ready to listen to and investigate a complaint and to enforce the payment of tribute or taxes so that the loss should not fall upon the collector. Thus, in one of his letters Hammurabi informs the governor of Larsam that a collector named Sheb-Sin had reported to him, saying " Enubi-Marduk hath laid hands upon the money for the temple of Bit-il-kittim (*i.e.* the great temple of the Sun-god at Larsam) which is due from the city of Dûr-gurgurri and from the (region round about the) Tigris, and he hath not rendered the full sum; and Gimil-Marduk hath laid hands upon the money for the temple of Bit-il-kittim which is due from the city of Rakhabu and from the region round about that city, and he hath not (paid) the full amount. But the palace hath exacted the full sum from me." It is probable that both Enubi-Marduk and Gimil-Marduk were money-lenders, for we know from another letter that the former had laid claim to certain property on which he had held a mortgage, although the mortgage had been redeemed. In the present case they had probably lent money or seed-corn to certain cultivators of land near **Dûr-gurgurri** and Rakhabu and along the Tigris, and in settlement of their claims they had seized the crops and had, moreover, refused to pay to the king's officer the proportion of the crops that was due to the state as taxes upon the land. The governor of Larsam, the principal city in the district, had rightly, as the representative of the palace (*i.e.* the king), caused the tax-collector to make up the deficiency, but Hammurabi, on receiving the subordinate officer's complaint, referred the matter back to the governor. The end of the letter is wanting, but we may infer that Hammurabi condemned the defaulting money-lenders to pay the taxes due, and fined them in addition, or ordered them to be sent to the capital for punishment.

On another occasion Sheb-Sin himself and a second

tax-collector named Sin-mushtal appear to have been in fault and to have evaded coming to Babylon when summoned thither by the king. It had been their duty to collect large quantities of sesame seed as well as taxes paid in money. When first summoned, they had made the excuse that it was the time of harvest and they would come after the harvest was over. But as they did not then make their appearance, Hammurabi wrote an urgent letter insisting that they should be despatched with the full amount of the taxes due, in the company of a trustworthy officer who would see that they duly arrived at the capital.

Tribute on flocks and herds was also levied by the king, and collectors or assessors of the revenue were stationed in each district, whose duty it was to report any deficit in the revenue accounts. The owners of flocks and herds were bound to bring the young cattle and lambs that were due as tribute to the central city of the district in which they dwelt, and they were then collected into large bodies and added to the royal flocks and herds; but, if the owners attempted to hold back any that were due as tribute, they were afterwards forced to incur the extra expense and trouble of driving the beasts to Babylon. The flocks and herds owned by the king and the great temples were probably enormous, and yielded a considerable revenue in themselves apart from the tribute and taxes due from private owners. Shepherds and herdsmen were placed in charge of them, and they were divided into groups under chief shepherds, who arranged the districts in which the herds and flocks were to be grazed, distributing them when possible along the banks and in the neighbourhood of rivers and canals which would afford good pasturage and a plentiful supply of water. The king received reports from the chief shepherds and herdsmen, and it was the duty of the governors of the chief cities and districts of Babylonia to make tours of inspection and see that due care was taken of the royal flocks and sheep. The sheep-shearing for all the flocks that were pastured near the capital took place in Babylon, and the king used to send out summonses to his chief shepherds to inform them of the day when the shearing would take place; and it is probable that the governors of the other great cities sent out similar orders to the shepherds of flocks under their charge. Royal and priestly flocks were often under the same chief officer, a fact which shows the very strict control the king exercised over the temple revenues.

The interests of the agricultural population were strictly looked after by the king, who secured a proper supply of water for purposes of irrigation by seeing that the canals and waterways were kept in a proper state of repair and cleaned out at regular intervals. There is also evidence that nearly every king of the First Dynasty of Babylon cut new canals, and extended the system of irrigation and transportation which had been handed down to him from his fathers. The draining of the marshes and the proper repair of the canals could only be carried out by careful and continuous supervision, and it was the duty of the local governors to see that the inhabitants of villages and owners of land situated on the banks of a canal should keep it in proper order. When this duty had been neglected complaints were often sent to the king, who gave orders to the local governor to remedy the defect. Thus on one occasion it had been ordered that a canal at Erech which had silted up should be deepened, but the dredging had not been carried out thoroughly, so that the bed of the canal soon silted up again and boats were prevented from entering the city. In these circumstances Hammuràbi gave pressing orders that the obstruction was to be removed and the canal made navigable within three days.

Damage was often done to the banks of canals by floods which followed the winter rains, and a letter of Abêshu' gives an interesting account of a sudden rise of the water in the Irnina canal so that it overflowed its banks. The king was building a palace at the city of Kâr-Irnina, which was supplied by the Irnina canal, and every year it was possible to put so much work into the building. But one year, when little more than a third of the year's work was done, the building operations were stopped by flood, the canal having overflowed its banks so that the water rose right up to the wall of the town. In return for the duty of keeping the canals in order, the villagers along the banks had the privilege of fishing in its waters in the portion which was in their charge, and any poaching by other villagers in this part of the stream was strictly forbidden. On one occasion, in the reign of Samsu-iluna, Hammurabi's son and successor, the fishermen of the district of Rabim went down in their boats to the district of Shakanim and caught fish there contrary to the law. So the inhabitants of Shakanim complained of this poaching to the king, who sent a palace official to the authorities of Sippar, near which city the districts in question lay, with orders to inquire into the matter and take steps to prevent all such poaching for the future.

The regulation of transportation on the canals was also under the royal jurisdiction. The method of reckoning the size of ships has already been described, and there is evidence that the king possessed numerous vessels of all sizes for the carrying of grain, wool, and dates, as well as for the wood and stone employed in his building operations. Each ship seems to have had its own crew, under the command of a captain, and it is probable that officials who regulated the transportation from the centres where they were stationed were placed in charge of separate sections of the rivers and of the canals.

It is obvious, from the account that has been given of the numerous operations directly controlled and superintended by the king, that he had need of a very large body of officials, by whose means he was enabled to carry out successfully the administration of the country. In the course of the account we have made mention of the judges and judicial officers, the assessors and collectors of revenue, and the officials of the palace who were under the king's direct orders. It is also obvious that different classes of officers were in charge of all the departments of the administration. Two classes of officials, who were placed in charge of the public works and looked after and controlled the public slaves, and probably also had a good deal to do with the collection of the revenue, had special privileges assigned to them, and special legislation was drawn up to protect them in the enjoyment of the same. As payment for their duties they were each granted land with a house and garden, they were assigned the use of certain sheep and cattle with which to stock their land, and in addition they received a regular salary. They were in a sense personal retainers of the king and were liable to be sent at any moment on a special mission to carry out the king's commands. Disobedience was severely punished; for, if such an officer, when detailed for a special mission, did not go but hired a substitute, he was liable to be put to death and the substitute he had hired could take his office. Sometimes an officer was sent for long periods some distance from his home to take charge of a garrison, and when this was done his home duties were performed by another man, who temporarily occupied his house and land, but gave it back to the officer on his return. If such an officer had a son old enough to perform his duty in his father's absence, he was allowed to do so and to till his father's lands; but if the son was too young, the substitute who took the officer's place had to pay one-third of the produce of the land to the child's mother for his education. Before departing on his journey to the garrison it was the officer's duty to arrange for the proper cultivation of his land and the discharge of his local duties during his absence. If he omitted to do so and left his land and duties neglected for more than a year, and another had meanwhile taken his place, on his return he could not reclaim his land and office. It will be obvious, therefore, that his position was a specially favoured one and much sought after, and these regulations ensured that the duties attaching to the office were not neglected.

In the course of his garrison duty or when on special service, these officers ran some risk of being captured by the enemy, and in that event regulations were drawn up for their ransom. If the captured officer was wealthy and could pay for his own ransom, he was bound to do so, but if he had not the necessary means his ransom was to be paid out of the local temple treasury, and, when the funds in the temple treasury did not suffice, he was to be ransomed by the state. It was specially enacted that his land and garden and house were in no case to be sold in order to pay for his ransom. These were inalienably attached to the office which he held, and he was not allowed to sell them or the sheep and cattle with which they were stocked. Moreover, he was not allowed to bequeath any of this property to his wife or daughter, so that his office would appear to have been hereditary and the property attached to it to have been entailed on his son if he succeeded him. Such succession would not, of course, have taken place if the officer by his own neglect or disobedience had forfeited his office and its privileges during his lifetime.

It has been suggested with considerable probability

that these officials were originally personal retainers and follows of Sumu-abu, the founder of the First Dynasty of Babylon. They were probably assigned lands throughout the country in return for their services to the king, and their special duties were to preserve order and uphold the authority of their master. In the course of time their duties were no doubt modified, but they retained their privileges and they must have continued to be a very valuable body of officers, on whose personal loyalty the king could always rely. In the preceding chapter we have already seen how grants of considerable estates were made by the Kassite kings of the Third Dynasty to followers who had rendered conspicuous services, and at the same time they received the privilege of holding such lands free of all liability to forced labour and the payment of tithes and taxes. We may conclude that the class of royal officers under the kings of the First Dynasty had a similar origin.

In the present chapter, from information recently made available, we have given some account of the system of administration adopted by the early kings of Babylon, and we have described in some detail the various classes of the Babylonian population, their occupations, and the conditions under which they lived. In the two preceding chapters we have dealt with the political history of Western Asia from the very earliest period of the Sumerian city-states down to the time of the Kassite kings. In the course of this account we have seen how Mesopotamia in the dawn of history was in the sole possession of the Sumerian race and how afterwards it fell in turn under the dominion of the Semites and the kings of Elam. The immigration of fresh Semitic tribes at the end of the third millennium before Christ resulted in the establishment in Babylon of the Semitic kings who are known as First Dynasty kings; and under the sway of Hammurabi, the greatest of this group of kings, the empire thus established in Western Asia had every appearance of permanence. Although Elam no longer troubled Babylon, a great danger arose from a new and unexpected quarter. In the Country of the Sea—which comprised the districts in the extreme south of Babylonia on the shores of the Persian Gulf—the Sumerians had rallied their forces, and they now declared themselves independent of Babylonian control. A period of conflict followed between the kings of the First Dynasty and the kings of the Country of the Sea, in which the latter more than held their own; and, when the Hittite tribes of Syria invaded Northern Babylonia in the reign of Samsu-ditana, Babylon's power of resistance was so far weakened that she fell an easy prey to the rulers of the Country of the Sea. But the reappearance of the Sumerians in the rôle of leading race in Western Asia was destined not to last long, and was little more than the last flicker of vitality exhibited by this ancient and exhausted race. Thus the Second Dynasty fell in its turn before the onslaught of the Kassite tribes who descended from the mountainous districts in the west of Elam, and, having overrun the whole of Mesopotamia, established a new dynasty at Babylon, and adopted Babylonian civilization.

With the advent of the Kassite kings a new chapter opens in the history of Western Asia. Up to that time Egypt and Babylon, the two chief centres of ancient civilization, had no doubt indirectly influenced one another, but they had not come into actual contact. During the period of the Kassite kings both Babylon and Assyria established direct relations with Egypt, and from that time forward the influence they exerted upon one another was continuous and unbroken. We have already traced the history of Babylon up to this point in the light of recent discoveries, and a similar task awaits us with regard to Assyria. Before we enter into a discussion of Assyria's origin and early history in the light of recent excavation and research, it is necessary that we should return once more to Egypt, and describe the course of her history from the period when Thebes succeeded in displacing Memphis as the capital city.

CHAPTER VII

TEMPLES AND TOMBS OF THEBES

WE have seen that it was in the Theban period that Egypt emerged from her isolation, and for the first time came into contact with Western Asia. This grand turning-point in Egyptian history seemed to be the appropriate place at which to pause in the description of our latest knowledge of Egyptian history, in order to make known the results of archæological discovery in Mesopotamia and Western Asia generally. The description has been carried down past the point of convergence of the two originally isolated paths of Egyptian and Babylonian civilization, and what new information the latest discoveries have communicated to us on this subject has been told in the preceding chapters. We now have to retrace our steps to the point where we left Egyptian history and resume the thread of our Egyptian narrative.

The Hyksos conquest and the rise of Thebes are practically contemporaneous. The conquest took place perhaps three or four hundred years after the first advancement of Thebes to the position of capital of Egypt, but it must be remembered that this position was not retained during the time of the XIIth Dynasty. The kings of that dynasty, though they were Thebans, did not reign at Thebes. Their royal city was in the North, in the neighbourhood of Lisht and Mêdûm, where their pyramids were erected, and their chief care was for the lake province of the Fayyûm, which was largely the creation of Amenemhat III, the Moeris of the Greeks. It was not till Thebes became the focus of the national resistance to the Hyksos that its period of greatness began. Henceforward it was the undisputed capital of Egypt, enlarged and embellished by the care and munificence of a hundred kings, enriched by the tribute of a hundred conquered nations.

But were we to confine ourselves to the consideration only of the latest discoveries of Theban greatness after the expulsion of the Hyksos, we should be omitting much that is of interest and importance. For the Egyptians the first grand climacteric in their history (after the foundation of the monarchy) was the transference of the royal power from Memphis and Herakleopolis to a Theban house. The second, which followed soon after, was the Hyksos invasion. The two are closely connected in Theban history; it is Thebes that defeated Herakleopolis and conquered Memphis; it is Theban power that was overthrown by the Hyksos; it is Thebes that expelled them and initiated the second great period of Egyptian history. We therefore resume our narrative at a point before the great increase of Theban power at the time of the expulsion of the Hyksos, and will trace this power from its rise, which followed the defeat of Herakleopolis and Memphis. It is upon this epoch—the beginning of Theban power—that the latest discoveries at Thebes have thrown some new light.

More than anywhere else in Egypt excavations have been carried on at Thebes, on the site of the ancient capital of the country. And here, if anywhere, it might have been supposed that there was nothing more to be found, no new thing to be exhumed from the soil, no new fact to be added to our knowledge of Egyptian history. Yet here, no less than at Abydos, has the archæological exploration of the last few years been especially successful, and we have seen that the ancient city of Thebes has a great deal more to tell us than we had expected.

The most ancient remains at Thebes were discovered by Mr. Newberry in the shape of two tombs of the VIth Dynasty, cut upon the face of the well-known hill of Shêkh Abd el-Kûrna, on the west bank of the Nile opposite Luxor. Every winter traveller to Egypt knows well the ride from the sandy shore opposite the Luxor temple, along the narrow pathway between the gardens and the canal, across the bridges and over the cultivated land to the Ramesseum, behind which rises Shêkh Abd el-Kûrna, with its countless tombs, ranged in serried rows along the scarred and scarped face of the hill. This hill, which is geologically a fragment of the plateau behind which some gigantic landslip was sent sliding in the direction of the river, leaving the picturesque gorge and cliffs of Dêr el-Bahari to mark the place from which it was riven, was evidently the seat of the oldest Theban necropolis. Here were the tombs of the Theban chiefs in the period of the Old Kingdom, two of which have been found by Mr. Newberry. In later times, it would seem, these tombs were largely occupied and remodelled by the great nobles of the XVIIIth Dynasty, so that now nearly all the tombs extant on Shêkh Abd el-Kûrna belong to that dynasty.

Of the Thebes of the IXth and Xth Dynasties, when the Herakleopolites ruled, we have in the British Museum two very remarkable statues—one of which is here illustrated—of the steward of the palace, Mera. The tomb from which they came is not known. Both are very beautiful examples of the Egyptian sculptor's art, and are executed in a style eminently characteristic of the transition period between the work of the Old and Middle Kingdoms. As specimens of the art of the Hierakonpolite period, of which we have hardly any examples, they are of the greatest interest. Mera is represented wearing a different head-dress in each figure; in one he has a short wig, in the other a skull-cap.

When the Herakleopolite dominion was finally overthrown, in spite of the valiant resistance of the princes of Asyût, and the Thebans assumed the Pharaonic dignity, thus founding the XIth Dynasty, the Theban necropolis was situated in the great bay in the cliffs, immediately north of Shêkh Abd el-Kûrna, which is known as Dêr el-Bahari. In this picturesque part of

Statue of Mera.

Western Thebes, in many respects perhaps the most picturesque place in Egypt, the greatest king of the XIth Dynasty, Neb-hapet-Rā Mentuhetep, excavated his tomb and built for the worship of his ghost a funerary temple, which he called *Akh-aset*, " Glorious-is-its-Situation," a name fully justified by its surroundings. This temple is an entirely new discovery, made by Prof. Naville and Mr. Hall in 1903. The results obtained up to date have been of very great importance, especially with regard to the history of Egyptian art and architecture, for our sources of information were few and we were previously not very well informed as to the condition of art in the time of the XIth Dynasty.

The new temple lies immediately to the south of the great XVIIIth Dynasty temple at Dêr el-Bahari, which has always been known, and which was excavated first by Mariette and later by Prof. Naville, for the Egypt Exploration Fund. To the results of the later excavations we shall return. When they were finally completed, in the year 1898, the great XVIIIth Dynasty temple, which was built by Queen Hatshepsu, had been entirely cleared of débris, and the colonnades had been partially restored (under the care of Mr. Somers Clarke) in order to make a roof under which to protect the sculptures on the walls. The whole mass of débris, consisting largely of fallen *talus* from the cliffs above, which had almost hidden the temple, was removed; but a large tract lying to the south of the temple, which was also covered with similar mounds of débris, was not touched, but remained to await further investigation. It was here, beneath these heaps of débris, that the new temple was found when work was resumed by the Egypt Exploration Fund in 1903. The actual tomb of the king has not yet been revealed, although that of Neb-hetep Mentuhetep, who may have been his immediate predecessor, was discovered by Mr. Carter in 1899. It was known, however, and still uninjured in the reign of Ramses IX of the XXth Dynasty. Then, as we learn from the report of the inspectors sent to examine the royal tombs, which is preserved in the Abbott Papyrus, they found " the *pyramid*-tomb of King Neb-hapet-Rā which is in Tjesret (the ancient Egyptian name for Dêr el-Bahari); it was intact." We know, therefore, that it was intact about 1000 B.C. The description of it as a pyramid-tomb is interesting, for in the inscription of Tetu, the priest of Akh-aset, who was buried at Abydos, Akh-aset is said to have been a pyramid. That the newly discovered temple was called Akh-aset we know from several inscriptions found in it. And the most remarkable thing about this temple is that in its centre there was a pyramid. This must be the pyramid-tomb which was found intact by the inspectors, so that the tomb itself must be close by. But it does not seem to have been beneath the pyramid, below which is only solid rock. It is perhaps a gallery cut in the cliffs at the back of the temple.

The pyramid was then a dummy, made of rubble within a revetment of heavy flint nodules, which was faced with fine limestone. It was erected on a pyloniform base with heavy cornice of the usual Egyptian pattern. This central pyramid was surrounded by a roofed hall or ambulatory of small octagonal pillars, the outside wall of which was decorated with coloured reliefs, depicting various scenes connected with the *sed-heb* or jubilee-festival of the king, processions of the warriors and magnates of the realm, scenes of husbandry, boat-building, and so forth, all of which were considered appropriate to the chapel of a royal tomb at that period. Outside this wall was an open colonnade of square pillars. The whole of this was built upon an artificially squared rectangular platform of natural rock, about fifteen feet high. To north and south of this were open courts. The southern is bounded by the hill; the northern is now bounded by the Great Temple of Hatshepsu, but, before this was built, there was evidently a very large open court here. The face of the rock platform is masked by a wall of large rectangular blocks of fine white limestone, some of which measure six feet by three feet six inches. They are beautifully squared and laid in bonded courses of alternate sizes, and the walls generally may be said to be among the finest yet found in Egypt. We have already remarked that the architects of the Middle Kingdom appear to have been specially fond of fine masonry in white stone. The contrast between these splendid XIth Dynasty walls, with their great base-stones of sandstone, and the bad rough masonry of the XVIIIth Dynasty temple close by, is striking. The XVIIIth Dynasty architects and masons had degenerated considerably from the standard of the Middle Kingdom.

This rock platform was approached from the east in the centre by an inclined plane or ramp, of which part of the original pavement of wooden beams remains *in situ*. To right and left of this ramp are colonnades, each of twenty-two square pillars, all inscribed with the

XIth DYNASTY WALL: DÊR EL-BAHARI.
Excavated by Mr. Hall, 1904, for the Egypt Exploration Fund.

name and titles of Mentuhetep. The walls masking the platform in these colonnades were sculptured with various scenes, chiefly representing boat processions and campaigns against the Aamu or nomads of the Sinaitic peninsula. The design of the colonnades is the same as that of the Great Temple, and the whole plan of

ARCHITECTURE OF DIFFERENT DYNASTIES 325

this part, with its platform approached by a ramp flanked by colonnades, is so like that of the Great Temple that we cannot but assume that the peculiar design of the latter, with its tiers of platforms approached by ramps flanked by colonnades, is not an original idea,

XVIIIth DYNASTY WALL, DÊR EL-BAHARI.
Excavated by M. Naville, 1896; repaired by Mr. Howard Carter, 1904.

but was directly copied by the XVIIIth Dynasty architects from the older XIth Dynasty temple which they found at Dêr el-Bahari when they began their work.

The supposed originality of Hatshepsu's temple is then non-existent; it was a copy of the older design, in fact, a magnificent piece of archaism. But Hatshepsu's architects copied this feature only; the actual arrangements *on* the platforms in the two temples are as different as they can possibly be. In the older we have a central pyramid with a colonnade round it, in the newer

EXCAVATION OF THE NORTH LOWER COLONNADE OF THE XIth DYNASTY TEMPLE, DÊR EL-BAHARI, 1904.

may be found an open court in front of rock-cave shrines.

Before the XIth Dynasty temple was set up a series of statues of King Mentuhetep and of a later king, Amenhetep I, in the form of Osiris, like those of Usertsen (Senusret) I at Lisht already mentioned. One of these statues is in the British Museum. In the south court were discovered six statues of King Usertsen

(Senusret) III, depicting him at different periods of his life. Four of the heads are preserved, and, as the expression of each differs from that of the other, it is

THE GRANITE THRESHOLD AND OCTAGONAL SANDSTONE PILLARS OF THE XIth DYNASTY TEMPLE AT DÊR EL-BAHARI.
About 2500 B.C.

quite evident that some show him as a young, others as an old, man. The face is of the well-known hard and lined type which is seen also in the portraits of Amenemhat III, and was formerly considered to be that of the Hyksos. Messrs. Newberry and Garstang, as we have seen, consider it to be so, indirectly, as they regard the type as having been introduced into the XIIth Dynasty by Queen Nefret, the mother of Usertsen (Senusret) III. This queen, they think, was a Hittite princess, and the Hittites were practically the same thing

EXCAVATION OF THE TOMB OF A PRIESTESS, ON THE PLATFORM OF THE XIth DYNASTY TEMPLE, DÊR EL-BAHARI, 1904.

as the Hyksos. We have seen, however, that there is very little foundation for this view, and it is more than probable that this peculiar physiognomy is of a type purely Egyptian in character.

On the platform, around the central pyramid, were buried in small chamber-tombs a number of priestesses of the goddess Hathor, the mistress of the desert and special deity of Dêr el-Bahari. They were all members of the king's harîm, and they bore the title of "King's Favourite." As told in a previous chapter, all were buried at one time, before the final completion of the temple, and it is by no means impossible that they were strangled at the king's death and buried round him in order that their ghosts might accompany him in the next world, just as the slaves were buried around the graves (or secondary graves) of the Ist Dynasty kings at Abydos. They themselves, as also already related, took with them to the next world little waxen figures which when called upon could by magic be turned into ghostly slaves. These images were *ushabtiu*, "answerers," the predecessors of the little figures of wood, stone, and pottery which are found buried with the dead in later times. The priestesses themselves were, so to speak, human *ushabtiu*, for royal use only, and accompanied the kings to their final resting-place.

With the priestesses was buried the usual funerary furniture characteristic of the period. This consisted of little models of granaries with the peasants bringing in the corn, models of bakers and brewers at work, boats with their crews, etc., just as we find them in the XIth and XIIth Dynasty tombs at el-Bersha and Beni Hasan. These models, too, were supposed to be transformed by magic into actual workmen who would work for the deceased, heap up grain for her, brew beer for her, ferry her over the ghostly Nile into the tomb-world, or perform any other services required.

Some of the stone sarcophagi of the priestesses are very elaborately decorated with carved and painted reliefs depicting each deceased receiving offerings from priests, one of whom milks the holy cows of Hathor to give her milk. The sarcophagi were let down into the tomb in pieces and there joined together, and they have been removed in the same way. The finest is a unique

CASES OF ANTIQUITIES LEAVING DÊR EL-BAHARI FOR TRANSPORT TO CAIRO.

example of XIth Dynasty art, and it is now preserved in the Museum of Cairo.

In memory of the priestesses there were erected on the platform behind the pyramid a number of small shrines, which were decorated with the most delicately coloured carvings in high relief, representing chiefly the same subjects as those on the sarcophagi. The peculiar style of these reliefs was previously unknown. In connection with them a most interesting possibility presents itself. We know the name of the chief artist of Mentuhetep's reign. He was called Mertisen, and he thus describes himself on his tombstone from Abydos, now in the Louvre: " I was an artist skilled in my art.

SHIPPING CASES OF ANTIQUITIES ON BOARD THE NILE STEAMER AT LUXOR, FOR THE EGYPT EXPLORATION FUND.

I knew my art, how to represent the forms of going forth and returning, so that each limb may be in its proper place. I knew how the figure of a man should walk and the carriage of a woman, the poising of the arm to bring the hippopotamus low, the going of the runner. I knew how to make amulets, which enable us to go without fire burning us and without the flood washing us away. No man could do this but I, and the eldest son of my body. Him has the god decreed to excel in art, and I have seen the perfections of the work of his hands in every kind of rare stone, in gold and silver, in ivory and ebony." Now since Mertisen and his son were the chief artists of their day, it is more than probable that they were employed to decorate their king's funerary chapel. So that in all probability the XIth Dynasty reliefs from Dêr el-Bahari are the work of Mertisen and his son, and in them we see the actual " forms of going forth and returning, the poising of the arm to bring the hippopotamus low, the going of the runner," to which he refers on his tombstone. This adds a note of personal interest to the reliefs, an interest which is often sadly wanting in Egypt, where we rarely know the names of the great artists whose works we admire so much. We have recovered the names of the sculptor and painter of Seti I's temple at Abydos and that of the sculptor of some of the tombs at Tell el-Amarna, but otherwise very few names of the artists are directly associated with the temples and tombs which they decorated, and of the architects we know little more. The great temple of Dêr el-Bahari was, however, we know, designed by Senmut, the chief architect to Queen Hatshepsu.

It is noticeable that Mertisen's art, if it is Mertisen's, is of a peculiar character. It is not quite so fully developed as that of the succeeding XIIth Dynasty. The drawing of the figures is often peculiar, strange lanky forms taking the place of the perfect proportions of the IVth-VIth and the XIIth Dynasty styles. Great elaboration is bestowed upon decoration, which is again of a type rather archaic in character when compared with that of the XIIth Dynasty. We are often reminded of the rude sculptures which used to be regarded as typical of the art of the XIth Dynasty, while at the same time we find work which could not be surpassed by the best XIIth Dynasty masters. In fact, the art of Neb-hapet-Rā's reign was the art of a transitional period. Under the decadent Memphites of the VIIth and VIIIth Dynasties, Egyptian art rapidly fell from the high estate which it had attained under the Vth Dynasty, and, though good work was done under the Hierakonpolites, the chief characteristic of Egyptian art at the time of the Xth and early XIth Dynasties is its curious roughness and almost barbaric appearance. When, however, the kings of the XIth Dynasty reunited the whole land under one sceptre, and the long reign of Neb-hapet-Rā Mentuhetep enabled the reconsolidation of the realm to be carried out by one hand, art began to revive, and, just as to Neb-hapet-Rā must be attributed the renascence of the Egyptian state under the hegemony of Thebes, so must the revival of art in his reign be attributed to his great artists, Mertisen and his son. They carried out in the realm of art what their king had carried out in the political realm, and to them must be attributed the origin of the art of the Middle Kingdom which under the XIIth Dynasty attained so high a pitch of excellence. The sculptures of the king's temple at

Dêr el-Bahari, then, are monuments of the renascence of Egyptian art, after the state of decadence into which it had fallen during the long civil wars between South and North; it is a reviving art, struggling out of barbarism to regain perfection, and therefore has much about it that seems archaic, stiff, and curious when compared with later work. To the XVIIIth Dynasty Egyptian it would no doubt have seemed hopelessly old-fashioned and even semi-barbarous, and he had no qualms about sweeping it aside whenever it appeared in the way of the work of his own time; but to us this very strangeness gives additional charm and interest, and we can only be thankful that Mertisen's work has lasted (in fragments only, it is true) to our own day, to tell us the story of a little known chapter in the history of ancient Egyptian art.

From this description it will have been seen that the temple is an important monument of the Egyptian art and architecture of the Middle Kingdom. It is the only temple of that period of which considerable traces have been found, and on that account the study of it will be of the greatest interest. It is the best preserved of the older temples of Egypt, and at Thebes it is by far the most ancient building recovered. Historically it has given us a new king of the XIth Dynasty, Sekhāhetep-Rā Mentuhetep, and the name of the queen of Nebhapet-Rā Mentuhetep, Aasheit, who seems to have been an Ethiopian, to judge from her portrait, which has been discovered. It is interesting to note that one of the priestesses was a negress.

The name Neb-hapet-Rā may be unfamiliar to those readers who are acquainted with the lists of the Egyptian kings. It is a correction of the former reading, "Neb-kheru-Rā," which is now known from these excavations to be erroneous. Neb-hapet-Rā (or, as he used to be called, Neb-kheru-Rā) is Mentuhetep III of Prof. Petrie's arrangement. Before him there seem to have come the kings Mentuhetep Neb-hetep (who is also commemorated in this temple) and Neb-taui-Rā; after him, Sekhāhetep-Rā Mentuhetep IV and Seānkhkarā Mentuhetep V, who were followed by an Antef, bearing the banner or hawk-name Uah-ānkh. This king was followed by Amenemhat I, the first king of the XIIth Dynasty. Antef Uah-ānkh may be numbered Antef I, as the prince Antefa, who founded the XIth Dynasty, did not assume the title of king.

Other kings of the name of Antef also ruled over Egypt, and they used to be regarded as belonging to the XIth Dynasty; but Prof. Steindorff has now proved that they really reigned after the XIIIth Dynasty, and immediately before the Sekenenrās, who were the fighters of the Hyksos and predecessors of the XVIIIth Dynasty. The second names of Antef III (Seshes-Rā-up-maat) and Antef IV (Seshes-Rā-her-her-maat) are exactly similar to those of the XIIIth Dynasty kings and quite unlike those of the Mentuheteps; also at Koptos a decree of Antef II (Nub-kheper-Rā) has been found inscribed on a doorway of Usertsen (Senusret) I; so that he cannot have preceded him. Prof. Petrie does not yet accept these conclusions, and classes all the

Antefs together with the Mentuheteps in the XIth Dynasty. He considers that he has evidence from Herakleopolis that Antef Nub-kheper-Rā (whom he numbers Antef V) preceded the XIIth Dynasty, and he supposes that the decree of Nub-kheper-Rā at Koptos is a later copy of the original and was inscribed during the XIIth Dynasty. But this is a difficult saying. The probabilities are that Prof. Steindorff is right. Antef Uah-ānkh must, however, have preceded the XIIth Dynasty, since an official of that period refers to his father's father as having lived in Uah-ānkh's time.

The necropolis of Dêr el-Bahari was no doubt used all through the period of the XIth and XIIth Dynasties, and many tombs of that period have been found there. A large number of these were obliterated by the building of the great temple of Queen Hatshepsu, in the northern part of the cliff-bay. We know of one queen's tomb of that period which runs right underneath this temple from the north, and there is another that is entered at the south side which also runs down underneath it. Several tombs were likewise found in the court between it and the XIth Dynasty temple. We know that the XVIIIth Dynasty temple was largely built over this court, and we can see now the XIth Dynasty maskwall on the west of the court running northwards underneath the mass of the XVIIIth Dynasty temple. In all probability, then, when the temple of Hatshepsu was built, the larger portion of the Middle Kingdom necropolis (of chamber-tombs reached by pits), which had filled up the bay to the north of the Mentuhetep temple, was covered up and obliterated, just as the older VIth Dynasty gallery tombs of Shêkh Abd el-Kûrna had been appropriated and altered at the same period.

The kings of the XIIth and XIIIth Dynasties were not buried at Thebes, as we have seen, but in the North, at Dashûr, Lisht, and near the Fayyûm, with which their royal city at Itht-taui had brought them into contact. But at the end of the XIIIth Dynasty the great invasion of the Hyksos probably occurred, and all Northern Egypt fell under the Arab sway. The native kings were driven south from the Fayyûm to Abydos, Koptos, and Thebes, and at Thebes they were buried, in a new necropolis to the north of Dêr el-Bahari (probably then full), on the flank of a long spur of hill which is now called Dra' Abu-'l-Negga, " Abu-'l-Negga's Arm." Here the Theban kings of the period between the XIIIth and XVIIth Dynasties, Upuantemsaf, Antef Nub-kheper-Rā, and his descendants, Antefs III and IV, were buried. In their time the pressure of foreign invasion seems to have been felt, for, to judge from their coffins, which show progressive degeneration of style and workmanship, poverty now afflicted Upper Egypt and art had fallen sadly from the high standard which it had reached in the days of the XIth and XIIth Dynasties. Probably the later Antefs and Sebekemsafs were vassals of the Hyksos. Their descendants of the XVIIth Dynasty were buried in the same necropolis of Dra' Abu-'l-Negga, and so were the first two kings of the XVIIIth Dynasty, Aahmes and Amenhetep I. The tombs of the last two have not yet been found, but we know from the Abbott Papyrus that Amenhetep's was here, for, like that of Mentuhetep III, it was found intact by the inspectors. It was a gallery-tomb of very great length, and will be a most interesting find when it is discovered, as it no doubt eventually will be. Aahmes had a tomb at Abydos, which was discovered by Mr. Currelly, working for the Egypt Exploration Fund. This, however, like the Abydene tomb of Usertsen (Senusret) III, was in all likelihood a sham or secondary tomb, the king having most probably been buried at Thebes, in the Dra' Abu-'l-Negga. The Abydos tomb is of interesting construction. The entrance is by a simple pit, from which a gallery runs round in a curving direction to a great hall supported by eighteen square pillars, beyond which is a further gallery which was never finished. Nothing was found in the tomb. On the slope of the mountain, due west of and in a line with the tomb, Mr. Currelly found a terrace-temple analogous to those of Dêr el-Bahari, approached not by means of a ramp but by stairways at the side. It was evidently the funerary temple of the tomb.

The secondary tomb of Usertsen (Senusret) III at Abydos, which has already been mentioned, was discovered in the preceding year by Mr. A. E. P. Weigall, and excavated by Mr. Currelly in 1903. It lies north of the Aahmes temple, between it and the main cemetery of Abydos. It is a great *bâb* or gallery-tomb, like those of the later kings at Thebes, with the usual apparatus of granite plugs, barriers, pits, etc., to defy plunderers. The tomb had been plundered, nevertheless, though it

is probable that the robbers were vastly disappointed with what they found in it. Mr. Currelly ascribes the absence of all remains to the plunderers, but the fact is that there probably never was anything in it but an empty sarcophagus. Near the tomb Mr. Weigall discovered some dummy mastabas, a find of great interest. Just as the king had a secondary tomb, so secondary mastabas, mere dummies of rubble like the XIth Dynasty pyramid at Dêr el-Bahari, were erected beside it to look like the tombs of his courtiers. Some curious sinuous brick walls which appear to act as dividing lines form a remarkable feature of this sham cemetery. In a line with the tomb, on the edge of the cultivation, is the funerary temple belonging to it, which was found by Mr. Randall-MacIver in 1900. Nothing remains but the bases of the fluted limestone columns and some brick walls. A headless statue of Usertsen was found.

We have an interesting example of the custom of building a secondary tomb for royalties in these two necropoles of Dra' Abu-'l-Negga and Abydos. Queen Teta-shera, the grandmother of Aahmes, a beautiful statuette of whom may be seen in the British Museum, had a small pyramid at Abydos, eastward of and in a line with the temple and secondary tomb of Aahmes. In 1901 Mr. Mace attempted to find the chamber, but could not. In the next year Mr. Currelly found between it and the Aahmes tomb a small chapel, containing a splendid stele, on which Aahmes commemorates his grandmother, who, he says, was buried at Thebes and had a *mer-āhāt* at Abydos, and he records his determination to build her also a pyramid at Abydos, out of his love and veneration for her memory. It thus appeared that the pyramid to the east was simply a dummy, like Usertsen's mastabas, or the Mentuhetep pyramid at Dêr el-Bahari. Teta-shera was actually buried at Dra' Abu-'l-Negga. Her secondary pyramid, like that of Aahmes himself, was in the " holy ground " at Abydos, though it was not an imitation *bâb*, but a dummy pyramid of rubble. This well illustrates the whole custom of the royal primary and secondary tombs, which, as we have seen, had obtained in the case of royal personages from the time of the Ist Dynasty, when Aha had two tombs, one at Nakâda and the other at Abydos. It is probable that all the Ist Dynasty tombs at Abydos are secondary, the kings being really buried elsewhere. After their time we know for certain that Tjeser and Snefru had duplicate tombs, possibly also Unas, and certainly Usertsen (Senusret) III, Amenemhat III, and Aahmes; while Mentuhetep III and Queen Teta-shera had dummy pyramids as well as their tombs. Ramses III also had two tombs, both at Thebes. The reasons for this custom were two: first, the desire to elude plunderers, and second, the wish to give the ghost a *pied-à-terre* on the sacred soil of Abydos or Sakkâra.

As the inscription of Aahmes which records the building of the dummy pyramid of Teta-shera is of considerable interest, it may here be translated. The text reads: " It came to pass that when his Majesty the king, even the king of South and North, Neb-pehti-Rā, Son of the Sun, Aahmes, Giver of Life, was taking his pleasure in the *tjadu*-hall, the hereditary princess greatly favoured and greatly prized, the king's daughter, the king's sister, the god's wife and great wife of the king, Nefret-ari-Aahmes, the living, was in the presence of his Majesty. And the one spake unto the other, seeking to do honour to Those There,[1] which consisteth in the pouring of water, the offering upon the altar, the painting of the stele at the beginning of each season, at the Festival of the New Moon, at the feast of the month, the feast of the going-forth of the *Sem*-priest, the Ceremonies of the Night, the Feasts of the Fifth Day of the Month and of the Sixth, the *Hak*-festival, the *Uag*-festival, the feast of Thoth, the beginning of every season of heaven and earth. And his sister spake, answering him: 'Why hath one remembered these matters, and wherefore hath this word been said? Prithee, what hath come into thy heart?' The king spake, saying: 'As for me, I have remembered the mother of my mother, the mother of my father, the king's great wife and king's mother Teta-shera, deceased, whose tomb-chamber and *mer-āhāt* are at this moment upon the soil of Thebes and Abydos. I have spoken thus unto thee because my Majesty desireth to cause a pyramid and chapel to be made for her in the Sacred Land, as a gift of a monument from my Majesty, and that its lake should be dug, its trees planted, and its offerings prescribed; that it should be provided with slaves, furnished with lands, and endowed with cattle, with *hen-ka* priests and *kher-heb* priests performing

[1] A polite periphrasis for the dead.

their duties, each man knowing what he hath to do.' Behold! when his Majesty had thus spoken, these things were immediately carried out. His Majesty did these things on account of the greatness of the love which he bore her, which was greater than anything. Never had ancestral kings done the like for their mothers. Behold! his Majesty extended his arm and bent his hand, and made for her the king's offering to Geb, to the Ennead of Gods, to the lesser Ennead of Gods . . . [to Anubis] in the God's Shrine, thousands of offerings of bread, beer, oxen, geese, cattle . . . to [the Queen Teta-shera]." This is one of the most interesting inscriptions discovered in Egypt in recent years, for the picturesqueness of its diction is unusual.

As has already been said, the king Amenhetep I was also buried in the Dra' Abu-'l-Negga, but the tomb has not yet been found. Amenhetep I and his mother, Queen Nefret-ari-Aahmes, who is mentioned in the inscription translated above, were both venerated as tutelary demons of the Western Necropolis of Thebes after their deaths, as also was Mentuhetep III. At Dêr el-Bahari both kings seem to have been worshipped with Hathor, the Mistress of the Waste. The worship of Amen-Rā in the XVIIIth Dynasty temple of Dêr el-Bahari was a novelty introduced by the priests of Amen at that time. But the worship of Hathor went on side by side with that of Amen in a chapel with a rock-cut shrine at the side of the Great Temple. Very possibly this was the original cave-shrine of Hathor, long before Mentuhetep's time, and was incorporated with the Great

Temple and beautified with the addition of a pillared hall before it, built over part of the XIth Dynasty north court and wall, by Hatshepsu's architects.

The Great Temple, the excavation of which for the Egypt Exploration Fund was successfully brought to an end by Prof. Naville in 1898, was erected by Queen Hatshepsu in honour of Amen-Rā, her father Thothmes I, and her brother-husband Thothmes II, and received a few additions from Thothmes III, her successor. He, however, did not complete it, and it fell into disrepair, besides suffering from the iconoclastic zeal of the heretic Akhunaten, who hammered out some of the beautifully painted scenes upon its walls. These were badly restored by Ramses II, whose painting is easily distinguished from the original work by the dulness and badness of its colour.

The peculiar plan and other remarkable characteristics of this temple are well known. Its great terraces, with the ramps leading up to them, flanked by colonnades, which, as we have seen, were imitated from the design of the old XIth Dynasty temple at its side, are familiar from a hundred illustrations, and the marvellously preserved colouring of its delicate reliefs is known to every winter visitor to Egypt, and can be realized by those who have never been there through the medium of Mr. Howard Carter's wonderful coloured reproductions, published in Prof. Naville's edition of the temple by the Egypt Exploration Fund. The Great Temple stands to-day clear of all the débris which used to cover it, a lasting monument to the work of the greatest of the societies which busy themselves with the unearthing of the relics of the ancient world. The two temples of Dêr el-Bahari will soon stand side by side, as they originally stood, and will always be associated with the name

THE TWO TEMPLES OF DÊR EL-BAHARI.
Excavated by Prof. Naville, 1893-8 and 1903-6, for the Egypt Exploration Fund.

of the society which rescued them from oblivion, and gave us the treasures of the royal tombs at Abydos. The names of the two men whom the Egypt Exploration Fund commissioned to excavate Dêr el-Bahari and Abydos, and for whose work it exclusively supplied the funds, Profs. Naville and Petrie, will live chiefly in connection with their work at Dêr el-Bahari and Abydos.

The Egyptians called the two temples *Tjeserti*, " the two holy places," the new building receiving the name of *Tjeser-tjesru*, " Holy of Holies," and the whole tract of Dêr el-Bahari the appellation *Tjesret*, " the Holy." The extraordinary beauty of the situation in which they are placed, with its huge cliffs and rugged hillsides, may be appreciated from the photograph which is taken from a steep path half-way up the cliff above the Great Temple. In it we see the Great Temple in the foreground with the modern roofs of two of its colonnades, devised in order to protect the sculptures beneath them, the great trilithon gate leading to the upper court, and the entrance to the cave-shrine of Amen-Rā, with the niches of the kings on either side, immediately at the foot of the cliff. In the middle distance is the duller form of the XIth Dynasty temple, with its rectangular platform, the ramp leading up to it, and the pyramid in the centre of it, surrounded by pillars, half-emerging from the great heaps of sand and débris all around. The background of cliffs and hills, as seen in the photograph, will serve to give some idea of the beauty of the surroundings,—an arid beauty, it is true, for all is desert. There is not a blade of vegetation near; all is salmon-red in colour beneath a sky of ineffable blue, and against the red cliffs the white temple stands out in vivid contrast.

The second illustration gives a nearer view of the great trilithon gate in the upper court, at the head of

346   TEMPLES AND TOMBS OF THEBES

the ramp. The long hill of Dra'Abu-'l-Negga is seen bending away northward behind the gate. This is the famous gate on which the jealous Thothmes III

THE UPPER COURT AND TRILITHON GATE OF THE XVIIIth DYNASTY TEMPLE AT DÊR EL-BAHARI.
About 1500 B.C.

chiselled out Hatshepsu's name in the royal cartouches and inserted his own in its place; but he forgot to alter the gender of the pronouns in the accompanying inscription, which therefore reads " King Thothmes III, she made this monument to her father Amen."

Among Prof. Naville's discoveries here one of the most important is that of the altar in a small court to the north, which, as the inscription says, was made in honour of the god Rā-Harmachis " of beautiful white stone of Anu." It is of the finest white limestone known. Here also were found the carved ebony doors of a shrine, now in the Cairo Museum. One of the most beautiful parts of the temple is the Shrine of Anubis, with its splendidly preserved paintings and perfect columns and roof of white limestone. The effect of the pure white stone and simplicity of architecture is almost Hellenic.

The Shrine of Hathor has been known since the time of Mariette, but in connection with it some interesting discoveries have been made during the excavation of the XIth Dynasty temple. In the court between the two temples were found a large number of small votive offerings, consisting of scarabs, beads, little figures of cows and women, etc., of blue glazed *faïence* and rough pottery, bronze and wood, and blue glazed ware ears, eyes, and plaques with figures of the sacred cow, and other small objects of the same nature. These are evidently the ex-votos of the XVIIIth Dynasty fellahin to the goddess Hathor in the rock-shrine above the court. When the shrine was full or the little ex-votos broken, the sacristans threw them over the wall into the court below, which thus became a kind of dust-heap. Over this heap the sand and débris gradually collected, and thus they were preserved. The objects found are of considerable interest to anthropological science.

The Great Temple was built, as we have said, in honour of Thothmes I and II, and the deities Amen-Rā and Hathor. More especially it was the funerary chapel of Thothmes I. His tomb was excavated, not in the Dra' Abu-'l-Negga, which was doubtless now too near the capital city and not in a sufficiently dignified position of aloofness from the common herd, but at the end of the long valley of the Wadiyên, behind the cliff-hill above Dêr el-Bahari. Hence the new temple was oriented in the direction of his tomb. Immediately behind the temple, on the other side of the hill, is the tomb which was discovered by Lepsius and cleared in 1904 for Mr. Theodore N. Davis by Mr. Howard Carter, then chief inspector of antiquities at Thebes. Its gallery is of very small dimensions, and it winds about in the hill in corkscrew fashion like the tomb of Aahmes at Abydos. Owing to its extraordinary length, the heat and foul air in the depths of the tomb were almost insupportable and caused great difficulty to the excavators. When the sarcophagus-chamber was at length reached, it was found to contain the empty sarcophagi of Thothmes I and of Hatshepsu. The bodies had been removed for safe-keeping in the time of the XXIst Dynasty, that of Thothmes I having been found with those of Seti I and Ramses II in the famous pit at Dêr el-Bahari, which was discovered by M. Maspero in 1881. Thothmes I seems to have had another and more elaborate tomb (No. 38) in the Valley of the Tombs of the

Kings, which was discovered by M. Loret in 1898. Its frescoes had been destroyed by the infiltration of water.

The fashion of royal burial in the great valley behind Dêr el-Bahari was followed during the XVIIIth, XIXth, and XXth Dynasties. Here in the eastern branch of the Wadiyên, now called the *Bibân el-Mulûk*, "the Tombs of the Kings," the greater number of the mightiest Theban Pharaohs were buried. In the western valley rested two of the kings of the XVIIIth Dynasty, who desired even more remote burial-places, Amenhetep III and Ai. The former chose for his last home a most kingly site. Ancient kings had raised great pyramids of artificial stone over their graves. Amenhetep, perhaps the greatest and most powerful Pharaoh of them all, chose to have a natural pyramid for his grave, a mountain for his tumulus. The illustration shows us the tomb of this monarch, opening out of the side of one of the most imposing hills in the Western Valley. No other king but Amenhetep rested beneath this hill, which thus marks his grave and his only.

It is in the Eastern Valley, the Valley of the Tombs of the Kings properly speaking, that the tombs of Thothmes I and Hatshepsu lie, and here the most recent discoveries have been made. It is a desolate spot. As we come over the hill from Dêr el-Bahari we see below us in the glaring sunshine a rocky cañon, with sides sometimes sheer cliff, sometimes sloped by great falls of rock in past ages. At the bottom of these slopes the square openings of the many royal tombs can be descried.[1] Far below we see the forms of tourists and the tomb-guards accompanying them, moving in and out of the openings like ants going in and out of an ants' nest. Nothing is heard but the occasional cry of a kite and the ceaseless rhythmical throbbing of the exhaust-

THE TOMB-MOUNTAIN OF AMENHETEP III, IN THE WESTERN VALLEY, THEBES.

pipe of the electric light engine in the unfinished tomb of Ramses XI. Above and around are the red desert hills. The Egyptians called it "The Place of Eternity."

In this valley some remarkable discoveries have been made during the last few years. In 1898 M. Grébaut

[1] See illustration.

discovered the tomb of Amenhetep II, in which was found the mummy of the king, intact, lying in its sarcophagus in the depths of the tomb. The royal body now lies there for all to see. The tomb is lighted with electricity, as are all the principal tombs of the kings. At the head of the sarcophagus is a single lamp, and, when the party of visitors is collected in silence around the place of death, all the lights are turned out, and then the single light is switched on, showing the royal head illuminated against the surrounding blackness. The effect is indescribably weird and impressive. The body has only twice been removed from the tomb since its burial, the second time when it was for a brief space taken up into the sunlight to be photographed by Mr. Carter, in January, 1902. The temporary removal was carefully carried out, the body of his Majesty being borne up through the passages of the tomb on the shoulders of the Italian electric light workmen, preceded and followed by impassive Arab candle-bearers. The workmen were most reverent in their handling of the body of "*il gran ré*," as they called him.

In the tomb were found some very interesting objects, including a model boat (afterwards stolen), across which lay the body of a woman. This body now lies, with others found close by, in a side chamber of the tomb. One may be that of Hatshepsu. The walls of the tomb-chamber are painted to resemble papyrus, and on them are written chapters of the "Book of What Is in the Underworld," for the guidance of the royal ghost.

In 1902-3 Mr. Theodore Davis excavated the tomb of Thothmes IV. It yielded a rich harvest of antiquities belonging to the funeral state of the king, including a chariot with sides of embossed and gilded leather, decorated with representations of the king's warlike deeds, and much fine blue pottery, all of which are now in the Cairo Museum. The tomb-gallery returns upon itself, describing a curve. An interesting point with regard to it is that it had evidently been violated even in the short time between the reigns of its owner and Horemheb, probably in the period of anarchy which prevailed at Thebes during the reign of the heretic Akhunaten; for in one of the chambers is a hieratic inscription recording the repair of the tomb in the eighth year of Horemheb by Maya, superintendent of works in the Tombs of the Kings. It reads as follows: " In the eighth year, the third month of summer, under the Majesty of King Tjeser-khepru-Rā Sotp-n-Rā, Son of the Sun, Horemheb Meriamen, his Majesty (Life, health, and wealth unto him!) commanded that orders should be sent unto the Fanbearer on the King's Left Hand, the King's Scribe and Overseer of the Treasury, the Overseer of the Works in the Place of Eternity, the Leader of the Festivals of Amen in Karnak, Maya, son of the judge Aui, born of the Lady Ueret, that he should renew the burial of King Men-khepru-Rā, deceased, in the August Habitation in Western Thebes." Men-khepru-Rā was the prenomen or throne-name of Thothmes IV. Tied round a pillar in the tomb is still a length of the actual rope used by the thieves for crossing the chasm, which, as in many of the tombs here, was left open in the gallery to bar the way to plunderers. The mummy of the king was found in the tomb of Amenhetep II, and is now at Cairo.

The discovery of the tomb of Thothmes I and Hatshepsu has already been described. In 1905 Mr. Davis made his latest find, the tomb of Iuaa and Tuaa, the father and mother of Queen Tii, the famous consort of Amenhetep III and mother of Akhunaten the heretic. Readers of Prof. Maspero's history will remember that Iuaa and Tuaa are mentioned on one of the large memorial scarabs of Amenhetep III, which commemorates his marriage. The tomb has yielded an almost incredible treasure of funerary furniture, besides the actual mummies of Tii's parents, including a chariot overlaid with gold. Gold overlay of great thickness is found on everything, boxes, chairs, etc. It was no wonder that Egypt seemed the land of gold to the Asiatics, and that even the King of Babylon begs this very Pharaoh Amenhetep to send him gold, in one of the letters found at Tell el-Amarna, " for gold is as water in thy land." It is probable that Egypt really attained the height of her material wealth and prosperity in the reign of Amenhetep III. Certainly her dominion reached its farthest limits in his time, and his influence was felt from the Tigris to the Sudan. He hunted lions for his pleasure in Northern Mesopotamia, and he built temples at Jebel Barkal beyond Dongola. We see the evidence of lavish wealth in the furniture of the tomb of Iuaa and Tuaa. Yet, fine as are many of these gold-overlaid and overladen objects of the XVIIIth Dynasty, they have neither the good taste nor the charm of the beautiful jewels from the XIIth Dynasty tombs at Dashûr. It is mere vulgar wealth. There is too much gold thrown about. "For gold is as water in thy land." In three hundred years' time Egypt was to know what poverty meant, when the poor priest-kings of the XXIst Dynasty could hardly keep body and soul together and make a comparatively decent show as Pharaohs of Egypt. Then no doubt the latter-day Thebans sighed for the good old times of the XVIIIth Dynasty, when their city ruled a considerable part of Africa and Western Asia and garnered their riches into her coffers. But the days of the XIIth Dynasty had really been better still. Then there was not so much wealth, but what there was (and there was as much gold then, too) was used sparingly, tastefully, and simply. The XIIth Dynasty, not the XVIIIth, was the real Golden Age of Egypt.

From the funeral panoply of a tomb like that of Iuaa and Tuaa we can obtain some idea of the pomp and state of Amenhetep III. But the remains of his Theban palace, which have been discovered and excavated by Mr. C. Tytus and Mr. P. E. Newberry, do not bear out this idea of magnificence. It is quite possible that the palace was merely a pleasure house, erected very hastily and destined to fall to pieces when its owner tired of it or died, like the many palaces of the late Khedive Ismail. It stood on the border of an artificial lake, whereon the Pharaoh and his consort Tii sailed to take their pleasure in golden barks. This is now the cultivated rectangular space of land known as the Birket Habû, which is still surrounded by the remains of the embankment built to retain its waters, and becomes a lake during the inundation. On the western shore of this lake Amenhetep erected the "stately pleasure dome," the remains of which still cover the sandy tract known as el-Malkata, "the Salt-pans," south of the great temple of Medinet Habû. These remains consist merely of the foundations and lowest wall-courses of a complicated and rambling building of many chambers, constructed of common unburnt brick and plastered with white stucco on walls and floors, on which were painted beautiful frescoes of fighting bulls, birds of the air, water-fowl, fish-ponds, etc., in much the same style as the frescoes of Tell el-Amarna executed in the next reign. There were small pillared halls, the columns of which were of wood, mounted on bases of white limestone. The majority still remain in position. In several chambers there are small daïses, and in one the remains of a throne, built of brick and mud covered with plaster and stucco, upon which the Pharaoh Amenhetep sat. This is the palace of him whom the Greeks called Memnon, who ruled Egypt when Israel was in bondage and when the dynasty of Minos reigned in Crete. Here by the side of his pleasure-lake the most powerful of Egyptian Pharaohs whiled away his time during the summer heats. Evidently the building was intended to be of the lightest construction, and never meant to last; but to our ideas it seems odd that an Egyptian Pharaoh should live in a mud palace. Such a building is, however, quite suited to the climate of Egypt, as are the modern crude brick dwellings of the fellahin. In the ruins of the palace were found several small objects of interest, and close by was an ancient glass manufactory of Amenhetep III's time, where much

THE TOMB-HILL OF SHÊKH 'ABD EL-KÛRNA, THEBES.

of the characteristic beautifully coloured and variegated opaque glass of the period was made.

The tombs of the magnates of Amenhetep III's reign and of the reigns of his immediate predecessors were excavated, as has been said, on the eastern slope of the hill of Shêkh 'Abd el-Kûrna, where was the earliest Theban necropolis. No doubt many of the early tombs of the time of the VIth Dynasty were appropriated and remodelled by the XVIIIth Dynasty magnates. We have an instance of time's revenge in this matter, in the case of the tomb of Imadua, a great priestly official of the time of the XXth Dynasty. This tomb previously belonged to an XVIIIth Dynasty worthy, but Imadua appropriated it three hundred years later and covered up all its frescoes with the much begilt decoration fashionable in his period. Perhaps the XVIIIth Dynasty owner had stolen it from an original owner of the time of the VIth Dynasty. The tomb has lately been cleared out by Mr. Newberry.

Much work of the same kind has been done here of late years by Messrs. Newberry and R. L. Mond, in succession. To both we are indebted for the excavation of many known tombs, as well as for the discovery of many others previously unknown. Among the former was that of Sebekhetep, cleared by Mr. Newberry. Sebekhetep was an official of the time of Thothmes III. From his tomb, and from others in the same hill, came many years ago the fine frescoes shown in the illustration, which are among the most valued treasures of the Egyptian department of the British Museum. They are typical specimens of the wall-decoration of an XVIIIth Dynasty tomb. On one may be seen a bald-headed peasant, with staff in hand, pulling an ear of corn from the standing crop in order to see if it is ripe. He is the "Chief Reaper," and above him is a prayer that the "great god in heaven" may increase the crop. To the right of him is a charioteer standing beside a car and reining back a pair of horses, one black, the other bay. Below is another charioteer with two white horses. He sits on the floor of the car with his back to them, eating or resting, while they nibble the branches of a tree close by. Another scene is that of a scribe keeping tally of offerings brought to the tomb, while fellahin are bringing flocks of geese and other fowl, some in crates. The inscription above is apparently addressed by the gooseherd to the man with the crates. It reads: "Hasten thy feet because of the geese! Hearken! thou knowest not the next minute what has been said to thee!" Above, a reïs with a stick bids other peasants squat on the ground before addressing the scribe, and he is saying to them: "Sit ye down to talk." The third scene is in another style; on it may be seen Semites bringing offerings of vases of gold, silver, and copper to the royal presence, bowing themselves to the ground and kissing the dust before the throne. The fidelity and accuracy with which the racial type of the tribute-bearers is given is most extraordinary; every face seems a portrait, and each one might be seen any day now in the Jewish quarters of Whitechapel.

The first two paintings are representative of a very common style of fresco-pictures in these tombs. The care with which the animals are depicted is remarkable. Possibly one of the finest Egyptian representations of an animal is the fresco of a goat in the tomb of Gen-Amen, discovered by Mr. Mond. There is even an attempt here at chiaroscuro, which is unknown to Egyptian art generally, except at Tell el-Amarna. Evidently

the Egyptian painters reached the apogee of their art towards the end of the XVIIIth Dynasty. The third, the representation of tribute-bearers, is of a type also well known at this period. In all the chief tombs we have processions of Egyptians, Westerners, Northerners, Easterners, and Southerners, bringing tribute to the Pharaoh. The North is represented by the Semites, the East by the Punites (when they occur), the South by negroes, the West by the Keftiu or people of Crete and Cyprus. The representations of the last-named people have become of the very highest interest during the last few years, on account of the discoveries in Crete, which have revealed to us the state and civilization of these very Keftiu. Messrs. Evans and Halbherr have discovered at Knossos and Phaistos the cities and palace-temples of the king who sent forth their ambassadors to far-away Egypt with gifts for the mighty Pharaoh; these ambassadors were painted in the tombs of their hosts as representative of the quarter of the world from which they came.

The two chief Egyptian representations of these people, who since they lived in Greece may be called Greeks, though their more proper title would be "Pelasgians," are to be found in the tombs of Rekhmarā and Senmut, the former a vizier under Thothmes III, the latter the architect of Hatshepsu's temple at Dêr el-Bahari. Senmut's tomb is a new rediscovery. It was known, as Rekhmarā's was, in the early days of Egyptological science, and Prisse d'Avennes copied its paintings. It was afterwards lost sight of until rediscovered

360 TEMPLES AND TOMBS OF THEBES

by Mr. Newberry and Prof. Steindorff. The tomb of Rekhmarā (No. 35) is well known to every visitor to Thebes, but it is difficult to get at that of Senmut

FRESCO IN THE TOMB OF SENMUT AT THEBES.
About 1500 B. C.

(No. 110); it lies at the top of the hill round to the left and overlooking Dêr el-Bahari, — an appropriate place for it, by the way. In some ways Senmut's representations are more interesting than Rekhmara's. They are more easily seen, since they are now in the open air, the fore hall of the tomb having been ruined; and they are better preserved, since they have not been subjected to a century of inspection with naked candles and pawing with greasy hands, as have Rekhmara's frescoes. Further, there is no possibility of mistaking what they represent. From right to left, walking in procession, we see the Minoan gift-bearers from Crete, carrying in their hands and on their shoulders great cups of gold and silver, in shape like the famous gold cups found at Vaphio in Lakonia, but much larger, also a ewer of gold and silver exactly like one of bronze discovered by Mr. Evans two years ago at Knossos, and a huge copper jug with four ring-handles round the sides. All these vases are specifically and definitely Mycenæan, or rather, following the new terminology, Minoan. They are of Greek manufacture and are carried on the shoulders of Pelasgian Greeks. The bearers wear the usual Mycenæan costume, high boots and a gaily ornamented kilt, and little else, just as we see it depicted in the fresco of the Cupbearer at Knossos and in other Greek representations. The coiffure, possibly the most characteristic thing about the Mycenæan Greeks, is faithfully represented by the Egyptians both here and in Rekhmara's tomb. The Mycenæan men allowed their hair to grow to its full natural length, like women, and wore it partly hanging down the back, partly tied up in a knot or plait (the κέρας of the dandy Paris in the Iliad) on the crown of the head. This was the universal fashion, and the Keftiu are consistently depicted by the XVIIIth Dynasty Egyptians as following it. The faces in the Senmut fresco are not so well portrayed as those in the Rekhmarā fresco. There it is evident that the first three' ambassadors are faithfully depicted, as the portraits are marked. The procession advances from left to right. The first man, "the Great Chief of the Kefti and the Isles of the Green Sea," is young, and has a remarkably small mouth with an amiable expression. His complexion is fair rather than dark, but his hair is dark brown. His lieutenant, the next in order, is of a different type,—elderly, with a most forbidding visage, Roman nose, and nutcracker jaws. Most of the others are very much alike,—young, dark in complexion, and with long black hair hanging below their waists and twisted up into fantastic knots and curls on the tops of their heads. One, carrying on his shoulder a great silver vase with curving handles and in one hand a dagger of early European Bronze Age type, is looking back to hear some remark of his next companion. Any one of these gift-bearers might have sat for the portrait of the Knossian Cupbearer, the fresco discovered by Mr. Evans in the palace-temple of Minos; he has the same ruddy brown complexion, the same long black hair dressed in the same fashion, the same parti-coloured kilt, and he bears his vase in much the same way. We have only to allow for the difference of Egyptian and Mycenæan ways of drawing. There is no doubt whatever that these Keftiu of the Egyptians were Cretans of the Minoan Age. They used to be considered Phœnicians, but this view was long ago exploded. They are not Semites, and that is quite enough. Neither are they Asiatics of any kind. They are purely and simply Mycenæan, or rather Minoan, Greeks of the pre-Hellenic period—Pelasgi, that is to say.

Probably no discovery of more far-reaching importance to our knowledge of the history of the world generally and of our own culture especially has ever been made than the finding of Mycenæ by Schliemann, and the further finds that have resulted therefrom, culminating in the discoveries of Mr. Arthur Evans at Knossos. Naturally, these discoveries are of extraordinary interest to us, for they have revealed the beginnings and first bloom of the European civilization of to-day. For our culture-ancestors are neither the Egyptians, nor the Assyrians, nor the Hebrews, but the Hellenes, and they, the Aryan-Greeks, derived most of their civilization from the pre-Hellenic people whom they found in the land before them, the Pelasgi or "Mycenæan" Greeks, "Minoans," as we now call them, the Keftiu of the Egyptians. These are the ancient Greeks of the Heroic Age, to which the legends of the Hellenes refer; in their day were fought the wars of Troy and of the Seven against Thebes, in their day the tragedy of the Atridæ was played out to its end, in their day the wise Minos ruled Knossos and the Ægean. And of all the events which are at the back of these legends we know nothing. The hieroglyphed tablets of the pre-Hellenic Greeks lie before us, but we cannot read them; we can only see that the Minoan writing in many ways resembled the

Egyptian, thus again confirming our impression of the original early connection of the two cultures.[1]

In view of this connection, and the known close relations between Crete and Egypt, from the end of the XIIth Dynasty to the end of the XVIIIth, we might have hoped to recover at Knossos a bilingual inscription in Cretan and Egyptian hieroglyphs which would give us the key to the Minoan script and tell us what we so dearly wish to know. But this hope has not yet been realized. Two Egyptian inscriptions have been found at Knossos, but no bilingual one. A list of Keftian names is preserved in the British Museum upon an Egyptian writing-board from Thebes with what is perhaps a copy of a single Cretan hieroglyph, a vase; but again, nothing bilingual. A list of "Keftian words" occurs at the head of a papyrus, also in the British Museum, but they appear to be nonsense, a mere imitation of the sounds of a strange tongue. Still we need not despair of finding the much desired Cretan-Egyptian bilingual inscription yet. Perhaps the double text of a treaty between Crete and Egypt, like that of Ramses II with the Hittites, may come to light. Meanwhile we can only do our best with the means at our hand to trace out the history of the relations of the oldest European culture with the ancient civilization of Egypt. The tomb-paintings at Thebes are very important material. For it is due to them that the voice of the doubter has finally ceased to be heard, and that now no archæologist questions that the Egyptians were in

[1] See above, p. 128.

direct communication with the Cretan Mycenæans in the time of the XVIIIth Dynasty, some fifteen hundred years before Christ, for no one doubts that the pictures of the Keftiu are pictures of Mycenæans.

As we have seen, we know that this connection was far older than the time of the XVIIIth Dynasty, but it is during that time and the Hyksos period that we have the clearest documentary proof of its existence, from the statuette of Abnub and the alabastron lid of King Khian, found at Knossos, down to the Mycenæan pottery fragments found at Tell el-Amarna, a site which has been utterly abandoned since the time of the heretic Akhunaten (B. C. 1430), so that there is no possibility of anything found there being later than his time. That the connection existed as late as the time of the XXth Dynasty we know from the representations of golden *Bügelkannen* or false-necked vases of Mycenæan form in the tomb of Ramses III in the Bibân el-Mulûk, and of golden cups of Vaphio type in the tomb of Imadua, already mentioned. This brings the connection down to about 1050 B. C.

After that date we cannot hope to find any certain evidence of connection, for by that time the Mycenæan civilization had probably come to an end. In the days of the XIIth and XVIIIth Dynasties a great and splendid power evidently existed in Crete, and sent its peaceful ambassadors, the Keftiu who are represented in the Theban tombs, to Egypt. But with the XIXth Dynasty the name of the Keftiu disappears from Egyptian records, and their place is taken by a congeries of warring seafaring tribes, whose names as given by the Egyptians seem to be forms of tribal and place names well known to us in the Greece of later days. We find the Akaivasha (Αχαιϝοὶ, Achaians), Shakalsha (Sagalassians of Pisidia), Tursha (Tylissians of Crete?), and Shardana (Sardians) allied with the Libyans and Mashauash (Maxyes) in a land attack upon Egypt in the days of Meneptah, the successor of Ramses II—just as in the later days of the XXVIth Dynasty the Northern pirates visited the African shore of the Mediterranean, and in alliance with the predatory Libyans attacked Egypt.

Prof. Petrie has lately[1] proffered an alternative view, which would make all these tribes Tunisians and Algerians, thus disposing of the identification of the Akaivasha with the Achaians, and making them the ancient representatives of the town of el-Aghwat (Roman Agbia) in Tunis. But several difficulties might be pointed out which are in the way of an acceptance of this view, and it is probable that the older identifications with Greek tribes must still be retained, so that Meneptah's Akaivasha are evidently the ancient representatives of the Achai(v)ans, the Achivi of the Roman poets. The terminations *sha* and *na*, which appear in these names, are merely ethnic and locative affixes belonging to the Asianic language system spoken by these tribes at that time, to which the language of the Minoan Cretans (which is written in the Knossian hieroglyphs) belonged. They existed in ancient Lycian in the forms

[1] *History of Egypt*, iii, pp. 111, 112.

azzi and *ñna*, and we find them enshrined in the Asia Minor place-names terminating in *assos* and *nda*, as Halikarnassos, Sagalassos (Shakalasha in Meneptah's inscription), Oroanda, and Labraunda (which, as we have seen, is the same as the Greek λαβύρινθος, a word of pre-Hellenic origin, both meaning " Place of the Double Axe "). The identification of these *sha* and *na* terminations in the Egyptian transliterations of the foreign names, with the Lycian affixes referred to, was made some five years ago,[1] and is now generally accepted. We have, then, to find the equivalents of these names, to strike off the final termination, as in the case of Akaiva-sha, where Akaiva only is the real name, and this seems to be the Egyptian equivalent of Αχαιϝοί, Achivi. It is strange to meet with this great name on an Egyptian monument of the thirteenth century B. C. But yet not so strange, when we recollect that it is precisely to that period that Greek legend refers the war of Troy, which was an attack by Greek tribes from all parts of the Ægean upon the Asianic city at Hissarlik in the Troad, exactly parallel to the attacks of the Northerners on Egypt. And Homer preserves many a reminiscence of early Greek visits, peaceful and the reverse, to the coast of Egypt at this period. The reader will have noticed that one no longer treats the siege of Troy as a myth. To do so would be to exhibit a most uncritical mind; even the legends of King Arthur have a historic foundation, and those of the Nibelungen are still more probable.

[1] See Hall, *Oldest Civilization of Greece*, p. 178 *f.*

In the eighth year of Ramses III the second Northern attack was made, by the Pulesta (*Pelishtim*, Philistines), Tjakaray, Shakalasha (Sagalassians), Vashasha, and Danauna or Daanau, in alliance with North Syrian tribes. The Danauna are evidently the ancient representatives of the Δαναοί, the Danaans who formed the bulk of the Greek army against Troy under the leadership of the long-haired Achaians, καρηκομόωντες 'Αχαιοί (like the Keftiu). The Vashasha have been identified by the writer with the Axians, the ϝαξίοι of Crete. Prof. Petrie compares the name of the Tjakaray with that of the (modern) place Zakro in Crete. Identifications with modern place-names are of doubtful value; for instance, we cannot but hold that Prof. Petrie errs greatly in identifying the name of the Pidasa (another tribe mentioned in Ramses II's time) with that of the river Pidias in Cyprus. "Pidias" is a purely modern corruption of the ancient Pediæus, which means the "plain-river" (because it flows through the central plain of the island), from the Greek πεδίον. If, then, we make the Pidasa Cypriotes we assume that pure Greek was spoken in Cyprus as early as 1100 B. C., which is highly improbable. The Pidasa were probably Leleges (Pedasians); the name of Pisidia may be the same, by metathesis. Pedasos is a name always connected with the much wandering tribe of the Leleges, wherever they are found in Lakonia or in Asia Minor. We believe them to have been known to the Egyptians as Pidasa. The identification of the Tjakaray with Zakro is very tempting. The name was formerly identified with that of the Teukrians, but the υ in the word Τεύκροι has always been a stumbling-block in the way. Perhaps Zakro is neither more nor less than the Τεύκρος-name, since the legendary Teucer, the archer, was connected with the eastern or Eteokretan end of Crete, where Zakro lies. In Mycenæan times Zakro was an important place, so that the Tjakaray may be the Teukroi, after all, and Zakro may preserve the name. At any rate, this identification is most alluring and, taken in conjunction with the other cumulative identifications, is very probable; but the identification of the Pidasa with the river Pediæus in Cyprus is neither alluring nor probable.

In the time of Ramses II some of these Asia Minor tribes had marched against Egypt as allies of the Hittites. We find among them the Luka or Lycians, the Dardenui (Dardanians, who may possibly have been at that time in the Troad, or elsewhere, for all these tribes were certainly migratory), and the Masa (perhaps the Mysians). With the Cretans of Ramses III's time must be reckoned the Pulesta, who are certainly the Philistines, then most probably in course of their traditional migration from Crete to Palestine. In Philistia recent excavations by Mr. Welch have disclosed the unmistakable presence of a late Mycenæan culture, and we can only ascribe this to the Philistines, who were of Cretan origin.

Thus we see that all these Northern tribal names hold together with remarkable persistence, and in fact refuse to be identified with any tribes but those of Asia Minor and the Ægean. In them we see the broken remnants of the old Minoan (Keftian) power, driven hither and thither across the seas by intestinal feuds, and "winding the skein of grievous wars till every man of them perished," as Homer says of the heroes after the siege of Troy. These were in fact the wanderings of the heroes, the period of *Sturm und Drang* which succeeded the great civilized epoch of Minos and his thalassocracy, of Knossos, Phaistos, and the Keftius. On the walls of the temple of Medinet Habû, Ramses III depicted the portraits of the conquered heroes who had fallen before the Egyptian onslaught, and he called them heroes, *tuher* in Egyptian, fully recognizing their Berserker gallantry. Above all in interest are the portraits of the Philistines, those Greeks who at this very time seized part of Palestine (which takes its name from them), and continued to exist there as a separate people (like the Normans in France) for at least two centuries. Goliath the giant was, then, a Greek; certainly he was of Cretan descent, and so a Pelasgian.

Such are the conclusions to which modern discovery in Crete has impelled us with regard to the pictures of the Keftiu at Shêkh 'Abd el-Kûrna. It is indeed a new chapter in the history of the relations of ancient Egypt with the outside world that Dr. Arthur Evans has opened for us. And in this connection some American work must not be overlooked. An expedition sent out by the University of Pennsylvania, under Miss Harriet Boyd, has discovered much of importance to Mycenæan study in the ruins of an ancient town at Gournia in

Crete, east of Knossos. Here, however, little has been found that will bear directly on the question of relations between Mycenæan Greece and Egypt.

The Theban necropoles of the New Empire are by no means exhausted by a description of the Tombs of the Kings and Shêkh 'Abd el-Kûrna; but few new discoveries have been made anywhere except in the picturesque valley of the Tombs of the Queens, south of Shêkh 'Abd el-Kûrna. Here the Italian Egyptologist, Prof. Schiaparelli, has lately discovered and excavated some very fine tombs of the XIXth and XXth Dynasties. The best is that of Queen Nefertari, one of the wives of Ramses II. The colouring of the reliefs upon these walls is extraordinarily bright, and the portraits of the queen, who has a very beautiful face, with aquiline nose, are wonderfully preserved. She was of the dark type, while another queen, Titi by name, who was buried close by, was fair, and had a retroussé nose. Prof. Schiaparelli also discovered here the tombs of some princes of the XXth Dynasty, who died young. All the tombs are much alike, with a single short gallery, on the walls of which are mythological scenes, figures of the prince and of his father, the king, etc., painted in a crude style, which shows a great degeneration from that of the XVIIIth Dynasty tombs.

We now leave the great necropolis and turn to the later temples of the Western Bank at Thebes. These were of a funerary character, like those of Dêr el-Bahari, already described. The most imposing of all in some respects is the Ramesseum, where lies the huge granite

372   TEMPLES AND TOMBS OF THEBES

colossus of Ramses II, prostrate and broken, which Diodorus knew as the statue of Osymandyas. This name is a late corruption of Ramses II's throne-name, User-maat-Rā, pronounced Ûsimare. The temple has been

THE VALLEY OF THE TOMBS OF THE QUEENS AT THEBES.
In which Prof. Schiaparelli discovered the tomb of Ramses II's wife (1904).

cleared by Mr. Howard Carter for the Egyptian government, and the small town of priests' houses, magazines, and cellars, to the west of it, has been excavated by him. This is quite a little Pompeii, with its small streets, its houses with the stucco still clinging to the walls, its public altar, its market colonnade, and its gallery of statues. The statues are only of brick like the walls, and roughly shaped and plastered, but they were portraits, undoubtedly, of celebrities of the time, though we do not know of whom. On either side are the long magazines in which were kept the possessions of the priests of the Ramesseum, the grain from the lands with which they were endowed, and everything meet to be offered to the ghost of the king whom they served. The plan of the place had evidently been altered after the time of Ramses II, as remains of overbuilding were found here and there. The magazines were first investigated in 1896 by Prof. Petrie, who also found in the neighbourhood the remains of a number of small royal funerary temples of the XVIIIth Dynasty, all looking in the direction of the hill, beyond which lay the tombs of the kings.

We may now turn to Luxor, where immediately above the landing-place of the steamers and dahabiyas rise the stately coloured colonnades of the Temple of Luxor. Unfortunately, modern excavations have not been allowed to pursue their course to completion here, as in the first great colonnaded court, which was added by Ramses II to the original building of Amenhetep III, Tutankhamen, and Horemheb, there still remains the Mohammedan Mosque of Abu-'l-Haggâg, which may not be removed. Abu-'l-Haggâg, " the Father of Pilgrims " (so called on account of the number of pilgrims to his shrine), was a very holy shêkh, and his memory is held in the greatest reverence by the Luksuris. It is unlucky that this mosque was built within the court of the Great Temple, and it cannot be removed till Moslem religious prejudices become at least partially ameliorated, and then the work of completely excavating the Temple of Luxor may be carried out.

Between Luxor and Karnak lay the temple of the goddess Mut, consort of Amen and protectress of

THE NILE-BANK AT LUXOR, WITH A DAHABÎYA AND A STEAMER OF THE ANGLO-AMERICAN NILE COMPANY.

Thebes. It stood in the part of the city known as Asheru. This building was cleared in 1895 at the expense and under the supervision of two English ladies, Miss Benson and Miss Gourlay. The temple had always been remarkable on account of the prodigious number of seated figures of the lioness-headed goddess Sekhemet, or Pakhet, which it contains, dedicated by

Amenhetep III and Sheshenk I; most of those in the British Museum were brought from this temple. The excavators found many more of them, and also some very interesting portrait-statues of the late period which had been dedicated there. The most important of these was the head and shoulders of a statue of Mentuemhat, governor of Thebes at the time of the sack of the city by Ashur-bani-pal of Assyria in 668 B. C. In Miss Benson's interesting book, *The Temple of Mut in Asher*, it is suggested, on the authority of Prof. Petrie, that his facial type is Cypriote, but this speculation is a dangerous one, as is also the similar speculation that the wonderful portrait-head of an old man found by Miss Benson[1] is of Philistine type. We have only to look at the faces of elderly Egyptians to-day to see that the types presented by Mentuemhat and Miss Benson's "Philistine" need be nothing but pure Egyptian. The whole work of the clearing was most efficiently carried out, and the Cairo Museum obtained from it some valuable specimens of Egyptian sculpture.

The Great Temple of Karnak is one of the chief cares of the Egyptian Department of Antiquities. Its paramount importance, so to speak, as the cathedral temple of Egypt, renders its preservation and exploration a work of constant necessity, and its great extent makes this work one which is always going on and which probably will be going on for many years to come. The Temple of Karnak has cost the Egyptian government much money, yet not a piastre of this can be

[1] Plate vii of her book.

grudged. For several years past the works have been under the charge of M. Georges Legrain, the well-known engineer and draughtsman who was associated with

THE GREAT TEMPLE OF KARNAK.
The left-hand obelisk is the highest in Egypt, and was erected by Hatshepsu; the right-hand obelisk was put up by Thothmes III.

M. de Morgan in the work at Dashûr. His task is to clear out the whole temple thoroughly, to discover in it what previous investigators have left undiscovered, and to restore to its original position what has fallen.

No general work of restoration is contemplated, nor would this be in the slightest degree desirable. Up to the present M. Legrain has certainly carried out all three branches of his task with great success. An unforeseen event has, however, considerably complicated and retarded the work. In October, 1899, one of the columns of the side aisles of the great Hypostyle Hall fell, bringing down with it several others. The whole place was a chaotic ruin, and for a moment it seemed as though the whole of the Great Hall, one of the wonders of the world, would collapse. The disaster was due to the gradual infiltration of water from the Nile beneath the structure, whose foundations, as is usual in Egypt, were of the flimsiest description. Even the most imposing Egyptian temples have jerry-built foundations; usually they are built on the top of the wall-stumps of earlier buildings of different plan, filled in with a confused mass of earlier slabs and weak rubbish of all kinds. Had the Egyptian buildings been built on sure foundations, they would have been preserved to a much greater extent even than they are. In such a climate as that of Egypt a stone building well built should last for ever.

M. Legrain has for the last five years been busy repairing the damage. All the fallen columns are now restored to the perpendicular, and the capitals and architraves are in process of being hoisted into their original positions. The process by which M. Legrain carries out this work has been already described. He works in the old Egyptian fashion, building great inclines or ramps of earth up which the pillar-drums, the capitals, and the architrave-blocks are hauled by manual labour, and then swung into position. This is the way in which the Egyptians built Karnak, and in this way, too, M. Legrain is rebuilding it. It is a slow process, but a sure one, and now it will not be long before we shall see the hall, except its roof, in much the same condition as it was when Seti built it. Lovers of the picturesque will, however, miss the famous leaning column, hanging poised across the hall, which has been a main feature in so many pictures and photographs of Karnak. This fell in the catastrophe of 1899, and naturally it has not been possible to restore it to its picturesque, but dangerous, position.

The work at Karnak has been distinguished during the last two years by two remarkable discoveries. Outside the main temple, to the north of the Hypostyle Hall, M. Legrain found a series of private sanctuaries or shrines, built of brick by personages of the XVIIIth Dynasty and later, in order to testify their devotion to Amen. In these small cells were found some remarkable statues, one of which is illustrated. It is one of the most perfect of its kind. A great dignitary of the XVIIIth Dynasty is seen seated with his wife, their daughter standing between them. Round his neck are four chains of golden rings, with which he had been decorated by the Pharaoh for his services. It is a remarkable group, interesting for its style and workmanship as well as for its subject. As an example of the formal hieratic type of portraiture it is very fine.

AMAZING DISCOVERIES

The other and more important discovery of the two was made by M. Legrain on the south side of the Hypostyle Hall. Tentative excavations, begun in an unoccu-

M. LEGRAIN'S EXCAVATION OF THE KARNAK STATUES IN PROGRESS.

pied tract under the wall of the hall, resulted in the discovery of parts of statues; the place was then regularly excavated, and the result has been amazing. The ground was full of statues, large and small, at some unknown period buried pell-mell, one on the top of another. Some are broken, but the majority are perfect, which is in itself unusual, and is due very much to the soft, muddy soil in which they have lain. Statues found on dry desert land are often terribly cracked, especially when they are of black granite, the crystals of which seem to have a greater tendency to disintegration than have those of the red syenite. The Karnak statues are figures of pious persons, who had dedicated portraits of themselves in the temple of Amen, together with those of great men whom the king had honoured by ordering their statues placed in the temple during their lives.

Of this number was the great sage Amenhetep, son of Hapi, the founder of the little desert temple of Dêr el-Medina, near Dêr el-Bahari, who was a sort of prime minister under Amenhetep III, and was venerated in later days as a demigod. His statue was found with the others by M. Legrain. Among them is a figure made entirely of green felspar, an unusual material for so large a statuette. 'A fine portrait of Thothmes III was also found. The illustration shows this wonderfully fruitful excavation in progress, with the diggers at work in the black mud soil, in the foreground the basket-boys carrying away the rubbish on their shoulders, and the massive granite walls of the Great Hypostyle Hall of Seti in the background. The huge size of the roof-blocks is noticeable. These are not the actual uppermost roof-blocks, but only the architraves from pillar

CONSTRUCTION OF A TEMPLE 381

to pillar; the original roof consisted of similar blocks laid across in the transverse direction from architrave to architrave. An Egyptian granite temple was in fact

PORTRAIT-GROUP OF A GREAT NOBLE AND HIS WIFE, OF THE TIME OF THE XVIIIth DYNASTY.
Discovered by M. Legrain at Karnak.

built upon the plan of a child's box of bricks; it was but a modified and beautified Stonehenge.

Other important discoveries have been made by

M. Legrain in the course of his work. Among them are statues of the late Middle Kingdom, including one of King Usertsen (Senusret) IV of the XIIIth Dynasty. There are also reliefs of the reign of Amenhetep I, which are remarkable for the delicacy of their workmanship and the sureness of their technique. We know that the

A TOMB FITTED UP AS AN EXPLORER'S RESIDENCE.

The Tomb of Pentu (No. 5) at Tell el-Amarna, inhabited by Mr. de G. Davies during his work for the Archæological Survey of Egypt (Egypt Exploration Fund). About 1400 B.C.

temple was built as early as the time of Usertsen, for in it have been found one or two of his blocks; and no doubt the original shrine, which was rebuilt in the time of Philip Arrhidæus, was of the same period, but hitherto no remains of the centuries between his time and that of Hatshepsu had been found. With M. Legrain's work in the greatest temple of Thebes we finish our account of the new discoveries in the chief city of ancient Egypt, as we began it with the work of M. Naville in the oldest temple there.

One of the most interesting questions connected with the archæology of Thebes is that which asks whether the heretical disk-worshipper Akhunaten (Amenhetep IV) erected buildings there, and whether any trace of them has ever been discovered. To those who are interested in Egyptian history and religion the transitory episode of the disk-worship heresy is already familiar. The precise character of the heretical dogma, which Amenhetep IV proclaimed and desired his subjects to accept, has lately been well explained by Mr. de Garis Davies in his volumes, published by the "Archæological Survey of Egypt" branch of the Egypt Exploration Fund, on the tombs of el-Amarna. He shows that the heretical doctrine was a monotheism of a very high order. Amenhetep IV (or as he preferred to call himself, Akhunaten, " Glory of the Disk ") did not, as has usually been supposed, merely worship the Sun-disk itself as the giver of life, and nothing more. He venerated the glowing disk merely as the visible emanation of the deity behind it, who dispensed heat and life to all living things through its medium. The disk was, so to speak, the window in heaven through which the unknown God, the " Lord of the Disk," shed a portion of his radiance on the world. Now, given an ignorance of the true astronomical character of the sun, we see how eminently rational a religion this was. In effect, the sun is the source of all life upon this earth, and so Akhunaten caused its rays to be depicted each with a hand holding out the sign of life to the earth. The monotheistic worship of the sun alone is certainly the highest form of pagan religion, but Akhunaten saw further than this. His doctrine was that there was a deity behind the sun, whose glory shone through it and gave us life. This deity was unnamed and unnamable; he was "the Lord of the Disk." We see in his heresy, therefore, the highest attitude to which religious ideas had attained before the days of the Hebrew prophets.

This religion seems to have been developed out of the philosophical speculations of the priests of the Sun at Heliopolis. Akhunaten with unwise iconoclastic zeal endeavoured to root out the worship of the ancient gods of Egypt, and especially that of Amen-Rā, the ruler of the Egyptian pantheon, whose primacy in the hearts of the people made him the most redoubtable rival of the new doctrine. But the name of the old Sun-god Rā-Harmachis was spared, and it is evident that Akhunaten regarded him as more or less identical with his god.

It has been supposed by Prof. Petrie that Queen Tii, the mother of Akhunaten, was of Mitannian (Armenian) origin, and that she brought the Aten religion to Egypt from her native land, and taught it to her son. Certainly it seems as though the new doctrine had made some headway before the death of Amenhetep III, but we have no reason to attribute it to Tii, or to suppose that she brought it with her from abroad. There is no proof whatever that she was not a native Egyptian, and the mummies of her parents, Iuaa and Tuaa, are purely

Egyptian in facial type. It seems undoubted that the Aten cult was a development of pure Egyptian religious thought.

At first **Akhunaten** tried to establish his religion at Thebes alongside that of Amen and his attendant pantheon. He seems to have built a temple to the Aten there, and we see that his courtiers began to make tombs for themselves in the new realistic style of sculptural art, which the king, heretical in art as in religion, had introduced. The tomb of Rāmes at Shêkh 'Abd el-Kûrna has on one side of the door a representation of the king in the old regular style, and on the other side one in the new realistic style, which depicts him in all the native ugliness in which this strange truth-loving man seems to have positively gloried. We find, too, that he caused a temple to the Aten to be erected in far-away Napata, the capital of Nubia, by Jebel Barkal in the Sudan. The facts as to the Theban and Napata temples have been pointed out by Prof. Breasted, of Chicago.

But the opposition of the Theban priesthood was too strong. Akhunaten shook the dust of the capital off his feet and retired to the isolated city of Akhet-aten, "the Glory of the Disk," at the modern Tell el-Amarna, where he could philosophize in peace, while his kingdom was left to take care of itself. He and his wife Nefret-iti, who seems to have been a faithful sharer of his views, reigned over a select court of Aten-worshipping nobles, priests, and artists. The artists had under Akhunaten an unrivalled opportunity for development, of which they had already begun to take considerable advantage before the end of his reign and the restoration of the old order of ideas. Their style takes on itself an almost bizarre freedom, which reminds us strongly of the similar characteristic in Mycenæan art. There is a strange little relief in the Berlin Museum of the king standing cross-legged, leaning on a staff, and languidly smelling a flower, while the queen stands by with her garments blown about by the wind. The artistic monarch's graceful attitude is probably a faithful transcript of a characteristic pose.

We see from this what an Egyptian artist could do when his shackles were removed, but unluckily Egypt never produced another king who was at the same time an original genius, an artist, and a thinker. When Akhunaten died, the Egyptian artists' shackles were riveted tighter than ever. The reaction was strong. The kingdom had fallen into anarchy, and the foreign empire which his predecessors had built up had practically been thrown to the winds by Akhunaten. The whole is an example of the confusion and disorganization which ensue when a philosopher rules. Not long after the heretic's death the old religion was fully restored, the cult of the disk was blotted out, and the Egyptians returned joyfully to the worship of their myriad deities. Akhunaten's ideals were too high for them. The débris of the foreign empire was, as usual in such cases, put together again, and customary law and order restored by the conservative reactionaries who succeeded him. Henceforth Egyptian civilization runs an uninspired and undeveloping course till the days of the Saïtes and the Ptolemies. This point in the history of Egypt, therefore, forms a convenient stopping-place at which to pause, while we turn once more to Western Asia, and ascertain to what extent recent excavations and research have thrown new light upon the problems connected with the rise and history of the Assyrian and Neo-Babylonian Empires.

CHAPTER VIII

THE ASSYRIAN AND NEO-BABYLONIAN EMPIRES IN THE LIGHT OF RECENT RESEARCH

THE early history of Assyria has long been a subject on which historians were obliged to trust largely to conjecture, in their attempts to reconstruct the stages by which its early rulers obtained their independence and laid the foundations of the mighty empire over which their successors ruled. That the land was colonized from Babylonia and was at first ruled as a dependency of the southern kingdom have long been regarded as established facts, but until recently little was known of its early rulers and governors, and still less of the condition of the country and its capital during the early periods of their existence. Since the excavations carried out by the British Museum at Kala Sherghat, on the western bank of the Tigris, it has been known that the mounds at that spot mark the site of the city of Ashur, the first capital of the Assyrians, and the monuments and records recovered during those excavations have hitherto formed our principal source of information for the early history of the country.[1] Some of the oldest records found in the course of these excavations were short votive texts inscribed by rulers who bore the title of *ishshakku*, corresponding to the Sumerian and early Babylonian title of patesi, and with some such meaning as " viceroy." It was rightly conjectured from the title which they bore that these early rulers owed allegiance to the kings of Babylon and were their nominees, or at any rate their tributaries. The names of a few of these early viceroys were recovered from their votive inscriptions and from notices in later historical texts, but it was obvious that our knowledge of early Assyrian history would remain very fragmentary until systematic excavations in Assyria were resumed. Three years ago (1902) the British Museum resumed excavations at Kuyunjik, the site of Nineveh. The work was begun and carried out under the direction of Mr. L. W. King, but since last summer has been continued by Mr. R. C. Thompson. Last year, too, excavations were reopened at Sherghat by the Deutsch-Orient Gesellschaft, at first under the direction of Dr. Koldewey, and afterwards under that of Dr. Andrae, by whom they are at present being carried on. This renewed activity on the sites of the ancient cities of Assyria is already producing results of considerable interest, and the veil which has so long concealed the earlier periods in the history of that country is being lifted.

Shortly before these excavations in Assyria were

[1] For the texts and translations of these documents, see Budge and King, *Annals of the Kings of Assyria*, pp. i *ff.*

set on foot an indication was obtained from an early Babylonian text that the history of Assyria as a dependent state or province of Babylon must be pushed back to a far more remote period than had hitherto been supposed. In one of Hammurabi's letters to Sin-idinnam, governor of the city of Larsam, to which reference has already been made,[1] directions are given for the despatch to the king of " two hundred and forty men of ' the King's Company ' under the command of Nannar-iddina ... who have left the country of Ashur and the district of Shitullum." From this most interesting reference it followed that the country to the north of Babylonia was known as Assyria at the time of the kings of the First Dynasty of Babylon, and the fact that Babylonian troops were stationed there by Hammurabi proved that the country formed an integral part of the Babylonian empire.

These conclusions were soon after strikingly confirmed by two passages in the introductory sections of Hammurabi's code of laws which was discovered at Susa.[2] Here Hammurabi records that he " restored his (*i. e.* the god Ashur's) protecting image unto the city of Ashur," and a few lines farther on he describes himself as the king " who hath made the names of Ishtar glorious in the city of Nineveh in the temple of E-mish-mish." That Ashur should be referred to at this period is what we might expect, inasmuch as it was known to have been the earliest capital of Assyria; more striking is the reference to Nineveh, proving as it does that

---

[1] See above, p. 301.   [2] See above, p. 267.

it was a flourishing city in Hammurabi's time and that the temple of Ishtar there had already been long established. It is true that Gudea, the Sumerian patesi of Shirpurla, records that he rebuilt the temple of the goddess Ninni (Ishtar) at a place called Nina. Now Nina may very probably be identified with Nineveh, but many writers have taken it to be a place in Southern Babylonia and possibly a district of Shirpurla itself. No such uncertainty attaches to Hammurabi's reference to Nineveh, which is undoubtedly the Assyrian city of that name. Although no account has yet been published of the recent excavations carried out at Nineveh by the British Museum, they fully corroborate the inference drawn with regard to the great age of the city. The series of trenches which were cut deep into the lower strata of Kuyunjik revealed numerous traces of very early habitations on the mound.

Neither in Hammurabi's letters, nor upon the stele inscribed with his code of laws, is any reference made to the contemporary governor or ruler of Assyria, but on a contract tablet preserved in the Pennsylvania Museum a name has been recovered which will probably be identified with that of the ruler of Assyria in Hammurabi's reign. In legal and commercial documents of the period of the First Dynasty of Babylon the contracting parties frequently swore by the names of two gods (usually Shamash and Marduk) and also that of the reigning king. Now it has been found by Dr. Ranke that on this document in the Pennsylvania Museum the contracting parties swear by the name of Hammurabi and also by that of Shamshi-Adad. As only gods and kings are mentioned in the oath formulæ of this period, it follows that Shamshi-Adad was a king, or at any rate a patesi or ishshakku. Now from its form the name Shamshi-Adad must be that of an Assyrian, not that of a Babylonian, and, since he is associated in the oath formula with Hammurabi, it is legitimate to conclude that he governed Assyria in the time of Hammurabi as a dependency of Babylon. An early Assyrian ishshakku of this name, who was the son of Ishme-Dagan, is mentioned by Tiglath-Pileser I, but he cannot be identified with the ruler of the time of Hammurabi, since, according to Tiglath-Pileser, he ruled too late, about 1800 B. C. A brick-inscription of another Shamshi-Adad, however, the son of Igur-kapkapu, is preserved in the British Museum, and it is probable that we may identify him with Hammurabi's Assyrian viceroy. Erishum and his son Ikunum, whose inscriptions are also preserved in the British Museum, should certainly be assigned to an early period of Assyrian history.

The recent excavations at Sherghat are already yielding the names of other early Assyrian viceroys, and, although the texts of the inscriptions in which their names occur have not yet been published, we may briefly enumerate the more important of the discoveries that have been made. Last year a small cone or cylinder was found which, though it bears only a few lines of inscription, restores the names of no less than seven early Assyrian viceroys whose existence was not previously known. The cone was inscribed by Ashir-rim-nishêshu, who gives his own genealogy and records the restoration of the wall of the city of Ashur, which he states had been rebuilt by certain of his predecessors on the throne. The principal portion of the inscription reads as follows: " Ashir-rim-nishêshu, the viceroy of the god Ashir, the son of Ashir-nirari, the viceroy of the god Ashir, the son of Ashir-rabi, the viceroy. The city wall which Kikia, Ikunum, Shar-kenkate-Ashir, and Ashir-nirari, the son of Ishme-Dagan, my forefathers, had built, was fallen, and for the preservation of my life . . . I rebuilt it." Perhaps no inscription has yet been recovered in either Assyria or Babylonia which contained so much new information packed into so small a space. Of the names of the early viceroys mentioned in it only one was previously known, *i.e.* the name of Ikunum, the son of Erishum, is found in a late copy of a votive text preserved in the British Museum. Thus from these few lines the names of three rulers in direct succession have been recovered, viz., Ashir-rabi, Ashir-nirari, and Ashur-rim-nishêshu, and also those of four earlier rulers, viz., Kikia, Shar-kenkate-Ashir, Ishme-Dagan, and his son Ashir-nirari. Another interesting point about the inscription is the spelling of the name of the national god of the Assyrians. In the later periods it is always written *Ashur*, but at this early time we see that the second vowel is changed and that at first the name was written *Ashir*, a form that was already known from the Cappadocian cuneiform inscriptions. The form Ashir is a good participial construction and signifies " the Beneficent," " the Merciful One."

Another interesting find, which was also made last year, consists of four stone tablets, each engraved with the same building-inscription of Shalmaneser I, a king who reigned over Assyria about 1300 B. C. In recording his rebuilding of E-kharsag-kurkura, the temple of the god Ashur in the city of Ashur, he gives a brief summary of the temple's history with details as to the length of time which elapsed between the different periods during which it had been previously restored. The temple was burned in Shalmaneser's time, and, when recording this fact and the putting out of the fire, he summarizes the temple's history in a long parenthesis, as will be seen from the following translation of the extract: "When E-kharsag-kurkura, the temple of Ashur, my lord, which Ushpia (variant *Aushpia*), the priest of Ashur, my forefather, had built aforetime,— and it fell into decay and Erishu, my forefather, the priest of Ashur, rebuilt it; 159 years passed by after the reign of Erishu, and that temple fell into decay, and Shamshi-Adad, the priest of Ashur, rebuilt it; (during) 580 years that temple which Shamshi-Adad, the priest of Ashur, had built, grew hoary and old—(when) fire broke out in the midst thereof . . . , at that time I drenched that temple (with water) in (all) its circuit."

From this extract it will be seen that Shalmaneser gives us, in Ushpia or Aushpia, the name of a very early Assyrian viceroy, who in his belief was the founder of the great temple of the god Ashur. He also tells us that 159 years separated Erishu from a viceroy named

Shamshi-Adad, and that 580 years separated Shamshi-Adad from his own time. When these inscriptions were first found they were hailed with considerable satisfaction by historians, as they gave what seemed to be valuable information for settling the chronology of the early patesis. But confidence in the accuracy of Shalmaneser's reckoning was somewhat shaken a few months afterwards by the discovery of a prism of Esarhaddon, who gave in it a history of the same temple, but ascribed totally different figures for the periods separating the reigns of Erishu and Shamshi-Adad, and the temple's destruction by fire. Esarhaddon agrees with Shalmaneser in ascribing the founding of the temple to Ushpia, but he states that only 126 years (instead of 159 years) separated Erishu (whom he spells Irishu), the son of Ilu-shumma, from Shamshi-Adad, the son of Bêl-kabi; and he adds that 434 years (instead of 580 years) elapsed between Shamshi-Adad's restoration of the temple and the time when it was burned down. As Shalmaneser I lived over six hundred years earlier than Esarhaddon, he was obviously in a better position to ascertain the periods at which the events recorded took place, but the discrepancy between the figures he gives and those of Esarhaddon is disconcerting. It shows that Assyrian scribes could make bad mistakes in their reckoning, and it serves to cast discredit on the absolute accuracy of the chronological notices contained in other late Assyrian inscriptions. So far from helping to settle the unsolved problems of Assyrian chronology, these two recent finds at Sherghat have introduced fresh confusion, and Assyrian chronology for the earlier periods is once more cast into the melting pot.

In addition to the recovery of the names of hitherto unknown early rulers of Assyria, the recent excavations at Sherghat have enabled us to ascertain the true reading of the name of Shalmaneser I's grandfather, who reigned a considerable time after Assyria had gained her independence. The name of this king has hitherto been read as Pudi-ilu, but it is now shown that the signs composing the first part of the name are not to be taken phonetically, but as ideographs, the true reading of the name being Arik-dên-ilu, the signification of which is "Long (*i. e.* far-reaching) is the judgment of God." Arik-dên-ilu was a great conqueror, as were his immediate descendants, all of whom extended the territory of Assyria. By strengthening the country and increasing her resources they enabled Arik-dên-ilu's great-grandson, Tukulti-Ninib I, to achieve the conquest of Babylon itself. Concerning Tukulti-Ninib's reign and achievements an interesting inscription has recently been discovered. This is now preserved in the British Museum, and before describing it we may briefly refer to another phase of the excavations at Sherghat.

The mounds of Sherghat rise a considerable height above the level of the plain, and are to a great extent of natural and not of artificial formation. In fact, the existence of a group of high natural mounds at this point on the bank of the Tigris must have led to its selection by the early Assyrians as the site on which

Stone Object Bearing a Votive Inscription of Arik-den-ilu.
An early independent King of Assyria, who reigned about B.C. 1350. Photograph by Messrs. Mansell & Co.

to build their first stronghold. The mounds were already so high, from their natural formation, that there was no need for the later Assyrian kings to increase their height artificially (as they raised the chief palace-mound at Nineveh), and the remains of the Assyrian buildings of the early period are thus only covered by a few feet of débris and not by masses of unburnt brick and arti-

ENTRANCE INTO ONE OF THE GALLERIES OR TUNNELS CUT INTO THE PRINCIPAL MOUND AT SHERGHAT.

ficially piled up soil. This fact has considerably facilitated the systematic uncovering of the principal mound that is now being carried out by Dr. Andrae. Work has hitherto been confined to the northwest corner of the mound around the ziggurat, or temple tower, and already considerable traces of Assyrian buildings have been laid bare in this portion of the site. The city wall on the northern side has been uncovered, as well as quays with steps leading down to the water along the river front. Part of the great temple of the god Ashur has been excavated, though a considerable portion of it must be still covered by the modern Turkish fort at the extreme northern point of the mounds; also part of a palace erected by Ashur-nasir-pal has been identified. In fact, the work at Sherghat promises to add considerably to our knowledge of ancient Assyrian architecture.

The inscription of Tukulti-Ninib I, which was referred to above as having been recently acquired by the trustees of the British Museum, affords valuable information for the reconstruction of the history of Assyria during the first half of the thirteenth century B. C.[1] It is seen from the facts summarized that for our knowledge of the earlier history of the country we have to depend to a large extent on short brick-inscriptions and votive texts supplemented by historical references in inscriptions of the later period. The only historical inscription of any length belonging to the early Assyrian period, which had been published up to a year ago, was the famous memorial slab containing an inscription of Adad-nirari I, which was acquired by the late Mr. George Smith some thirty years ago. Although purchased in Mosul, the slab had been found by the natives in the mounds at Sherghat, for the text engraved upon it in archaic Assyrian characters records the restoration of a part of the temple of the god Ashur in the ancient city of Ashur, the first

---

[1] For the text and translation of the inscription, see King, *Studies in Eastern History*, i (1904).

capital of the Assyrians, now marked by the mounds of Sherghat, which have already been described. The object of Adad-nirari in causing the memorial slab to be inscribed was to record the restoration of the portion of the temple which he had rebuilt, but the most important part of the inscription was contained in the introductory phrases with which the text opens. They recorded the conquests achieved not only by Adad-nirari but by his father Arik-dên-ilu, his grandfather Bêl-nirari, and his great-grandfather Ashur-uballit. They thus enabled the historian to trace the gradual extension and consolidation of the Assyrian empire during a critical period in its early history.

The recently recovered memorial slab of Tukulti-Ninib I is similar to that of his grandfather Adad-nirari I, and ranks in importance with it for the light it throws on the early struggles of Assyria. Tukulti-Ninib's slab, like that of Adad-nirari, was a foundation memorial intended to record certain building operations carried out by order of the king. The building so commemorated was not the restoration of a portion of a temple, but the founding of a new city, in which the king erected no less than eight temples dedicated to various deities, while he also records that he built a palace therein for his own habitation, that he protected the city by a strongly fortified wall, and that he cut a canal from the Tigris by which he ensured a continuous supply of fresh water. These were the facts which the memorial was primarily intended to record, but, like the text of Adad-nirari I, the most interesting events for the historian are those referred to in the introductory portions of the inscription. Before giving details concerning the founding of the new city, named Kar-Tukulti-Ninib, "the Fortress of Tukulti-Ninib," the king supplies an account of the military expeditions which he had conducted during the course of his reign up to the time when the foundation memorial was inscribed. These introductory paragraphs record how the king gradually conquered the peoples to the north and northeast of Assyria, and how he finally undertook a successful campaign against Babylon, during which he captured the city and completely subjugated both Northern and Southern Babylonia. Tukulti-Ninib's reign thus marks an epoch in the history of his country.

We have already seen how, during the early ages of her history, Assyria had been merely a subject province of the Babylonian empire. Her rulers had been viceroys owing allegiance to their overlords in Babylon, under whose orders they administered the country, while garrisons of Babylonian soldiers, and troops commanded by Babylonian officers, served to keep the country in a state of subjection. Gradually, however, the country began to feel her feet and long for independence. The conquest of Babylon by the kings of the Country of the Sea [1] afforded her the opportunity of throwing off the Babylonian yoke. In the fifteenth century the Assyrian kings were powerful enough to have independent relations with the kings of Egypt, and, during the two centuries which preceded Tukulti-Ninib's reign,

[1] See above, Chapter V, p. 251.

Assyria's relations with Babylon were the cause of constant friction due to the northern kingdom's growth in power and influence. The frontier between the two countries was constantly in dispute, and, though sometimes rectified by treaty, the claims of Assyria often led to war between the two countries.. The general result of these conflicts was that Assyria gradually extended her authority farther southwards, and encroached upon territory which had previously been Babylonian. The successes gained by Ashur-uballit, Bêl-nirari, and Adad-nirari I against the contemporary Babylonian kings had all resulted in the cession of fresh territory to Assyria and in an increase of her international importance. Up to the time of Tukulti-Ninib no Assyrian king had actually seated himself upon the Babylonian throne. This feat was achieved by Tukulti-Ninib, and his reign thus marks an important step in the gradual advance of Assyria to the position which she later occupied as the predominant power in Western Asia.

Before undertaking his campaign against Babylon, Tukulti-Ninib secured himself against attack from other quarters, and his newly discovered memorial inscription supplies considerable information concerning the steps he took to achieve this object. In his inscription the king does not number his military expeditions, and, with the exception of the first one, he does not state the period of his reign in which they were undertaken. The results of his campaigns are summarized in four paragraphs of the text, and it is probable that they are not described in chronological order, but are arranged rather according to the geographical position of the districts which he invaded and subdued. Tukulti-Ninib records that his first campaign took place at the beginning of his sovereignty, in the first year of his reign, and it was directed against the tribes and peoples inhabiting the territory on the east of Assyria. Of the tribes which he overran and conquered on this occasion the most important was the Kuti, who probably dwelt in the districts to the east of the Lower Zâb. They were a turbulent race and they had already been conquered by Arik-dên-ilu and Adad-nirari I, but on neither occasion had they been completely subdued, and they had soon regained their independence. Their subjugation by Tukulti-Ninib was a necessary preliminary to any conquest in the south, and we can well understand why it was undertaken by the king at the beginning of his reign. Other conquests which were also made in the same region were the Ukumanî and the lands of Elkhunia, Sharnida, and Mekhri, mountainous districts which probably lay to the north of the Lower Zâb. The country of Mekhri took its name from the mekhru-tree, a kind of pine or fir, which grew there in abundance upon the mountainsides, and was highly esteemed by the Assyrian kings as affording excellent wood for building purposes. At a later period Ashur-nasir-pal invaded the country in the course of his campaigns and brought back beams of mekhru-wood, which he used in the construction of the temple dedicated to the goddess Ishtar in Nineveh.

The second group of tribes and districts enumerated by Tukulti-Ninib as having been subdued in his early years, before his conquest of Babylon, all lay probably to the northwest of Assyria. The most powerful among these peoples were the Shubarî, who, like the Kuti on the eastern border of Assyria, had already been conquered by Adad-nirari I, but had regained their independence and were once more threatening the border on this side. The third group of his conquests consisted of the districts ruled over by forty kings of the lands of Na'iri, which was a general term for the mountainous districts to the north of Assyria, including territory to the west of Lake Van and extending eastwards to the districts around Lake Urmi. The forty kings in this region whom Tukulti-Ninib boasts of having subdued were little more than chieftains of the mountain tribes, each one possessing authority over a few villages scattered among the hills and valleys. But the men of Na'iri were a warlike and hardy race, and, if left long in undisturbed possession of their native fastnesses, they were tempted to make raids into the fertile plains of Assyria. It was therefore only politic for Tukulti-Ninib to traverse their country with fire and sword, and, by exacting heavy tribute, to keep the fear of Assyrian power before their eyes. From the king's records we thus learn that he subdued and crippled the semi-independent races living on his borders to the north, to the northwest, and to the east. On the west was the desert, from which region he need fear no organized attack when he concentrated his army elsewhere, for his permanent garrisons were strong enough to repel and punish any incursion of nomadic tribes. He was thus in a position to try conclusions with his hereditary foe in the south, without any fear of leaving his land open to invasion in his absence.

The campaign against Babylon was the most important one undertaken by Tukulti-Ninib, and its successful issue was the crowning point of his military career. The king relates that the great gods Ashur, Bêl, and Shamash, and the goddess Ishtar, the queen of heaven and earth, marched at the head of his warriors when he set out upon the expedition. After crossing the border and penetrating into Babylonian territory he seems to have had some difficulty in forcing Bitiliashu, the Kassite king who then occupied the throne of Babylon, to a decisive engagement. But by a skilful disposition of his forces he succeeded in hemming him in, so that the Babylonian army was compelled to engage in a pitched battle. The result of the fighting was a complete victory for the Assyrian arms. Many of the Babylonian warriors fell fighting, and Bitiliashu himself was captured by the Assyrian soldiers in the midst of the battle. Tukulti-Ninib boasts that he trampled his lordly neck beneath his feet, and on his return to Assyria he carried his captive back in fetters to present him with the spoils of the campaign before Ashur, the national god of the Assyrians.

Before returning to Assyria, however, Tukulti-Ninib marched with his army throughout the length and breadth of Babylonia, and achieved the subjugation of the whole of the Sumer and Akkad. He destroyed the fortifications of Babylon to ensure that they should not again be used against himself, and all the inhabitants who did not at once submit to his decrees he put to the sword. He then appointed his own officers to rule the country and established his own system of administration, adding to his previous title of "King of Assyria," those of "King of Karduniash (*i. e.* Babylonia)" and "King of Sumer and Akkad." It was probably from this period that he also adopted the title of "King of the Four Quarters of the World." As a mark of the complete subjugation of their ancient foe, Tukulti-Ninib and his army carried back with them to Assyria not only the captive Babylonian king, but also the statue of Marduk, the national god of Babylon. This they removed from E-sagila, his sumptuous temple in Babylon, and they looted the sacred treasures from the treasure-chambers, and carried them off together with the spoil of the city.

Tukulti-Ninib no doubt left a sufficient proportion of his army in Babylon to garrison the city and support the governors and officials into whose charge he committed the administration of the land, but he himself returned to Assyria with the rich spoil of the campaign, and it was probably as a use for this large increase of wealth and material that he decided to found another city which should bear his own name and perpetuate it for future ages. The king records that he undertook this task at the bidding of Bêl (*i. e.* the god Ashur), who commanded that he should found a new city and build a dwelling-place for him therein. In accordance with the desire of Ashur and the gods, which was thus conveyed to him, the king founded the city of Kar-Tukulti-Ninib, and he erected therein temples dedicated not only to Ashur, but also to the gods Adad, and Shamash, and Ninib, and Nusku, and Nergal, and Imina-bi, and the goddess Ishtar. The spoils from Babylon and the temple treasures from E-sagila were doubtless used for the decoration of these temples and the adornment of their shrines, and the king endowed the temples and appointed regular offerings, which he ordained should be their property for ever. He also built a sumptuous palace for his own abode when he stayed in the city, which he constructed on a mound or terrace of earth, faced with brick, and piled high above the level of the city. Finally, he completed its fortification by the erection of a massive wall around it, and the completion of this wall was the occasion on which his memorial tablet was inscribed.

The memorial tablet was buried and bricked up within the actual structure of the wall, in order that in future ages it might be read by those who found it, and so it might preserve his name and fame. After finishing the account of his building operations in the new city and recording the completion of the city wall from its foundation to its coping stone, the king makes an appeal to any future ruler who should find it, in the following words: " In the days that are to come, when this wall shall have grown old and shall have fallen into ruins, may a future prince repair the damaged parts thereof, and may he anoint my memorial tablet with oil, and may he offer sacrifices and restore it unto its place, and then Ashur will hearken unto his prayers. But whosoever shall destroy this wall, or shall remove my memorial tablet or my name that is inscribed thereon, or shall leave Kar-Tukulti-Ninib, the city of my dominion, desolate, or shall destroy it, may the lord Ashur overthrow his kingdom, and may he break his weapons, and may he cause his warriors to be defeated, and may he diminish his boundaries, and may he ordain that his rule shall be cut off, and on his days may he bring sorrow, and his years may he make evil, and may he blot out his name and his seed from the land!"

By such blessings and curses Tukulti-Ninib hoped to ensure the preservation of his name and the rebuilding of his city, should it at any time be neglected and fall into decay. Curiously enough, it was in this very city that Tukulti-Ninib met his own fate less than seven years after he had founded it. At that time one of his own sons, who bore the name of Ashur-nasir-pal, conspired against his father and stirred up the nobles to revolt. The insurrection was arranged when Tukulti-Ninib was absent from his capital and staying in Kar-Tukulti-Ninib, where he was probably protected by only a small bodyguard, the bulk of his veteran warriors remaining behind in garrison at Ashur. The insurgent nobles, headed by Ashur-nasir-pal, fell upon the king without warning when he was passing through the city without any suspicion of risk from a treacherous attack. The king defended himself and sought refuge in a neighbouring house, but the conspirators surrounded the building and, having forced an entrance, slew him with the sword. Thus Tukulti-Ninib perished in the city he had built and beautified with the spoils of his campaigns, where he had looked forward to passing a peaceful and secure old age. Of the fate of the city itself we know little except that its site is marked to-day by a few mounds which rise slightly above the level of the surrounding desert. The king's memorial tablet only has survived. For some 3,200 years it rested undisturbed in the foundations of the wall of unburnt brick, where it was buried by Tukulti-Ninib on the completion of the city wall.. Thence it was removed by the hands of modern Arabs, and it is now preserved in the British Museum, where the characters of the inscription may be seen to be as sharp and uninjured as on the day when the Assyrian graver inscribed them by order of the king.

In the account of his first campaign, which is preserved upon the memorial tablet, it is stated that the peoples conquered by Tukulti-Ninib brought their yearly tribute to the city of Ashur. This fact is of considerable interest, for it proves that Tukulti-Ninib restored the capital of Assyria to the city of Ashur, removing it from Calah, whither it had been transferred by his father Shalmaneser I. The city of Calah had been founded and built by Shalmaneser I in the same way that his son Tukulti-Ninib built the city of Kar-Tukulti-Ninib, and the building of both cities is striking evidence of the rapid growth of Assyria and her need of expansion

Stone Tablet.
Bearing an inscription of Tukulti-Ninib I, King of Assyria, about B.C. 1275.

around fresh centres prepared for administration and defence. The shifting of the Assyrian capital to Calah by Shalmaneser I was also due to the extension of Assyrian power in the north, in consequence of which there was need of having the capital nearer the centre of the country so enlarged. Ashur's recovery of her old position under Tukulti-Ninib I was only a temporary check to this movement northwards, and, so long as Babylon remained a conquered province of the Assyrian empire, obviously the need for a capital farther north than Ashur would not have been

THE ZIGGURAT, OR TEMPLE TOWER, OF THE ASSYRIAN CITY OF CALAH.

pressing. But with Tukulti-Ninib's death Babylon regained her independence and freed herself from Assyrian control, and the centre of the northern kingdom was once more subject to the influences which eventually resulted in the permanent transference of her capital to Nineveh. To the comparative neglect into which Ashur and Calah consequently fell, we may probably trace the extensive remains of buildings belonging to the earlier periods of Assyrian history which have been recovered and still remain to be found, in the mounds that mark their sites.

We have given some account of the results already achieved from the excavations carried out during the last two years at Sherghat, the site of the city of Ashur. That much remains to be done on the site of Calah, the other early capital of Assyria, is evident from even a cursory examination of the present condition of the mounds that mark the location of the city. These mounds are now known by the name of Nimrûd and are situated on the left or eastern bank of the Tigris, a short distance above the point at which it is joined by the stream of the Upper Zâb, and the great mound which still covers the remains of the ziggurat, or temple tower, can be seen from a considerable distance across the plain. During the excavations formerly carried out here for the British Museum, remains of palaces were recovered which had been built or restored by Shalmaneser I, Ashur-nasir-pal, Shalmaneser II, Tiglathpileser III, Sargon, Esarhaddon, and Ashur-etil-ilâni. After the conclusion of the diggings and the removal of many of the sculptures to England, the site was covered again with earth, in order to protect the remains of Assyrian buildings which were left in place. Since that time the soil has sunk and been washed away by the rains so that many of the larger sculptures are now protruding above the soil, an example of which is seen in the two winged bulls in the palace of Ashur-nasir-pal. It is improbable that the mounds of Nimrûd will yield such rich results as Sherghat, but the site would probably well repay prolonged and systematic excavation.

We have hitherto summarized and described the principal facts, with regard to the early history of Babylonia and Assyria and the neighbouring countries, which have been obtained from the excavations conducted recently on the sites of ancient cities. From the actual remains of the buildings that have been unearthed we have secured information with regard to the temples and palaces of ancient rulers and the plans on which they were designed. From the objects of daily life and of religious use which have been recovered, such as weapons of bronze and iron, and vessels of metal, stone, and clay, it is possible for the archæologist to draw conclusions with regard to the customs of these early peoples; while from a study of their style and workmanship and of such examples of their sculpture as have been brought to light, he may determine the stage of artistic development at which they had arrived. The clay tablets and stone monuments that have been recovered reveal the family life of the people, their commercial undertakings, their system of legislation and land tenure, their epistolary correspondence, and the administration under which they lived, while the royal inscriptions and foundation-memorials throw light on the religious and historical events of the period in which they were inscribed. Information on all these points has been acquired as the result of excavation, and is based on the discoveries in the ruins of early cities which have remained buried beneath the soil for some thousands of years. But for the history of Assyria and of the other nations in the north there is still another source of information to which reference must now be made.

The kings of Assyria were not content with recording their achievements on the walls of their buildings, on stelæ set up in their palaces and temples, on their tablets of annals preserved in their archive-chambers, and on their cylinders and foundation-memorials concealed within the actual structure of the buildings themselves. They have also left records graven in the living rock, and these have never been buried, but have been exposed to wind and weather from the moment they were engraved. Records of irrigation works and military operations successfully undertaken by Assyrian kings remain to this day on the face of the mountains to the north and east of Assyria. The kings of one great mountain race that had its capital at Van borrowed from the Assyrians this method of recording their achievements, and, adopting the Assyrian character, have left numerous rock-inscriptions in their own language in the mountains of Armenia and Kurdistan. In some instances the action of rain and frost has nearly if not quite obliterated the record, and a few have been defaced by the hand of man. But as the majority are engraved in panels cut on the sheer face of the rock, and are inaccessible except by means of ropes and tackle, they have escaped mutilation. The photograph reproduced will serve to show the means that must be adopted for reaching such rock-inscriptions in order to examine or copy them. The inscription shown in the photograph is one of those cut by Sennacherib in

WORK IN PROGRESS ON ONE OF THE ROCK-INSCRIPTIONS OF SENNACHERIB, IN THE GORGE OF THE RIVER GOMEL, NEAR BAVIAN.

the gorge near Bavian, through which the river Gomel flows, and can be reached only by climbing down ropes fixed to the top of the cliff. The choice of such positions by the kings who caused the inscriptions to be engraved was dictated by the desire to render it difficult to destroy them, but it has also had the effect of delaying to some extent their copying and decipherment by modern workers. Considerable progress, however,

THE PRINCIPAL ROCK SCULPTURES IN THE GORGE OF THE GOMEL NEAR BAVIAN IN ASSYRIA.

has recently been made in identifying and copying these texts, and we may here give a short account of what has been done and of the information furnished by the inscriptions that have been examined.

Recently considerable additions have been made to

our knowledge of the ancient empire of Van and of its relation to the later kings of Assyria by the labours of Prof. Lehmann and Dr. Belck on the inscriptions which the kings of that period caused to be engraved

THE ROCK AND CITADEL OF VAN.
The flat roofs of the houses of the city of Van may be seen to the left of the photograph nestling below the rock.

upon the rocks among the mountains of Armenia. The centre and capital of this empire was the ancient city which stood on the site of the modern town of Van at the southwest corner of the lake which bears the same name. The city was built at the foot of a natural rock which rises precipitously from the plain, and must have formed an impregnable stronghold against the attack of the foe.

In this citadel at the present day remain the ancient galleries and staircases and chambers which were cut in the living rock by the kings who made it their fortress, and their inscriptions, engraved upon the face of the rock on specially prepared and polished surfaces, enable us to reconstruct in some degree the history of that ancient empire. From time to time there have been found and copied other similar texts, which are cut on the mountainsides or on the massive stones which formed part of the construction of their buildings and fortifications. A complete collection of these texts, together with translations, will shortly be published by Prof. Lehmann. Meanwhile, this scholar has discussed and summarized the results to be obtained from much of his material, and we are thus already enabled to sketch the principal achievements of the rulers of this mountain race, who were constantly at war with the later kings of Assyria, and for two centuries at least disputed her claim to supremacy in this portion of Western Asia.

The country occupied by this ancient people of Van was the great table-land which now forms Armenia. The people themselves cannot be connected with the Armenians, for their language presents no characteristics of those of the Indo-European family, and it is equally certain that they are not to be traced to a Semitic origin. It is true that they employed the

Assyrian method of writing their inscriptions, and their art differs only in minor points from that of the Assyrians, but in both instances this similarity of culture was directly borrowed at a time when the less civilized

ANCIENT FLIGHT OF STEPS AND GALLERY ON THE FACE OF THE ROCK-CITADEL OF VAN.

race, having its centre at Van, came into direct contact with the Assyrians. The exact date at which this influence began to be exerted is not certain, but we have records of immediate relations with Assyria in the second half of the ninth century before Christ. The district inhabited by the Vannic people was known to the Assyrians by the name of Urartu, and although the inscriptions of the earlier Assyrian kings do not record expeditions against that country, they frequently make mention of campaigns against princes and petty rulers of the land of Na'iri. They must therefore for long have exercised an indirect, if not a direct, influence on the peoples and tribes which lay more to the north.

The earliest evidence of direct contact between the Assyrians and the land of Urartu which we at present possess dates from the reign of Ashur-nasir-pal, and in the reign of his son Shalmaneser II three expeditions were undertaken against the people of Van. The name of the king of Urartu at this time was Arame, and his capital city, Arzasku, probably lay to the north of Lake Van. On all three occasions the Assyrians were victorious, forcing Arame to abandon his capital and capturing his cities as far as the sources of the Euphrates. Subsequently, in the year 833 B.C., Shalmaneser II made another attack upon the country, which at that time was under the sway of Sarduris I. Under this monarch the citadel of Van became the great stronghold of the people of Urartu, for he added to the natural strength of the position by the construction of walls built between the rock of Van and the harbour. The massive blocks of stone of which his fortifications were composed are standing at the present day, and they bear eloquent testimony to the energy with which this monarch devoted himself to the task of rendering his new citadel impregnable. The fortification and strengthening of Van and its citadel was carried on during the reigns of his direct successors and descendants, Ispuinis, Menuas, and Argistis I, so that when Tiglath-pileser III brought fire and sword into the country and

PART OF THE ANCIENT FORTIFICATIONS OF THE CITY OF VAN, BETWEEN THE CITADEL AND THE LAKE.

laid siege to Van in the reign of Sarduris II, he could not capture the citadel. It was not difficult for the Assyrian king to assault and capture the city itself, which lay at the foot of the citadel as it does at the present day, but the latter, within the fortifications of which Sarduris and his garrison withdrew, proved itself able to withstand the Assyrian attack. The expedition of Tiglath-pileser III did not succeed in crushing the Vannic empire, for Rusas I, the son and successor of Sarduris II, allied himself to the neighbouring mountain races and gave considerable trouble to Sargon, the Assyrian king, who was obliged to undertake an expedition to check their aggressions.

It was probably Rusas I who erected the buildings on Toprak Kala, the hill to the east of Van, traces of which remain to the present day. He built a palace and a temple, and around them he constructed a new city with a reservoir to supply it with water, possibly because the slopes of Toprak Kala rendered it easier of defence than the city in the plain (beneath the rock and citadel) which had fallen an easy prey to Tiglath-pileser III. The site of the temple on Toprak Kala has been excavated by the trustees of the British Museum, and our knowledge of Vannic art is derived from the shields and helmets of bronze and small bronze figures and fittings which were recovered from this building. One of the shields brought to the British Museum from the Toprak Kala, where it originally hung with others on the temple walls, bears the name of Argistis II, who was the son and successor of Rusas I, and who attempted to give trouble to the Assyrians by stirring the inhabitants of the land of Kummukh (Kommagene) to revolt against Sargon. His son, Rusas II, was the contemporary of Esarhaddon, and from some recently discovered rock-inscriptions we learn that he extended the limits of his kingdom on the west and secured victories against Mushki (Meshech) to the southeast of the Halys and against the Hittites in Northern Syria. Rusas III rebuilt the temple on Toprak Kala, as we know from an inscription of his on one of the shields from that place in the British Museum. Both he and Sarduris III were on friendly terms with the Assyrians, for we know that they both sent embassies to Ashur-bani-pal.

By far the larger number of rock-inscriptions that have yet been found and copied in the mountainous districts bordering on Assyria were engraved by this ancient Vannic people, and Drs. Lehmann and Belck have done good service by making careful copies and collations of all those which are at present known. Work on other classes of rock-inscriptions has also been carried on by other travellers. A new edition of the inscriptions of Sennacherib in the gorge of the Gomel, near the village of Bavian, has been made by Mr. King, who has also been fortunate enough to find a number of hitherto unknown inscriptions in Kurdistan on the Judi Dagh and at the sources of the Tigris. The inscriptions at the mouth of the Nahr el-Kelb, "the Dog River," in Syria, have been reëxamined by Dr. Knudtzon, and the long inscription which Nebuchadnezzar II cut on the rocks at Wadi Brissa in the Lebanon, formerly published by M. Pognon, has been recopied by Dr. Weissbach. Finally, the great trilingual inscription of Darius Hystaspes on the rock at Bisutun in Persia, which was formerly copied by the late Sir Henry Rawlinson and used by him for the successful decipherment of the cuneiform inscriptions, was completely copied last year by Messrs. King and Thompson.[1]

The main facts of the history of Assyria under her later kings and of Babylonia during the Neo-Babylonian and Persian periods were many years ago correctly ascertained, and recent excavation and research have done little to add to our knowledge of the history of these periods. It was hoped that the excavations conducted by Dr. Koldewey at Babylon would result in the recovery of a wealth of inscriptions and records referring to the later history of the country, but unfortunately comparatively few tablets or inscriptions have been found, and those that have been recovered consist mainly of building-inscriptions and votive texts. One such building-inscription contains an interesting historical reference. It occurs on a barrel-cylinder of clay inscribed with a text of Nabopolassar, and it was found in the temple of Ninib and records the completion and restoration of the temple by the king. In addition to recording the building operations he had carried out in the temple, Nabopolassar boasts of his opposition to the Assyrians. He says: " As for the Assyrians who had ruled all peoples from distant days and had set the people of the land under a heavy yoke, I, the weak and humble man who worshippeth the Lord of Lords (*i. e.* the god Marduk), through the mighty power of Nabû and Marduk, my lords, held back their feet from the land of Akkad and cast off their yoke."

---

[1] Messrs. King and Thompson are preparing a new edition of this inscription.

It is not yet certain whether the Babylonians under Nabopolassar actively assisted Cyaxares and the Medes in the siege and in the subsequent capture of Nineveh in 606 B. C., but this newly discovered reference to the Assyrians by Nabopolassar may possibly be taken to imply that the Babylonians were passive and not active allies of Cyaxares. If the cylinder were inscribed after the fall of Nineveh we should have expected Nabopolassar, had he taken an active part in the capture of the city, to have boasted in more definite terms of his achievement. On his stele which is preserved at Constantinople, Nabonidus, the last king of the Neo-Babylonian empire, who himself suffered defeat at the hands of Cyrus, King of Persia, ascribed the fall of Nineveh to the anger of Marduk and the other gods of Babylon because of the destruction of their city and the spoliation of their temples by Sennacherib in 689 B. C. We see the irony of fate in the fact that Cyrus also ascribed the defeat and deposition of Nabonidus and the fall of Babylon to Marduk's intervention, whose anger he alleges was aroused by the attempt of Nabonidus to concentrate the worship of the local city-gods in Babylon.

Thus it will be seen that recent excavation and research have not yet supplied the data for filling in such gaps as still remain in our knowledge of the later history of Assyria and Babylon. The closing years of the Assyrian empire and the military achievements of the great Neo-Babylonian rulers, Nabopolassar, Neriglissar, and Nebuchadnezzar II, have not yet been found recorded in any published Assyrian or Babylonian inscription, but it may be expected that at any moment some text will be discovered that will throw light upon the problems connected with the history of those periods which still await solution. Meanwhile, the excavations at Babylon, although they have not added much to our knowledge of the later history of the country, have been of immense service in revealing the topography of the city during the Neo-Babylonian period, as well as the positions, plans, and characters of the principal buildings erected by the later Babylonian kings. The discovery of the palaces of Nebuchadnezzar II on the mound of the Kasr, of the small but complete temple E-makh, of the temple of the goddess Nin-makh to the northeast of the palaces, and of the sacred road dividing them and passing through the Great Gate of Ishtar (adorned with representations of lions, bulls, and dragons in raised brick upon its walls) has enabled us to form some conception of the splendour and magnificence of the city as it appeared when rebuilt by its last native rulers. Moreover, the great temple E-sagila, the famous shrine of the god Marduk, has been identified and partly excavated beneath the huge mound of Tell Amran ibn-Ali, while a smaller and less famous temple of Ninib has been discovered in the lower mounds which lie to the eastward. Finally, the sacred way from E-sagila to the palace mound has been traced and uncovered. We are thus enabled to reconstitute the scene of the most solemn rite of the Babylonian festival of the New Year, when the statue of the god Marduk was carried in solemn procession along this road from the temple to the palace, and the Babylonian king made his yearly obeisance to the national god, placing his own hands within those of Marduk, in token of his submission to and dependence on the divine will.

Though recent excavations have not led to any startling discoveries with regard to the history of Western

WITHIN THE SHRINE OF E-MAKH, THE TEMPLE OF THE GODDESS NIN-MAKH.

Asia during the last years of the Babylonian empire, research among the tablets dating from the Neo-Babylonian and Persian periods has lately added considerably to our knowledge of Babylonian literature. These periods were marked by great literary activity on the part of the priests at Babylon, Sippar, and elsewhere, who, under the royal orders, scoured the country for all remains of the early literature which was preserved in the ancient temples and archives of the country, and made careful copies and collections of all they found. Many of these tablets containing Neo-Babylonian copies of earlier literary texts are preserved in the British Museum, and have been recently published, and we have thus recovered some of the principal grammatical, relig-

TRENCH IN THE BABYLONIAN PLAIN, BETWEEN THE MOUND OF THE KASR AND TELL AMRAN IBN-ALI, SHOWING A SECTION OF THE PAVED SACRED WAY.

ious, and magical compositions of the earlier Babylonian period. Among the most interesting of such recent finds is a series of tablets inscribed with the Babylonian legends concerning the creation of the world and man, which present many new and striking parallels to the beliefs on these subjects embodied in Hebrew literature. We have not space to treat this subject at greater length in the present work, but we may here note that discovery and research in its relation to the later empires that ruled at Babylon have produced results of literary rather than of historical importance. But we should exceed the space at our disposal if we attempted even to skim this fascinating field of study in which so much has recently been achieved. For it is time we turned once more to Egypt and directed our inquiry towards ascertaining what recent research has to tell us with regard to her inhabitants during the later periods of her existence as a nation of the ancient world.

CHAPTER IX

THE LAST DAYS OF ANCIENT EGYPT

BEFORE we turned from Egypt to summarize the information, afforded by recent discoveries, upon the history of Western Asia under the kings of the Assyrian and Neo-Babylonian periods, we noted that the Asiatic empire of Egypt was regained by the reactionary kings of the XIXth Dynasty, after its temporary loss owing to the vagaries of Akhunaten. Palestine remained Egyptian throughout the period of the judges until the foundation of the kingdom of Judah. With the decline of military spirit in Egypt and the increasing power of the priesthood, authority over Asia became less and less a reality. Tribute was no longer paid, and the tribes wrangled without a restraining hand, during the reigns of the successors of Ramses III. By the time of the priest-kings of Thebes (the XXIst Dynasty) the authority of the Pharaohs had ceased to be exercised in Syria. Egypt was itself divided into two kingdoms, the one ruled by Northern descendants of the Ramessids at Tanis, the other by the priestly monarchs at Thebes, who reigned by right of inheritance as a result of the marriage of the daughter of Ramses with the high priest Amenhetep, father of Herhor, the first priest-king. The Thebans fortified Gebelên in the South and el-Hêbi in the North against attack, and evidently their relations with the Tanites were not always friendly.

In Syria nothing of the imperial power remained. The prestige of the god Amen of Thebes, however, was still very great. We see this clearly from a very interesting papyrus of the reign of Herhor, published in 1899 by Mr. Golenischeff, which describes the adventures of Uenuamen, an envoy sent (about 1050 B.C.) to Phœnicia to bring wood from the mountains of Lebanon for the construction of a great festival bark of the god Amen at Thebes. In the course of his mission he was very badly treated (We cannot well imagine Thothmes III or Amenhetep III tolerating ill-treatment of their envoy!) and eventually shipwrecked on the coast of the land of Alashiya or Cyprus. He tells us in the papyrus, which seems to be the official report of his mission, that, having been given letters of credence to the Prince of Byblos from the King of Tanis, " to whom Amen had given charge of his North-land," he at length reached Phœnicia, and after much discussion and argument was able to prevail upon the prince to have the wood which he wanted brought down from Lebanon to the seashore.

Here, however, a difficulty presented itself,—the harbour was filled with the piratical ships of the Cretan Tjakaray, who refused to allow Uenuamen to return to

Egypt. "They said, 'Seize him; let no ship of his go unto the land of Egypt!' Then," says Uenuamen in the papyrus, "I sat down and wept. The scribe of the prince came out unto me; he said unto me, 'What aileth thee?' I replied, 'Seest thou not the birds which fly, which fly back unto Egypt? Look at them, they go unto the cool canal, and how long do I remain abandoned here? Seest thou not those who would prevent my return?' He went away and spoke unto the prince, who began to weep at the words which were told unto him and which were so sad. He sent his scribe out unto me, who brought me two measures of wine and a deer. He sent me Tentnuet, an Egyptian singing-girl who was with him, saying unto her, 'Sing unto him, that he may not grieve!' He sent word unto me, 'Eat, drink, and grieve not! To-morrow shalt thou hear all that I shall say.' On the morrow he had the people of his harbour summoned, and he stood in the midst of them, and he said unto the Tjakaray, 'What aileth you?' They answered him, 'We will pursue the piratical ships which thou sendest unto Egypt with our unhappy companions.' He said unto them, 'I cannot seize the ambassador of Amen in my land. Let me send him away and then do ye pursue after him to seize him!' He sent me on board, and he sent me away ... to the haven of the sea. The wind drove me upon the land of Alashiya. The people of the city came out in order to slay me. I was dragged by them to the place where Hatiba, the queen of the city, was. I met her as she was going out of one of her houses into the other. I greeted her and said unto the people who stood by her, 'Is there not one among you who understandeth the speech of Egypt?' One of them replied, 'I understand it.' I said unto him, 'Say unto thy mistress: even as far as the city in which Amen dwelleth (*i.e.* Thebes) have I heard the proverb, "In all cities is injustice done; only in Alashiya is justice to be found," and now is injustice done here every day!' She said, 'What is it that thou sayest?' I said unto her, 'Since the sea raged and the wind drove me upon the land in which thou livest, therefore thou wilt not allow them to seize my body and to kill me, for verily I am an ambassador of Amen. Remember that I am one who will be sought for always. And if these men of the Prince of Byblos whom they seek to kill (are killed), verily if their chief finds ten men of thine, will he not kill them also?' She summoned the men, and they were brought before her. She said unto me, 'Lie down and sleep . . .'"

At this point the papyrus breaks off, and we do not know how Uenuamen returned to Egypt with his wood. The description of his casting-away and landing on Alashiya is quite Homeric, and gives a vivid picture of the manners of the time. The natural impulse of the islanders is to kill the strange castaway, and only the fear of revenge and of the wrath of a distant foreign deity restrains them. Alashiya is probably Cyprus, which also bore the name Yantinay from the time of Thothmes III until the seventh century, when it is called Yatnan by the Assyrians. A king of Alashiya corresponded with Amenhetep III in cuneiform on terms of perfect equality, three hundred years before: "Brother," he writes, "should the small amount of the copper which I have sent thee be displeasing unto thy heart, it is because in my land the hand of Nergal my lord slew all the men of my land (*i. e.* they died of the plague), and there was no working of copper; and this was, my brother, not pleasing unto thy heart. Thy messenger with my messenger swiftly will I send, and whatsoever amount of copper thou hast asked for, O my brother, I, even I, will send it unto thee." The mention by Herhor's envoy of Nesibinebdad (Smendes), the King of Tanis, a powerful ruler who in reality constantly threatened the existence of the priestly monarchy at Thebes, as "him to whom Amen has committed the wardship of his North-land," is distinctly amusing. The hard fact of the independence of Lower Egypt had to be glozed somehow.

The days of Theban power were coming to an end and only the prestige of the god Amen remained strong for two hundred years more. But the alliance of Amen and his priests with a band of predatory and destroying foreign conquerors, the Ethiopians (whose rulers were the descendants of the priest-kings, who retired to Napata on the succession of the powerful Bubastite dynasty of Shishak to that of Tanis, abandoning Thebes to the Northerners), did much to destroy the prestige of Amen and of everything connected with him. An Ethiopian victory meant only an Assyrian reconquest, and between them Ethiopians and Assyrians had well-nigh ruined Egypt. In the Saïte period Thebes had declined greatly in power as well as in influence, and all its traditions were anathema to the leading people of the time, although not of course in Akhunaten's sense.

With the Saïte period we seem almost to have retraced our steps and to have reëntered the age of the Pyramid Builders. All the pomp and glory of Thothmes, Amenhetep, and Ramses were gone. The days of imperial Egypt were over, and the minds of men, sickened of foreign war, turned for peace and quietness to the simpler ideals of the IVth and Vth Dynasties. We have already seen that an archaistic revival of the styles of the early dynasties is characteristic of this late period, and that men were buried at Sakkâra and at Thebes in tombs which recall in form and decoration those of the courtiers of the Pyramid Builders. Everywhere we see this fashion of archaism. A Theban noble of this period named Aba was buried at Thebes. Long ago, nearly three thousand years before, under the VIth Dynasty, there had lived a great noble of the same name, who was buried in a rock-tomb at Dêr el-Gebrâwî, in Middle Egypt. This tomb was open and known in the days of the second Aba, who caused to be copied and reproduced in his tomb in the Asasif at Thebes most of the scenes from the bas-relief with which it had been decorated. The tomb of the VIth Dynasty Aba has lately been copied for the Archæological Survey of Egypt (Egypt Exploration Fund) by Mr. de Garis Davies, who has found the reliefs of the XXVIth Dynasty Aba of considerable use to him in reconstituting destroyed portions of their ancient originals.

During late years important discoveries of objects of this era have been few. One of the most noteworthy is that of a contemporary inscription describing the battle of Momemphis, which is mentioned by Herodotus (ii, 163, 169). We now have the official account of this battle, and know that it took place in the third year of the reign of Amasis—not before he became king. This was the fight in which the unpatriotic king, Apries, who had paid for his partiality for the Greeks of Naukratis with the loss of his throne, was finally defeated. As we see from this inscription, he was probably murdered by the country people during his flight.

The following are the most important passages of the inscription: " His Majesty (Amasis) was in the Festival-Hall, discussing plans for his whole land, when one came to say unto him, ' Hāā-ab-Rā (Apries) is rowing up; he hath gone on board the ships which have crossed over. Haunebu (Greeks), one knows not their number, are traversing the North-land, which is as if it had no master to rule it; he (Apries) hath summoned them, they are coming round him. It is he who hath arranged their settlement in the Peh-ān (the Andropolite name); they infest the whole breadth of Egypt, those who are on thy waters fly before them!' . . . His Majesty mounted his chariot, having taken lance and bow in his hand . . . (the enemy) reached Andropolis; the soldiers sang with joy on the roads . . . they did their duty in destroying the enemy. His

Majesty fought like a lion; he made victims among them, one knows not how many. The ships and their warriors were overturned, they saw the depths as do the fishes. Like a flame he extended, making a feast of fighting. His heart rejoiced. . . . The third year, the 8th Athyr, one came to tell Majesty: ' Let their vileness be ended! They throng the roads, there are thousands there ravaging the land; they fill every road. Those who are in ships bear thy terror in their hearts. But it is not yet finished!' Said his Majesty unto his soldiers: '. . . Young men and old men, do this in the cities and nomes! . . . Going upon every road, let not a day pass without fighting their galleys!' . . . The land was traversed as by the blast of a tempest, destroying their ships, which were abandoned by the crews. The people accomplished their fate, killing the prince (Apries) on his couch, when he had gone to repose in his cabin. When he saw his friend overthrown . . . his Majesty himself buried him (Apries), in order to establish him as a king possessing virtue, for his Majesty decreed that the hatred of the gods should be removed from him."

This is the event to which we have already referred in a preceding chapter, as proving the great amelioration of Egyptian ideas with regard to the treatment of a conquered enemy, as compared with those of other ancient nations. Amasis refers to the deposed monarch as his " friend," and buries him in a manner befitting a king at the charges of Amasis himself. This act warded off from the spirit of Apries the just anger of the gods at his partiality for the "foreign devils," and ensured his reception by Osiris as a king *neb menkh*, " possessing virtues."

The town of Naukratis, where Apries established himself, had been granted to the Greek traders by Psametik I a century or more before. Mr. D. G. Hogarth's recent exploration of the site has led to a considerable modification of our first ideas of the place, which were obtained from Prof. Petrie's excavations. Prof. Petrie was the discoverer of Naukratis, and his diggings told us what Naukratis was like in the first instance, but Mr. Hogarth has shown that several of his identifications were erroneous and that the map of the place must be redrawn. The chief error was in the placing of the Hellenion (the great meeting-place of the Greeks), which is now known to be in quite a different position from that assigned to it by Prof. Petrie. The " Great Temenos " of Prof. Petrie has now been shown to be non-existent. Mr. Hogarth has also pointed out that an old Egyptian town existed at Naukratis long before the Greeks came there. This town is mentioned on a very interesting stele of black basalt (discovered at Tell Gaif, the site of Naukratis, and now in the Cairo Museum), under the name of " Permerti, which is called Nukrate." The first is the old Egyptian name, the second the Greek name adapted to Egyptian hieroglyphs. The stele was erected by Nekhtnebf, the last native king of Egypt, to commemorate his gifts to the temples of Neïth on the occasion of his accession at Saïs. It is beautifully cut, and the inscription is written in a curious manner, with alphabetic spellings instead of ideographs, and ideographs instead of alphabetic spellings, which savours fully of the affectation of the learned pedant who drafted it; for now, of course, in the fourth century before Christ, nobody but a priestly antiquarian could read hieroglyphics. Demotic was the only writing for practical purposes.

We see this fact well illustrated in the inscriptions of the Ptolemaïc temples. The accession of the Ptolemies marked a great increase in the material wealth of Egypt, and foreign conquest again came in fashion. Ptolemy Euergetes marched into Asia in the grand style of a Ramses and brought back the images of gods which had been carried off by Esarhaddon or Nebuchadnezzar II centuries before. He was received on his return to Egypt with acclamations as a true successor of the Pharaohs. The imperial spirit was again in vogue, and the archaistic simplicity and independence of the Saïtes gave place to an archaistic imperialism, the first-fruits of which were the repair and building of temples in the great Pharaonic style. On these we see the Ptolemies masquerading as Pharaohs, and the climax of absurdity is reached when Ptolemy Auletes (the Piper) is seen striking down Asiatic enemies in the manner of Amenhetep or Ramses! This scene is directly copied from a Ramesside temple, and we find imitations of reliefs of Ramses II so slavish that the name of the earlier king is actually copied, as well as the relief, and appears above the figure of a Ptolemy. The names of the nations who were conquered by Thothmes III are repeated on Ptolemaïc sculptures to do duty for the conquered of Euergetes, with all sorts of mistakes in spelling, naturally, and also with later interpolations. Such an inscription is that in the temple of Kom Ombo, which Prof. Sayce has held to contain the names of "Caphtor and Casluhim" and to prove the knowledge of the latter name in the fourteenth century before Christ. The name of Caphtor is the old Egyptian Keftiu (Crete); that of Casluhim is unknown in real Old Egyptian inscriptions, and in this Ptolemaïc list at Kom Ombo it may be quite a late interpolation in the lists, perhaps no older than the Persian period, since we find the names of Parsa (Persia) and Susa, which were certainly unknown to Thothmes III, included in it. We see generally from the Ptolemaïc inscriptions that nobody could read them but a few priests, who often made mistakes. One of the most serious was the identification of Keftiu with Phœnicia in the Stele of Canopus. This misled modern archæologists down to the time of Dr. Evans's discoveries at Knossos, though how these utterly un-Semitic looking Keftiu could have been Phœnicians was a puzzle to everybody. We now know, of course, that they were Mycenæan or Minoan Cretans, and that the Ptolemaïc antiquaries made a mistake in identifying the land of Keftiu with Phœnicia.

We must not, however, say too much in dispraise of the Ptolemaïc Egyptians and their works. We have to be grateful to them indeed for the building of the temples of Edfu and Dendera, which, owing to their later date, are still in good preservation, while the best preserved of the old Pharaonic fanes, such as Medinet Habû, have suffered considerably from the ravages of time. For these temples show us to-day what an old Egyptian temple, when perfect, really looked like. They are, so to speak, perfect mummies of temples, while of the old buildings we have nothing but the disjointed and damaged skeletons.

A good deal of repairing has been done to these buildings, especially to that at Edfu, of late years. But the main archæological interest of Ptolemaïc and Roman times has been found in the field of epigraphy and the study of papyri, with which the names of Messrs. Kenyon, Grenfell, and Hunt are chiefly connected. The treasures which have lately been obtained by the British Museum in the shape of the manuscripts of Aristotle's "Constitution of Athens," the lost poems of Bacchylides, and the Mimes of Herondas, all of which have been published for the trustees of that institution by Mr. Kenyon, are known to those who are interested in these subjects. The long series of publications of Messrs. Grenfell and Hunt, issued at the expense of the Egypt Exploration Fund (Græco-Roman branch), with the exception of the volume of discoveries at Tebtunis, which was issued by the University of California, is also well known.

The two places with which Messrs. Grenfell and Hunt's work has been chiefly connected are the Fayyûm and Behnesâ, the site of the ancient Pemje or Oxyrrhynchus. The lake-province of the Fayyûm, which attained such prominence in the days of the XIIth Dynasty, seems to have had little or no history during the whole period of the New Empire, but in Ptolemaïc times it revived and again became one of the richest and most important provinces of Egypt. The town of Arsinoë was founded at Crocodilopolis, where are now the mounds of Kom el-Fâris (The Mound of the Horseman), near Medinet el-Fayyûm, and became the capital of the province. At Illahûn, just outside the entrance to the Fayyûm, was the great Nile harbour and entrepôt of the lake-district, called Ptolemaïs Hormos.

The explorations of Messrs. Hogarth, Grenfell, and Hunt in the years of 1895 - 6 and 1898 - 9 resulted in the identification of the sites of the ancient cities of Karanis (Kom Ushim), Bacchias (Ûmm el-'Atl), Euhemeria (Kasr el-Banât), Theadelphia (Harit), and Philoteris (Wadfa). The work for the University of California in 1899 - 1900 at Umm el-Baragât showed that this place was Tebtunis. Dimê, on the northern coast of the Birket Karûn, the modern representative of the ancient Lake Moeris, is now known to be the ancient Soknopaiou Nesos (the Isle of Soknopaios), a local form of Sebek, the crocodile-god of the Fayyûm. At Karanis this god was worshipped under the name of Petesuchos ("He whom Sebek has given"), in conjunction with Osiris•Pnepherōs (P-nefer-ho, "the beautiful of face"); at Tebtunis he became Seknebtunis, *i. e.* Sebek-neb-Teb-tunis (Sebek, lord of Tebtunis). This is a typical example of the portmanteau pronunciations of the latter-day Egyptians.

Many very interesting discoveries were made during the course of the excavations of these places (besides Mr. Hogarth's find of the temple of Petesuchos and Pnepherōs at Karanis), consisting of Roman pottery of varied form and Roman agricultural implements, including a perfect plough.[1] The main interest of all, however, lies, both here and at Behnesâ, in the papyri. They consist of Greek and Latin documents of all ages from the early Ptolemaïc to the Christian. In fact, Messrs. Grenfell and Hunt have been unearthing and sifting the contents of the waste-paper baskets of the ancient Ptolemaïc and Roman Egyptians, which had been thrown out on to dust-heaps near the towns. Nothing perishes in the dry climate and soil of Egypt, so the contents of the ancient dust-heaps have been preserved intact until our own day, and have been found by Messrs. Grenfell and Hunt, just as the contents of the houses of the ancient Indian rulers of Chinese Turkestan, at Niya and Khotan, with their store of Kharoshthi documents, have been preserved intact in the dry Tibetan desert climate and have been found by Dr. Stein.[2] There is much analogy between the discoveries of Messrs. Grenfell and Hunt in Egypt and those of Dr. Stein in Turkestan.

The Græco-Egyptian documents are of all kinds, consisting of letters, lists, deeds, notices, tax-assessments, receipts, accounts, and business records of every sort and kind, besides new fragments of classical authors

---

[1] Illustrated on Plate IX of *Fayûm Towns and Their Papyri*.
[2] See Dr. Stein's *Sand-buried Ruins of Khotan*, London, 1903.

and the important "Sayings of Jesus," discovered at Behnesâ, which have been published in a special popular form by the Egypt Exploration Fund.[1]

These last fragments of the oldest Christian literature, which are of such great importance and interest to all Christians, cannot be described or discussed here. The other documents are no less important to the student of ancient literature, the historian, and the sociologist. The classical fragments include many texts of lost authors, including Menander. We will give a few specimens of the private letters and documents, which will show how extremely modern the ancient Egyptians were, and how little difference there actually is between our civilization and theirs, except in the matter of mechanical invention. They had no locomotives and telephones; otherwise they were the same. We resemble them much more than we resemble our mediæval ancestors or even the Elizabethans.

This is a boy's letter to his father, who would not take him up to town with him to see the sights: "Theon to his father Theon, greeting. It was a fine thing of you not to take me with you to the city! If you won't take me with you to Alexandria, I won't write you a letter, or speak to you, or say good-bye to you; and if you go to Alexandria I won't take your hand or ever greet you again. That is what will happen if you won't take me. Mother said to Archelaus, 'It quite upsets him to be left behind.' It was good of you to send me presents on the 12th, the day you sailed. Send me a

[1] Λογία 'Ιησοῦ, 1897, and *New Sayings of Jesus*, 1904.

lyre, I implore you. If you don't, I won't eat, I won't drink: there now!" Is not this more like the letter of a spoiled child of to-day than are the solemnly dutiful epistles of even our grandfathers and grandmothers when young? The touch about " Mother said to Archelaus, ' It quite upsets him to be left behind ' " is delightfully like the modern small boy, and the final request and threat are also eminently characteristic.

Here is a letter asking somebody to redeem the writer's property from the pawnshop: " Now please redeem my property from Sarapion. It is pledged for two minæ. I have paid the interest up to the month Epeiph, at the rate of a stater per mina. There is a casket of incense-wood, and another of onyx, a tunic, a white veil with a real purple border, a handkerchief, a tunic with a Laconian stripe, a garment of purple linen, two armlets, a necklace, a coverlet, a figure of Aphrodite, a cup, a big tin flask, and a wine-jar. From Onetor get the two bracelets. They have been pledged since the month Tybi of last year for eight . . . at the rate of a stater per mina. If the cash is insufficient owing to the carelessness of Theagenis, if, I say, it is insufficient, sell the bracelets and make up the money."

Here is an affectionate letter of invitation: " Greeting, my dear Serenia, from Petosiris. Be sure, dear, to come up on the 20th for the birthday festival of the god, and let me know whether you are coming by boat or by donkey, that we may send for you accordingly. Take care not to forget."

Here is an advertisement of a gymnastic display:

"The assault-at-arms by the youths will take place to-morrow, the 24th. Tradition, no less than the distinguished character of the festival, requires that they should do their utmost in the gymnastic display. Two performances." Signed by Dioskourides, magistrate of Oxyrrhynchus.

Here is a report from a public physician to a magistrate: "To Claudianus, the mayor, from Dionysos, public physician. I was to-day instructed by you, through Herakleides your assistant, to inspect the body of a man who had been found hanged, named Hierax, and to report to you my opinion of it. I therefore inspected the body in the presence of the aforesaid Herakleides at the house of Epagathus in the Broadway ward, and found it hanged by a noose, which fact I accordingly report." Dated in the twelfth year of Marcus Aurelius (A. D. 173).

The above translations are taken, slightly modified, from those in *The Oxyrrhynchus Papyri*, vol. i. The next specimen, a quaint letter, is translated from the text in Mr. Grenfell's *Greek Papyri* (Oxford, 1896), p. 69: "To Noumen, police captain and mayor, from Pokas son of Onōs, unpaid policeman. I have been maltreated by Peadius the priest of the temple of Sebek in Crocodilopolis. On the first epagomenal day of the eleventh year, after having abused me about . . . in the aforesaid temple, the person complained against sprang upon me and in the presence of witnesses struck me many blows with a stick which he had. And as part of my body was not covered, he tore my shirt, and this fact I called upon the bystanders to bear witness to. Wherefôre I request that if it seems proper you will write to Klearchos the headman to send him to you, in order that, if what I have written is true, I may obtain justice at your hands."

A will of Hadrian's reign, taken from the *Oxyrrhynchus Papyri* (i, p. 173), may also be of interest: "This is the last will and testament, made in the street (*i. e.* at a street notary's stand), of Pekysis, son of Hermes and Didyme, an inhabitant of Oxyrrhynchus, being sane and in his right mind. So long as I live, I am to have powers over my property, to alter my will as I please. But if I die with this will unchanged, I devise my daughter Ammonous whose mother is Ptolema, if she survive me, but if not then her children, heir to my shares in the common house, court, and rooms situate in the Cretan ward. All the furniture, movables, and household stock and other property whatever that I shall leave, I bequeath to the mother of my children and my wife Ptolema, the freedwoman of Demetrius, son of Hermippus, with the condition that she shall have for her lifetime the right of using, dwelling in, and building in the said house, court, and rooms. If Ammonous should die without children and intestate, the share of the fixtures shall belong to her half-brother on the mother's side, Anatas, if he survive, but if not, to . . . . No one shall violate the terms of this my will under pain of paying to my daughter and heir Ammonous a fine of 1,000 drachmæ and to the treasury an equal sum." Here follow the signatures of testator and witnesses, who are described, as in a passport, one of them as follows: " I, Dionysios, son of Dionysios of the same city, witness the will of Pekysis. I am forty-six years of age, have a curl over my right temple, and this is my seal of Dionysoplaton."

During the Roman period, which we have now reached in our survey, the temple building of the Ptolemies was carried on with like energy. One of the best-known temples of the Roman period is that at Philæ, which is known as the " Kiosk," or " Pharaoh's Bed." Owing to the great picturesqueness of its situation, this small temple, which was built in the reign of Trajan, has been a favourite subject for the painters of the last fifty years, and next to the Pyramids, the Sphinx, and Karnak, it is probably the most widely known of all Egyptian buildings. Recently it has come very much to the front for an additional reason. Like all the other temples of Philæ, it had been archæologically surveyed and cleared by Col. H. G. Lyons and Dr. Borchardt, but further work of a far-reaching character was rendered necessary by the building of the great Aswân dam, below the island of Philæ, one of the results of which has been the partial submergence of the island and its temples, including the picturesque Kiosk. The following account, taken from the new edition (1906) of Murray's *Guide to Egypt and the Sûdân*, will suffice better than any other description to explain what the dam is, how it has affected Philæ, and what work has been done to obviate the possibility of serious damage to the Kiosk and other buildings.

THE GREAT NILE DAM 447

"In 1898 the Egyptian government signed a contract with Messrs. John Aird & Co. for the construction of the great reservoir and dam at Shellâl, which serves for the storage of water at the time of the flood Nile. The river is 'held up' here sixty-five feet above its old normal level. A great masonry dyke, 150 feet high in places, has been carried across the Bab el-Kebir of the First Cataract, and a canal and four locks, two hundred feet long and thirty feet wide, allow for the passage of traffic up and down the river.

THE GREAT DAM OF ASWÂN, SHOWING WATER RUSHING THROUGH THE SLUICES.

The dam is 2,185 yards long and over ninety feet thick at the base; in places it rises one hundred feet above the bed of the river. It is built of the local red granite, and at each end the granite dam is built into the granite hillside. Seven hundred and eight thousand cubic yards of masonry were used. The sluices are 180 in number, and are arranged at four different levels. The sight of the great volume of water pouring through them is a very fine one. The Nile begins to rise in July, and at the end of November it is necessary to begin closing the sluice-gates to hold up the water. By the end of February the reservoir is usually filled and Philæ partially submerged, so that boats can sail in and out of the colonnades and Pharaoh's Bed. By the beginning of July the water has been distributed, and it then falls to its normal level.

"It is of course regrettable that the engineers were unable to find another site for the dam, as it seemed inevitable that some damage would result to the temples of Philæ from their partial submergence. Korosko was proposed as a site, but was rejected for cogent reasons, and apparently Shellâl was the only possible place. Further, no serious person, who places the greatest good of the greatest number above considerations of the picturesque and the 'interesting,' will deny that if it is necessary to sacrifice Philæ to the good of the people of Egypt, Philæ must go. 'Let the dead bury their dead.' The concern of the rulers of Egypt must be with the living people of Egypt rather than with the dead bones of the past; and they would not be doing their duty did they for a moment allow artistic and archæological considerations to outweigh in their minds the practical necessities of the country. This does not in the least imply that they do not owe a lesser duty to the monuments of Egypt, which are among the most precious relics of the past history of mankind. They do owe this lesser duty, and with regard to Philæ it has been conscientiously fulfilled. The whole temple, in order that its stability may be preserved under the stress of submersion, has been braced up and underpinned, under the superintendence of Mr. Ball, of the Survey Department, who has most efficiently carried out this important work, at a cost of £22,000. Steel girders have been fixed across the island from quay to quay, and these have been surrounded by cement masonry, made water-tight by forcing in cement grout. Pharaoh's Bed and the colonnade have been firmly underpinned in cement masonry, and there is little doubt that the actual stability of Philæ is now more

THE KIOSK AT PHILÆ IN PROCESS OF UNDERPINNING AND RESTORATION, JANUARY, 1902.

certain than that of any other temple in Egypt. The only possible damage that can accrue to it is the partial discolouration of the lower courses of the stonework of Pharaoh's Bed, etc., which already bear a distinct highwater mark. Some surface disintegration from the formation of salt crystals is perhaps inevitable here, but the effects of this can always be neutralized by careful washing, which it should be an important charge of the Antiquities Department to regularly carry out."

The photographs accompanying the present chapter

THE ANCIENT QUAY OF PHILÆ, NOVEMBER, 1904.
This is entirely covered when the reservoir is full, and the palm-trees are farther submerged.

show the dam, the Kiosk in process of conservation and underpinning (1902), and the shores of the island as they now appear in the month of November, with the water nearly up to the level of the quays. A view is also given of the island of Konosso, with its inscriptions, as it is now. The island is simply a huge granite boulder of the kind characteristic of the neighbourhood of Shellâl (Philæ) and Aswân.

On the island of Elephântinê, opposite Aswân, an interesting discovery has lately been made by Mr. Howard Carter. This is a remarkable well, which was supposed by the ancients to lie immediately on the tropic. It formed the basis of Eratosthenes' calculations of the measurement of the earth. Important finds of documents written in Aramaic have also been made here; they show that there was on the island in Ptolemaïc times a regular colony of Syrian merchants.

South of Aswân and Philæ begins Nubia. The Nubian language, which is quite different from Arabic, is spoken by everybody on the island of Elephántinê, and its various dialects are used as far south as Dongola, where Arabic again is generally spoken till we reach the land of the negroes, south of Khartûm. In Ptolemaïc and Roman days the Nubians were a powerful people, and the whole of Nubia and the modern North Sûdân formed an independent kingdom, ruled by queens who bore the title or name of Candace. It was the eunuch of a Candace who was converted to Christianity as he was returning from a mission to Jerusalem to salute Jehovah. "Go and join thyself unto his chariot" was the command to Philip, and when the Ethiopian had heard the gospel from his lips he went on his way rejoicing. The capital of this Candace was at Meroë, the

452   THE LAST DAYS OF ANCIENT EGYPT

modern Bagarawîya, near Shendi. Here, and at Naga not far off, are the remains of the temples of the Candaces, great buildings of semi-barbaric Egyptian style. For the civilization of the Nubians, such as it was, was of Egyptian origin. Ever since Egyptian rule had been extended southwards to Jebel Barkal, beyond Dongola, in the time of Amenhetep II, Egyptian culture had influenced the Nubians. Amenhetep III built a temple to Amen at Napata, the capital of Nubia, which lay

THE ROCK OF KONOSSO IN JANUARY, 1902, BEFORE THE BUILDING OF THE DAM AND FORMATION OF THE RESERVOIR.

under the shadow of Mount Barkal; Akhunaten erected a sanctuary of the Sun-Disk there; and Ramses II also built there.

The place in fact was a sort of appanage of the priests of Amen at Thebes, and when the last priest-king evacuated Thebes, leaving it to the Bubastites of the XXIId Dynasty, it was to distant Napata that he retired. Here a priestly dynasty continued to reign until, two centuries later, the troubles and misfortunes of Egypt seemed to afford an opportunity for the reassertion of the exiled Theban power. Piankhi Meramen returned to Egypt in triumph as its rightful sovereign, but his successors, Shabak, Shabatak, and Tirhakah, had to contend constantly with the Assyrians. Finally Urdamaneh, Tirhakah's successor, returned to Nubia, leaving Egypt, in the decadence of the Assyrian might, free to lead a quiet existence under Psametik I and the succeeding monarchs of the XXVIth Dynasty. When Cambyses conquered Egypt he aspired to conquer Nubia also, but his army was routed and destroyed by the Napatan king, who tells us in an inscription how he defeated " the man Kambasauden," who had attacked him. At Napata the Nubian monarchs, one of the greatest of whom in Ptolemaïc times was Ergamenes, a contemporary of Ptolemy Philopator, continued to reign. But the first Roman governor of Egypt, Ælius Gallus, destroyed Napata, and the Nubians removed their capital to Meroë, where the Candaces reigned.

The monuments of this Nubian kingdom, the temples of Jebel Barkal, the pyramids of Nure close by, the pyramids of Bagarawîya, the temples of Wadi Ben Naga, Mesawwarat en-Naga, and Mesawwarat es-Sufra (" Mesawwarat " proper), were originally investigated by Cailliaud and afterwards by Lepsius. During the last few years they and the pyramids excavated by Dr. E. A. Wallis Budge, of the British Museum, for the Sûdân government, have been again explored. As the results of his work are not yet fully published, it is possible at present only to quote the following description from Cook's *Handbook for Egypt and the Sûdân* (by Dr. Budge), p. 6, of work on the pyramids of Jebel Barkal: "The writer excavated the shafts of one of the pyramids here in 1897, and at the depth of about twenty-five cubits found a group of three chambers, in one of which were a number of bones of the sheep which was sacrificed there about two thousand years ago, and also portions of a broken amphora which had held Rhodian wine. A second shaft, which led to the mummy-chamber, was partly emptied, but at a further depth of twenty cubits water was found, and, as there were no means for pumping it out, the mummy-chamber could not be entered." With regard to the Bagarawîya pyramids, Dr. Budge writes, on p. 700 of the same work, *à propos* of the story of the Italian Ferlini that he found Roman jewelry in one of these pyramids: "In 1903 the writer excavated a number of the pyramids of Meroë for the Governor-General of the Sûdân, Sir F. R. Wingate, and he is convinced that the statements made by Ferlini are the result of misapprehension on his part. The pyramids are solid throughout, and the bodies are buried under them. When the details are complete the proofs for this view

THE ISLE OF KONOSSO, WITH ITS INSCRIPTIONS, NOVEMBER, 1904
The high-water mark of the reservoir when full is visible.

will be published." Dr. Budge has also written upon the subject of the orientation of the Jebel Barkal and Nure pyramids.

It is very curious to find the pyramids reappearing in Egyptian tomb-architecture in the very latest period of Egyptian history. We find them when Egyptian civilization was just entering upon its vigorous manhood, then they gradually disappear, only to revive in its decadent and exiled old age. The Ethiopian pyramids are all of much more elongated form than the old Egyptian ones. It is possible that they may be a survival of the archaistic movement of the XXVIth Dynasty, to which we have already referred.

These are not the latest Egyptian monuments in the Sûdân, nor are the temples of Naga and Mesawwarat the most ancient, though they belong to the Roman period and are decidedly barbarian as to their style and, especially, as to their decoration. The southernmost as well as latest relic of Egypt in the Sûdân is the Christian church of Soba, on the Blue Nile, a few miles above Khartûm. In it was found a stone ram, an emblem of Amen-Rā, which had formerly stood in the temple of Naga and had been brought to Soba perhaps under the impression that it was the Christian Lamb. It was removed to the garden of the governor-general's palace at Khartûm, where it now stands.

The church at Soba is a relic of the Christian kingdom of Alua, which succeeded the realm of the Candaces. One of its chief seats was at Dongola, and all Nubia is covered with the ruins of its churches. It was, of course, an offshoot of the Christianity of Egypt, but a late one, since Isis was still worshipped at Philæ in the sixth century, long after the Edict of Theodosius had officially abolished paganism throughout the Roman world, and the Nubians were at first zealous votaries of the goddess of Philæ. So also when Egypt fell beneath the sway of the Moslem in the seventh century, Nubia remained an independent Christian state, and continued so down to the twelfth century, when the soldiers of Islam conquered the country.

Of late pagan and early Christian Egypt very much that is new has been discovered during the last few years. The period of the Lower Empire has yielded much to the explorers of Oxyrrhynchus, and many papyri of interest belonging to this period have been published by Mr. Kenyon in his *Catalogue of the Greek Papyri in the British Museum*, especially the letters of Flavius Abinnæus, a military officer of the fourth century. The papyri of this period are full of the high-flown titles and affected phraseology which was so beloved of Byzantine scribes. " Glorious Dukes of the Thebaïd," " most magnificent counts and lieutenants," " all-praiseworthy secretaries," and the like strut across the pages of the letters and documents which begin " In the name of Our Lord and Master, Jesus Christ, the God and Saviour of us all, in the year x of the reign of the most divine and praised, great, and beneficent Lord Flavius Heraclius (or other) the eternal Augustus and Autokrator, month x, year x of the Indiction." It is an extraordinary period, this of the sixth and seventh centuries, which we have now entered, with its bizarre combination of the official titulary of the divine and eternal Cæsars Imperatores Augusti with the initial invocation of Christ and the Trinity. It is the transition from the ancient to the modern world, and as such has an interest all its own.

In Egypt the struggle between the adherents of Chalcedon, the "Melkites" or Imperialists of the orthodox Greek rite, and the Eutychians or Monophysites, the followers of the patriarch Dioskoros, who rejected Chalcedon, was going on with unabated fury, and was hardly stopped even by the invasion of the pagan Persians. The last effort of the party of Constantinople to stamp out the Monophysite heresy was made when Cyril was patriarch and governor of Egypt. According to an ingenious theory put forward by Mr. Butler, in his *Arab Conquest of Egypt*, it is Cyril the patriarch who was the mysterious Mukaukas, the μεγαυχὴς, or "Great and Magnificent One," who played so doubtful a part in the epoch-making events of the Arab conquest by 'Amr in A. D. 639 - 41. Usually this Mukaukas has been regarded as a "noble Copt," and the Copts have generally been credited with having assisted the Islamites against the power of Constantinople. This was a very natural and probable conclusion, but Mr. Butler will have it that the Copts resisted the Arabs valiantly, and that the treacherous Mukaukas was none other than the Constantinopolitan patriarch himself.

In the papyri it is interesting to note the gradual

increase of Arab names after the conquest, more especially in those of the Archduke Rainer's collection from the Fayyûm, which was so near the new capital city, Fustât. In Upper Egypt the change was not noticeable for a long time, and in the great collection of Coptic *ostraka* (inscriptions on slips of limestone and sherds of pottery, used as a substitute for paper or parchment), found in the ruins of the Coptic monastery established on the temple site of Dêr el-Bahari, we find no Arab names. These documents, part of which have been published by Mr. W. E. Crum for the Egypt Exploration Fund, while another part will shortly be issued for the trustees of the British Museum by Mr. Hall, date to the seventh and eighth centuries. Their contents resemble those of the earlier papyri from Oxyrrhynchus, though they are not of so varied a nature and are generally written by persons of less intelligence, *i. e.* the monks and peasants of the monasteries and villages of Tjēme, or Western Thebes. During the late excavation of the XIth Dynasty temple of Dêr el-Bahari, more of these *ostraka* were found, which will be published for the Egypt Exploration Fund by Messrs. Naville and Hall. Of actual buildings of the Coptic period the most important excavations have been those of the French School of Cairo at Bâwit, north of Asyût. This work, which was carried on by M. Jean Clédat, has resulted in the discovery of very important frescoes and funerary inscriptions, belonging to the monastery of a famous martyr, St. Apollo.

With these new discoveries of Christian Egypt our

work reaches its fitting close. The frontier which divides the ancient from the modern world has almost been crossed. We look back from the monastery of Bâwit down a long vista of new discoveries until, four thousand years before, we see again the Great Heads coming to the Tomb of Den, Narmer inspecting the bodies of the dead Northerners, and, far away in Babylonia, Narâm-Sin crossing the mountains of the East to conquer Elam, or leading his allies against the prince of Sinai.

THE END.

INDEX

A

Aahmes, king XVIIIth Dynasty, 337, 340
Aba, a noble, 433
Abêshu, Babylonian king, 249
   Letters of, 295, 310
Abnub, statuette of, 365
Abû Ghuraib, temple at, 102, 103
Abû Hatab, excavations at, 165
Abû-'l-Haggâg, Moslem shêkh, 373
Abusir, pyramids at, 95, 101, 103
Abydos, 59, 340, 344
Abyssinia, connection with Egypt, 40, 133
Adad-nirari, Assyrian king, 398, 402
Administration in Babylon, 314
Agriculture in Babylon, 286
Agum, Kassite ruler, 253, 254
Aha, king, tomb of, 49, 57, 61, 83
   Identified with Sma (?), 73 ; with Mena, 74, 76, 80
Aha-f-ka, priest of Snefru, 120
Ahnas, 131
Aı, king XVIIIth Dynasty, 349
Akaivasha = Achaians, 366
Akh-aset, pyramid temple, 322
Akhet-aten, city, 385
Akhunaten (Amenhetep IV), heretic king, 37, 99, 101, 133, 452
   Destroys temples of Amen, 343
   Mother of, 353
   Doctrine of, 383
   Neglects kingdom, 385
Alashiya = Cyprus, 429, 431
Alua, Christian King of Nubia, 455
Alu-usharshid, King of Kish, 224, 228
Amasis, 70, 434
Amelineau, discoveries of, 59, 62, 63, 64, 72, 73, 87
Amen-Ra, or Amen, deity, temple of, 342–345, 384, 429, 431, 452, 455
Amenemhat II, pyramid of, 118, 122
Amenemhat III, pyramid of, 118, 121, 124
   Descent of, 137
   = Moeris, 318

Amenhetep I, tomb of, 337
Amenhetep II, tomb of, 351, 452
Amenhetep III, tomb of, 349, 354
   = Memnon, 355, 452
Amenhetep IV = Akhunaten
Ammiditana, king First Dynasty, letter of, 303
An, city, 78
Ana, Sumerian deity, 183, 214
Andrae, Dr., discoveries of, 166, 167, 389, 397
Annunaki, spirits, 308
Antef, name of Egyptian kings, 335, 337
Anu, Northerners, 47, 54
Anubis, Egyptian deity, 49, 61, 105, 347
Apis, 81
Apries, conquered by Amasis, 70, 434
Arame, King of Van, 418
Archaism of XXVIth Dynasty, 105
Architecture, IVth Dynasty, 123
   XIIth, 123
Arik-dên-ilu, Assyrian ruler, 396, 399, 402
Armenia, 416
Arsaphes (Herakles). *See* Hershefi
Art, Vth Dynasty, 101
Asaru, Sumerian deity, 209
Ashir = Ashur
Ashur, city, excavations at, 167, 408, 409
Ashur, deity, 393, 394
   = Bêl, 405
Ashur-bani-pal, library of, 146
Ashur-nasir-pal, King of Assyria, 408, 410, 418
Assyria, gains independence, 400
   Buildings of, 396
   Culture of, 412
Astrologers in Babylon, 303
Aswân dam, 446
Asyut, chiefs of, 132
Ata, early King of Egypt, 56, 74
Aten, the Sun-god, 383. *See* Akhunaten
Ateth, early king, 56
   = Tja Ati (?), 74
Attitude toward death in Egypt, 69
Auabra Hor, identification of, 119
Ayrton, discoveries of, 8, 89

B

Babylon, excavations at, 166
  Administration in, 314
  Rise of Second Dynasty, 246
  Captured by Tukulti-Ninib, 404
  Culture of, 219, 411
Babylonia, influence on Egypt, 35, 134, 316
  Influenced by Sumerians, 145
  Religion of, 208, 219
  Methods of dating, 241
  Calendar of, 304
Bau, Sumerian deity, 193, 205, 209, 214
Beadnell, H. J. L., discoveries of, 12
Bêl, Babylonian deity, 235, 404, 405. *See* Ashur
Benson, Mrs., discoveries of, 374, 375
Bêt Allam, cemetery, 22
Betjumer = Narmer (?), 76
Bêt Khallâf, tombs at, 81, 82, 85
Binothris = Neneter, 79
Bitiliashi, 253, 254, 259, 404
Blankenhorn, discoveries of, 8, 11
Boats in Babylonia, 297
Borchardt, discoveries of, 97, 98, 110, 111
Boundary-stones, 255
Boyd, Harriet, discoveries of, 370
Bubastis, town, 137
Budge, Wallis, discoveries of, 87
Building regulations in Babylon, 284
Burial customs, 22, 33, 38, 66
Bur-Sin, King of Ur, 225
Buto, city, 44-46

C

Calah, capital of Assyria, 408, 410
Canals in Babylonia, 309
Candace, Queen of Nubia, 451
Carter, Howard, discoveries of, 322, 343, 348, 372
Castes in Babylon, 375
Chalcolithic period, implements of, 13
  Data of, 18
Chaldæan chronology, 185
Cheops = Khufu, 99
Code of Hammurabi, 266
  On marriage, 269
  Castes, 275
  Slaves, 277
  Commercial usages, 279
  Building, 284
  Agriculture, 286
  Irrigation, 294
  Transportation, 297
Copper, introduction into Egypt, 18
"Country of the Sea," 251
  Sumerian origin of inhabitants, 252
  Rebellion against Babylon, 315
Crete, relations with Egypt, 128, 130
Crocodile-god, 440
Cros, Gaston, discoveries of, 151-154, 178, 189-192
Currelly, C. T., discoveries of, 46, 338, 339
Cyprus, 429, 431
Cyrus, King of Persia, 423

D

Darius, inscription of, 421
Dashur, necropolis, 95, 98
Dauda, Sumerian king, 164
Davis, Theodore, discoveries of, 348, 352
Den, king, tomb of, 65, 73
Dêr el-Bahari, excavations at, 321, 336-338, 342, 344, 348
Dimgalabzu, Sumerian deity, 213
Double-Axe, place of, 125
Dra' Abu-'l-Neyga, necropolis, 337, 339
Dumuzi (Tammuz), Sumerian deity, 195
Dungi, King of Ur, 191, 225, 300
Dunshaga, Sumerian deity, 211

E

Ea, Babylonian deity, 235
Ea-gamil, king Second Dynasty, 253
Eannadu, ruler of Shirpurla, 36, 157, 172
E-bab-bara, temple of Sun-god, 272
Edfu, centre of sun-worship, 40, 44, 49, 438
Egypt, early invasions of, 34, 139
  Relations with Babylon, 35, 316
  With Bedawîn, 135
  Conquers Assyria, 140
  Division of, 428
Egyptians, origin of, 30
  Two races, 33
  One race, 43
  Language of, 35
Elam, 172, 203
  Geography, 221
  Relations with Babylon, 222, 223
  Rulers, 233, 236
  Not "Country of the Sea," 251
Elamite, civilization, 162
  Origin and culture, 226-233
El-'Amra cemetery, 22, 43
Elephántinê, island, 451
Embalming introduced, 38
Emutbal, district of Elam, 244
Enakilli, patesi of Gishkhu, 172
Enannadu I and II, rulers of Shirpurla, 173, 177
E-ninnû, temple of Ningirsu, 196-220
Enki, Sumerian deity, 183, 205, 210, 214
Enlil, Babylonian deity, 171, 176, 180, 183, 193, 196, 214
Enlulim, Sumerian deity, 212

INDEX 463

Ensignun, Sumerian deity, 212
Entemena, ruler Shirpurla, 154, 173-175
   Cones of, 176
Enzu, Sumerian deity, 183, 214
Erech, city, 183, 190, 191
Eridu, Babylonian city, 191, 212
Erosion, effects of, 6, 11
E-sagida, temple of Marduk, 273
Ethiopian stone = embalming knife, 14
Evans, Arthur, discoveries of, 359, 361,
   362, 370

F

Fâra, excavations at, 165
Fayyûm, the, 29, 126
Flint implements, 5, 11, 15

G

Galalim, Sumerian deity, 211
Gamil-Sin, King of Ur, 153, 225
Garstang, discoveries of, 63, 81, 137, 328
Gatumdug, Sumerian deity, 193, 198, 205
Gautier, discoveries of, 123, 124
Gebelên, cemetery, 22
Geese, fresco of, 358
Gemnika = Kagemna
Ghosts, habits of, 68
Gilgamesh, Babylonian hero, 222
Gishbare, Sumerian deity, 213
Gishkhu, Babylonian city, 169-190
Giza, pyramids of, 95
Golénischeff, theory of, 137
Gourlay, Miss, discoveries of, 374
Greek and Egyptian, common origin of,
   129
   Communication, 359
   Culture, 363
Greek literature discovered, 441
Grébaut, discoveries of, 104, 350
Gudea, Sumerian ruler, 153, 154, 191, 196
Gu-edin, district, 171, 177, 202, 213
Gurob, excavations at, 131

H

Halbherr, discoveries of, 359
Hall, discoveries of, 8, 321
Hammurabi, ruler of Babylon, 139, 163
   Defeats Elamites, 243
   Letters of, 264, 299, 390
   Code of, 266, 304, 390
Harim, slain with king, 71
Harper, R. F., discoveries of, 164, 165
Hathor, nurse of Horus, 40, 44, 328, 342,
   347
Hatshepsu, queen XVIIIth Dynasty, 321,
   336
   Builds temple, 343, 346
   Tomb of, 348, 351

Hatshepsut, 44
Hawara, tombs and temples at, 119, 124
Haynes, discoveries of, 164, 183
Heliopolis, centre of sun-worship, 40, 44
   Conquered by Narmer, 47
Hemaka, viceroy, 78
Henensu = Herakleopolis
Hen-neter = God's servant, 51
Herakleopolis, kings of, 95, 102, 318
   Excavations at, 131, 132
Herhor, first priest-king, 429, 432
Herodotus, 92, 434
Hershefi (Arsaphes), 131
Hesepti, early king, 73, 74, 77
Hierakonpolis (Nekheb-Nekhen), centre of
   sun-worship, 40, 41, 44, 46
Hittites, possibly Mycenæans, 137
Hor. See Auabra Hor
Horemheb, King of Egypt, 352
Horus, the Sun-god, 40, 49
Hyksos, shepherd kings, 96
   Origin, 136-139
   Invasion and conquest of, 317, 337

I

Ibis-mummies, 89
Ili, priest and ruler, 174
Iluma-ilu, king Second Dynasty, 246, 248
   = Dingir-a-an, 252
Ine-Sin, King of Ur, 225
Iron, knowledge of in Egypt, 112
Irrigation and civilization, 4
   In Babylon, 290
   In Egypt, 294
Isin, Babylonian city, 190
Iuaa, father of Queen Tii, 353

J

Jéquier, discoveries of, 119, 123, 124
Jewelry in Egyptian tombs, 120

K

Kadi, Kishite deity, 171
Kagemna (Gemnika), mastaba of, 104
Kahun, flints of, 15
Kal, Sumerian deity, 213
Karibu-sha-Shushinak, ruler of Elam, 233
Karnak, temple of, 375, 378
Kar-Tukulti-Ninib, city, 406
Kashakti-Shugab, inscription of, 256, 258
Kassites, conquer "Country of the Sea"
   and Babylon, 251, 253
Keftiu (Cretans), 359, 363
Khafra = Chephren, 1, 84
Khasekhemui, early King of Egypt, 46,
   47, 51, 76, 77
   Tomb of, 85, 93

INDEX

Khent = Tjer
Khentamerti, god of the dead, 61, 93.
   See Osiris
Kheta (Hittites), 137
Kheti, king, 132
Khian, king, 138, 365
Khnumhetep, prince, 136
Khufu (Cheops), IVth Dynasty, 1, 84, 88, 99
   Dress of, 101
Khumbaba, Elamite ruler, 222
King, L. W., discoveries of, 167, 389
Kings, lists of, 55, 72
   Identification of, 73
Kish, 156, 224
Knossos, labyrinth at, 125
   Vessels of, 361
Koldewey, discoveries of, 165, 166, 389
Kom es-Sultan, "Mound of the King," 88
Koptos, excavations at, 42
Kudur-mabug, Elamite ruler, 242-243
Kudurru, 225
Kutir-Nakhkhunte, liberates Elam, 236
Kuyunjik (Nineveh), excavations at, 167, 389

L

Labyrinth of Amenemhat III, 125
Lakhamu, monster, 206
Land tenure in Babylon, 261-263
Larsam, Elamite city, 191, 243
Legrain, Georges, discoveries of, 117-120, 376-382
Lepsius, discoveries of, 110, 111, 348
Lisht, pyramid, 95-98, 123
Loret, discoveries of, 349
Lugalenuruazagakam, Sumerian deity, 213
Lugaligikhusam, Sumerian deity, 212
Lugalkigubnidudu, 189
Lugalkurdub, Sumerian deity, 211
Lugalsisa, Sumerian deity, 212
Lugalzaggisi, ruler of Gishkhu, 182-190
Luxor, temple of, 373
Lythgoe, discoveries of, 28

M

Mace, discoveries of, 28, 59, 97, 339
MacIver, Randall, discoveries of, 21, 28, 32, 339
Magan, 158
Manes, 41
Manetho, dynastic annalist, 55, 59, 63, 73, 79, 81, 83, 92
Manishtusu, obelisk of, 156
Manlum, 158
Marduk, Babylonian deity, 191, 256, 422
   Statue taken by Assyrians, 405
Marduk-aplu-iddina, king Third Dynasty, 258, 259, 262
Marriage in First Dynasty, 269
   Among Sumerians, 271
Maspero, G., discoveries of, 95, 97, 107, 124, 150, 190, 266, 348, 353
Mastabat el-Fara'ûn, 107
Maya, Egyptian official, 352
Mêdûm, cemetery, 33, 95
Mekhu, district, 402
Melishikhu, Third Dynasty, 258, 259, 262
Melukhkha, land of, 203
Memnon = Amenhetep III
Memphis, founding of, 54, 56, 91
   Burial place, 61
Mena (Menes), identification of, 53, 56, 74, 92
Meneptah, successor of Ramses II, 366
Menes. *See* Mena
Menkaura, IVth Dynasty, 84
Mentuemhat, statue of, 375
Mentuhetep III, 123, 342
Mera, steward of palace, 320
Merbap (Merpeba Atjab), 73, 74, 91
Mereruka (Mera), tomb of, 104
Merikara, inscriptions of, 132
Merit, jewels of, 120
Merneit, 74, 77
Meroë, capital of Nubia, 451, 453, 454
Mertisen, Egyptian artist, 331
Mesilim, King of Kish, 157, 171
Mesniu, followers of Horus, 41, 43
Mesopotamia, different masters of, 314
Middle Kingdom, intercourse with foreigners of, 133
Min, deity, 42, 49
Minos, King of Crete, 125, 370
Moeris = Amenemhat III, 318
Momemphis, battle of, 434
Monarchy, origin of, 32
Mond, R. L., discoveries of, 357
Mongol origin of Hyksos, theory of, 136
Montelius, Prof. O., on antiquity of use of iron in Egypt, 113
Months, Babylonian, 304
Morgan, M. J. de, discoveries of, 21, 22, 24, 28, 32, 57, 58, 63, 115, 119, 122, 124, 155, 162, 221, 223, 225, 239, 255, 376
Mukayyar = Ur, burials at, 2
Mut, deity, 374
Mycenæans, represented, 137, 361

N

Nabonidus, 185, 423
Nabopolassar, 422
Nabû, Babylonian deity, 166, 168
Nag' ed-Dêr, excavations at, 27

INDEX 465

Na'iri, district of Assyria, 403, 418
Nakâda, cemetery, 22, 24, 49
  Tomb of Aha at, 57, 62
Napata, capital of Nubia, 452
Narâm-Sin, invades Egypt, 133
  Inscriptions of, 157
  Son of Sargon I, 186, 190, 223, 228, 300
Narmer, early King of Egypt, 46, 47
  Founded Memphis, 54
  Tomb of, 61
  Identification of, 74, 76
Nati, Babylonian deity, 235
Naukratis, 434, 436
Naville, discoveries of, 63, 138, 321, 343, 345, 347, 383
Nazimaruttash, Third Dynasty, 256
Nebhapet-Rā, wives buried, 71, 321, 322
  = Mentuhetep III, 335
Neb-hetep Mentuhetep, XIth Dynasty, 322, 335
Nebkaurā, 132
Nebuchadnezzar II, palace of, 166, 423–424
Necherophes, 83
Necropoles, prehistoric, 22
Neferarikarā, Vth Dynasty, 98
Nefertari, queen, tomb of, 371
Nefret, queen of Usertsen II, 137
Nefret-ari-Aahmes, worshipped, 341–342
Nefret-iti, queen of Akhunaten, 385
Neit-hetep, princess, 63
Nekhebet, deity, 44
Nekhen, shrine, 47
Nekhtnebf, king, 436
Ne-maat-hap, 81
Neneter, IId Dynasty, 79
Neolithic age, 5
  Pottery of, 15
  Population of, 32
Ne-user-Rā, Vth Dynasty, temple of, 98, 102
  Dress of, 101
Newberry, P. E., discoveries of, 63, 137, 138, 319, 320, 328, 354, 357, 360
Nidaba, deity of Gishkhu, 182, 183
Ninâ, deity of Shirpurla, 172–174, 181, 194, 198, 210, 391
Ninaza, Babylonian deity, 193, 194
Nindub, Sumerian deity, 199, 210
Nineveh, excavations at, 167, 389
Ningirsu, god of Shirpurla, 171, 174, 180, 181, 193, 196
Ningishzida, Sumerian deity, 193, 194, 199
Ninib, Babylonian god, 166, 422
Ninkharsag, Sumerian deity, 183, 193, 214, 235
Ninmakh, Sumerian deity, 166, 214
Ninni (Ishtar), 181, 183, 193, 203, 235, 391

Nin-tu-kalama, Sumerian deity, 303
Nippur, excavations at, 183, 186
Nomes, 45
  Standard of, 49
Nubhetep, princess, 122
Nubia, 451, 455

O

Osiris, Egyptian deity, 61
  Tomb of, 62, 65
  Presided over ghosts, 69
  Worship of, 78
  Sculptures, 86, 88, 105

P

Palæolithic age, habitations in, 5
  Climate, 6
  Flints of, 11
Palestine, relations with Egypt, 141, 428
Pepi I, 47
Perabsen = Sekhem-ab, 80
Petesuchos (Sebek), crocodile-god, 440
Petrie, Prof. Flinders, discoveries of, 11, 12 n, 16, 19, 20, 21, 24, 28, 29, 32, 42, 51 n, 58, 59, 61, 62, 63, 64, 72, 74, 77, 78, 83, 84, 89, 97, 99, 101, 111, 115, 116, 117, 123, 130, 131, 335, 345, 366, 368, 373, 375, 384
Philæ, temple at, 446, 456
Philistines, 369, 370
Phtah, god of Memphis, 93, 94
Phtahhetep, author, 104
Piankhi Meramen, 453
Piehl, discoveries of, 115
Pitt-Rivers, discoveries of, 10, 11
Portch, discoveries of, 8
Pottery, Neolithic, 15
  "Sequence dating" from, 19, 20
  Cretan, 87, 130
Psametik I, 453
Ptolemies, the, 140, 437, 453
Ptolemy Philadelphus, 93
Puenet = Punt
Punt = Abyssinia, 40, 133
Pyramids, Old and Middle Kingdom, 108
  The Step, 82
  Of Mêdûm, 83
  Method of building, 110, 117

Q

Qebh, early king, 73, 74
Quibell, J., discoveries of, 24, 28, 29, 51, 52, 58

INDEX

R

Rā, the Sun-god, temple at er-Rîgha, 102
  Rā Harmachis, the rising sun, 37, 103, 347
  Tum-Rā, the setting sun, 37, 103
Rā-Harmachis. *See* Rā
Ramesseum, 319, 371
Ramses I, 75
Ramses II, 133
  Dress of, 101
  Body of, 348
  Colossus of, 372
Ramses III, tombs of, 340, 365
  Attacked from North, 368
Reisner, discoveries of, 27, 28, 29, 97
Rekhmara, tomb of, 359
Rîm-Sin, Elamite ruler, 243, 249
Rusas I, II, III, Kings of Van, 420

S

Saghel el Baglieh, cemetery, 22
Sahura, Vth Dynasty, 98
Sakkâra, necropolis, 1, 94, 103, 105
Samsu-abu, First Dynasty, 314
Samsu-ditana, First Dynasty, 250
Samsu-iluna, ruler Babylon, 240, 245, 249, 300
Sanehat, 135
Sa-nekht, IIId Dynasty, 81, 83
Sargon I, King of Agade, 35, 185–190
  Conquers Elam, 223, 228, 300
Sarzec, M. de, discoveries of, 148, 150–154, 190 n, 193, 195, 300
Sayce, A. H., 146
"Sayings of Jesus," 442
Schafer, discoveries of, 98
Schiaparella, discoveries of, 371
Schweinfurth, Prof., 8
Sebek (Seknebtunis), crocodile-god, 440
Sebekhetep, official, 357
Sebekneferura, daughter of Amenemhat III, 119
Seker, god of the dead, 61, 94
Sekhāhetep-Rā Mentuhetep, XIth Dynasty, 334
Sekhem-ab (Perabsen), 81
Sekhemet (Pakhet), 374
Sekri = Seker
Semerkha, Ist Dynasty, 84
Semitic element in Egyptian language and culture, 39, 103
  Invasion of Egypt, 43
  Descent of Northerners, 48
  Conquest of Babylon and Elam, 228, 240
Semti-Den = Onsaphaïs, 73
Senmut, tomb of, 359
Sennacherib, 423

"Sequence dating," 42
Serapeum, 106
Sergi, discoveries of, 32
Sesokhris (Sa-nekht ?), 82
Set, deity, 81
Seti I, 75
  Built temple at Abydos, 92
  Body of, 348
Seton-Karr, excavations of, 8, 15
Shadduf, for raising water, 295
Shakanshabar, Sumerian deity, 212
Shalmaneser I, 394, 396
Shalmaneser II, 410, 418
Shamash, Babylonian deity, 222, 235
Shamshi-Adad, Assyrian ruler, 392, 395
Sheb-Sin, a tax collector, 306, 307
Shêkh-'Abd el-Kûrna, excavations at, 319, 371
Shemsu, early king, 73, 74
Shemsu-Heru, 41
Sherghat, excavations at, 410
Shirpurla (Telloh), excavations at, 148, 152, 178
  History of, 169, 190, 196
Shubari, people, 403
Shûnet ez Zebîb, city, 88
Shushinak, deity of Elam, 234
Shutruk-Nakhkhunte, Elamite king, 159
Sin, deity, 235
Sit-hathor, jewels of, 120
Sin-idinnam, governor of Larsam, 300, 304
Sin-muballit, Babylonian king, 243
Slaves, buried with masters, 68
  In Babylon, 277
Snefru, IIId Dynasty, tombs of, 56, 83, 108
  Invades Sinai, 133, 340
"Sons of the Sun," 102
Sphinx, emblem of Rā-Harmachis, 103
Steindorff, discoveries of, 97, 335, 336, 360
Stela = gravestone, 105
Stele of Palermo, 46, 79
  Of Victory, 157
  Of Vultures, 36, 38, 154
Step-Pyramid, 84, 86
Stone age, implements of, 3, 8
  Settlements in, 4
Sturge, Allen, 8
Sumerian people, 134
  Influence, 134, 145, 191
  Civilization, 141, 145, 146, 149, 191
  Religion, 195–220
  Relations with Babylon, 228
Susa, excavations at, 155, 160, 203

T

Tancheres = Tatkarā Assa
Ta-neter = Abyssinia, 40, 44
Tanis, Sphinxes of, 136

INDEX 467

Tatkarā Assa, 104
Taxes in Babylon, 306
Tell el-Amarna, 365, 385
Telloh (Shirpurla), 148, 150, 178, 191, 195
Temples, Assyrian and Babylonian
  Of Ashur in Ashur, 394
  Of Ashur in Kar-Tukulti-Ninib, 406
  Of Elamite deities, 301
  E-ninnû of Ningirsu, 194, 196
  E-sagila of Marduk at Babylon, 424
  Of Marduk sacked, 191
  Of Nin-makh, 424
  Of Shushinak, 233
  Of various Sumerian deities mentioned, 180, 181, 193
  At Toprak Kala, 420
Temples, Egyptian
  Akh-aset, 321
  Of Amen at Napata, 452
  Of Amen-Rā and Thothmes I and II, 343, 347
  Of the Candaces, 452
  At Dendera and Edfu, 438
  The Great, 336, 343
  Of Hathor, 347
  By Queen Hatshepsu, 321, 336, 343
  At Hawara, 124
  Of Hershefi, 131
  At Karnak, 375
  At Luxor, 373
  Of Medînet Habû, 370
  Of Mut, 374
  Of Neith, 436
  Of Nekhen, 47
  Of Ne-user-Rā, 98
  Of Nubia generally, 453, 455
  Of Petesuchos and Pnepherōs, 441
  At Philæ, 446
  Of Queens of Thebes, 371
  Of Rā near Gîza, 102
  By Seti I, 92
  By Snefru at Mêdûm, 88
Temti-agun, Elamite ruler, 237
Teta, legendary king, 56, 74
Teta-shera, queen, tomb of, 339
Thebes, the dominant power, 132, 318
This, 59
Thompson, R. C., discoveries of, 167, 389
Thot, 49
Thothmes I, 343, 348
Thothmes II, 343
Thothmes III, 343, 346
Thothmes IV, tomb of, 352
Tiglath-Pileser I, 392
Tiglath-Pileser III, 419, 420
Tii, Queen of Amenhetep III, 353, 384
Tjakaray, 429
Tjer, tomb of, 86, 87

Tjeser, invades Sinai, 133, 340
Tjeser, Khetneter, 81, 83
Tombs, Egyptian
  Of Aahmes at Abydos, 338
  Of Aba, 433
  Of Aha, 49, 57, 62, 63, 64
  Of Aha-f-ka, 120
  Of Amenemhat II, 118, 351
  Of Antef III and IV, 337
  Of A'uabra Hor, 119, 121
  At Dashûr, 108, 118
  Of King Den, 65, 85
  Of Ist and IId Dynasties, 60
  Of Gen-Amen, 358
  Of Herakleopolite kings, 95
  Of Hyksos kings, 96
  Of Imadua, 357
  Of Iuaa and Tuaa, 353
  Of Kagemna, 104
  Of Khāsekhemui, 85
  Of Khent or Tjer, 86
  Of Merpeba Atjab, 73, 74, 91
  Of Middle Empire, 96, 108
  Of Neb-hapet-Rā Mentuhetep, **71**, 321
  Of Neb-hetep Mentuhetep, 322
  Of Neferarikarā, 98
  Of Neithetep, a princess, 63
  Of Ne-user-Rā, 98
  Of Osiris at Abydos, 69
  Of Princesses, 120, 122
  Of priestesses of Hathor, 328
  Of Rekhmarā, 359
  Of Sahurā, 98
  Of Sa-nekht, 81, 84
  Of Sebekhetep, 357
  Of Senmut, 359
  In Shêkh Abd el-Kûrna, 319
  Of Snefru, 83, 95
  Of Queen Teta-shera, 339
  Of Theban kings, 96
  Of Tjeser Khetneter, 81, 84, 85
  Of Thothmes I, 348
  Of Thothmes IV, 352
  Of IIId and IVth Dynasties, 60
  Of Uerarina, 104
  At Umm el-Ga'ab, 75, 87
  Of Usertsen I, 123
  Of Usertsen III, 118, 338
Tombs, secondary, 340
Toprak Kala, citadel of Van, 420
Trade-routes, 283
Tuaa, mother of Queen Tii, 353
Tûkh, cemetery, 22, 24, 58
Tukulti-Ninib, King of Assyria, inscriptions of, 396, 398
  Conquéror, 402, 404
  Removes statue of Marduk, 405
Tum-Ra or Tum, the Sun-god, 37, 103
Turnure, list of, 92
Tytus, C., 354

U

Uenuamen, envoy of Herhor, 429
Uerarina, 104
Ukush, ruler of Gishkhu, 183, 189
Ulam-Buriash, defeats Ea-gamil, 253
Umm el-Ga'ab, cemetery, 64, 74, 75
   Pottery at, 87, 88
Unas, King of Egypt, 340
Ur, Elamite city, 190, 225, 243
Urartu = Vannic territory, 418
Ur-Engur, 191
Urizu, Sumerian deity, 212
Urkagina, ruler Shirpurla, 154, **177**
Urlumma, ruler Gishkhu, 172
Ur-nina, King of Babylon, 153
Usertsen (Senusret) I, statues of, 123
Usertsen II, pyramid of, 15, 62, 124
Usertsen III, portrait and statues of, 100, 326
   Pyramid of, 108, 118
   Jewels of, 121
   Invades Palestine, 136
   Possible Hittite descent, 137
   Tomb of, 338
Usertsen IV, 382

Ush, patesi of Gishkhu, 171
Ushabtiu = "Answerers," 72, 329
Ushpia, Assyrian ruler, 394–395
Ushumgabkalama, Sumerian deity

V

Van, empire of, 415–422
   = Armenia, 416
Vaphio, cups of, 361, 365

W

Wadi esh-Shêkh, 8, 15
Wadi Hammamat, 40, 43, 135
Wadiyên, valley of, 348, 349
Wealth in XIIth and XVIIth Dynasties, 353
Weigall, A. E. P., discoveries of, 338, 339
Welsh, discoveries of, 369
Writing, Sumerian, 149

Y

Yatnan (Yantinay) = Cyprus, 431

www.ingramcontent.com/pod-product-compliance
Lightning Source LLC
Chambersburg PA
CBHW062020290426
44108CB00024B/2723